Phoenix Web Development

Create rich web applications using functional programming
techniques with Phoenix and Elixir

Brandon Richey

BIRMINGHAM - MUMBAI

Phoenix Web Development

Commissioning Editor: Kunal Chaudhari
Acquisition Editor: Larissa Pinto
Content Development Editor: Mohammed Yusuf Imaratwale
Technical Editor: Ralph Rosario
Copy Editor: Safis Editing
Project Coordinator: Hardik Bhinde
Proofreader: Safis Editing
Indexer: Priyanka Dhadke
Graphics: Jason Monteiro
Production Coordinator: Shantanu Zagade

First published: April 2018

Production reference: 1250418

Published by Packt Publishing Ltd.
Livery Place
35 Livery Street
Birmingham
B3 2PB, UK.

ISBN 978-1-78728-419-7

www.packtpub.com

`mapt.io`

Mapt is an online digital library that gives you full access to over 5,000 books and videos, as well as industry leading tools to help you plan your personal development and advance your career. For more information, please visit our website.

Why subscribe?

- Spend less time learning and more time coding with practical eBooks and Videos from over 4,000 industry professionals

- Improve your learning with Skill Plans built especially for you

- Get a free eBook or video every month

- Mapt is fully searchable

- Copy and paste, print, and bookmark content

PacktPub.com

Did you know that Packt offers eBook versions of every book published, with PDF and ePub files available? You can upgrade to the eBook version at `www.PacktPub.com` and as a print book customer, you are entitled to a discount on the eBook copy. Get in touch with us at `service@packtpub.com` for more details.

At `www.PacktPub.com`, you can also read a collection of free technical articles, sign up for a range of free newsletters, and receive exclusive discounts and offers on Packt books and eBooks.

Contributors

About the author

Brandon Richey is a software engineer and Elixir enthusiast who has written a large number of popular Elixir tutorials. He has been doing professional and hobby programming projects spanning topics from healthcare, personal sites, recruiting, and game development for nearly 20 years! When not programming, Brandon enjoys spending time with his family, playing (and making) video games and working on his drawings and paintings!

I want to acknowledge the hard work put in by some friends and family who helped make this book a reality: Larry Rohrs, for his fantastic work in reviewing and editing a huge number of chapters as well as Mikhail Volozin and Rami Massoud, who also contributed reviews and edits!

About the reviewers

Atul S. Khot is a self-taught programmer and learned from reading C and C++ code. A Linux aficionado and a command-line guy at heart, Atul has dabbled in multiple languages. He is deeply interested in functional languages and massively parallel software systems. Atul speaks at software conferences, and he is a past Dr. Dobb's Jolt award judge. He was the author of *Learning functional Data Structures & Algorithms* and *Scala Functional Programming Patterns*, both published by Packt Publishing.

> *I would want to thank my parents—late Sushila S. Khot (Aai) and late Shriniwas V. Khot (Anna), for teaching me the value of continuous learning and sharing - and the importance of being human, first and foremost. You lit the lamp in so many lives! Heart of hearts, I know you are watching over me and silently feeling proud.*

Larry Rohrs worked for a large financial firm as an IT professional for 25 years. Professional coding projects were focused on infrastructure in APL-derivative languages, C, and C++. As a senior manager, Larry managed a large, global, IT team responsible for collecting, verifying, organizing, and expanding key reference data available through large, distributed databases. He is currently retired and enjoys spending more time with family and hobbies.

Packt is searching for authors like you

If you're interested in becoming an author for Packt, please visit `authors.packtpub.com` and apply today. We have worked with thousands of developers and tech professionals, just like you, to help them share their insight with the global tech community. You can make a general application, apply for a specific hot topic that we are recruiting an author for, or submit your own idea.

Table of Contents

Preface

With Elixir and Phoenix, you build your application the right way the first way: ready to scale and ready for the increasing demands of real-time web applications.

This book will cover the bare basics of the Phoenix web framework through building a community voting application and, in the course, discuss the new structure changes introduced in Phoenix v1.3. We'll cover the initial challenges of getting started with our app, working with the generators to learn more about the structure of a standard Phoenix app. From there, we'll build our application and work with Channels, Schemas, Contexts, and even dive into more advanced topics such as working with Tasks/Async and GenServers. By the end of this book, we'll have a strong grasp of all the core fundamentals of the Phoenix framework, and we'll have built a full production-ready web application from nothing!

Who this book is for

This is for people who have started messing around with Elixir and have enjoyed what they've seen! We'll take those skills and apply them to building a full web application. If you have some knowledge of Elixir and have experience with other web frameworks in other languages and want to see what it's like to build a web application where concurrency and performance are first-class citizens, you're in the right place!

What this book covers

Chapter 1, *A Brief Introduction to Elixir and Phoenix,* goes over the basics of developing in Elixir and Phoenix and makes the readers understand some of the basic constructs available.

Chapter 2, *Building Controllers, Views, and Templates,* covers working with the fundamentals of every Phoenix application.

Chapter 3, *Storing and Retrieving Vote Data with Ecto Pages,* discusses working with data in our database.

Chapter 4, *Introducing User Accounts and Sessions,* begins to introduce the concept of Users into our system and introduces working with login, logout, and session management.

Chapter 5, *Validations, Errors, and Tying Loose Ends,* explores working on tightening up our application through validation, error-handling, and general tweaks.

Chapter 6, *Live Voting with Phoenix,* starts building out a real-time application with Phoenix and JavaScript.

Chapter 7, *Improving Our Application and Adding Features,* continues to build upon the solid foundation of our application and brings it closer to production-ready.

Chapter 8, *Adding Chat to Your Phoenix Application,* adds even more real-time feature support.

Chapter 9, *Using Presence and ETS in Phoenix,* teaches readers to use Phoenix's new Presence support to keep track of what users are logged in or logged out of our system.

Chapter 10, *Working with Elixir's Concurrency Model,* takes readers through how Elixir handles concurrency implementations at a deeper level.

Chapter 11, *Implementing OAuth in Our Application,* implements a new way for users to sign in with providers such as Twitter and Google.

Chapter 12, *Building an API and Deploying,* outlines finishing reading our application, adding an API to interact with our application, and finally finishing deploying our application to production.

To get the most out of this book

1. Readers should already have at least a basic understanding of the Elixir programming language and some beginner-level knowledge of common web development terms and techniques
2. You will also need an internet-capable programming environment where you can install required software such as Elixir, Phoenix, Node.js, and Postgres

Download the example code files

You can download the example code files for this book from your account at `www.packtpub.com`. If you purchased this book elsewhere, you can visit `www.packtpub.com/support` and register to have the files emailed directly to you.

You can download the code files by following these steps:

1. Log in or register at `www.packtpub.com`.
2. Select the **SUPPORT** tab.
3. Click on **Code Downloads & Errata**.
4. Enter the name of the book in the **Search** box and follow the onscreen instructions.

Once the file is downloaded, please make sure that you unzip or extract the folder using the latest version of:

- WinRAR/7-Zip for Windows
- Zipeg/iZip/UnRarX for Mac
- 7-Zip/PeaZip for Linux

The code bundle for the book is also hosted on GitHub at `https://github.com/PacktPublishing/Phoenix-Web-Development`. In case there's an update to the code, it will be updated on the existing GitHub repository.

We also have other code bundles from our rich catalog of books and videos available at `https://github.com/PacktPublishing/`. Check them out!

Conventions used

There are a number of text conventions used throughout this book.

`CodeInText`: Indicates code words in text, database table names, folder names, filenames, file extensions, pathnames, dummy URLs, user input, and Twitter handles. Here is an example: "Let's use `String.Chars` as an example, where we'll call the `h` helper on `String.Chars` to learn more about the module from its documentation."

A block of code is set as follows:

```
person = %{ name: "Brandon" }
person = %{ name: "Richey" }
```

Any command-line input or output is written as follows:

```
iex(1)> greeting = "Hello There"
"Hello There"
```

Bold: Indicates a new term, an important word, or words that you see onscreen. For example, words in menus or dialog boxes appear in the text like this. Here is an example: "Select **System info** from the **Administration** panel."

 Warnings or important notes appear like this.

 Tips and tricks appear like this.

Get in touch

Feedback from our readers is always welcome.

General feedback: Email feedback@packtpub.com and mention the book title in the subject of your message. If you have questions about any aspect of this book, please email us at questions@packtpub.com.

Errata: Although we have taken every care to ensure the accuracy of our content, mistakes do happen. If you have found a mistake in this book, we would be grateful if you would report this to us. Please visit www.packtpub.com/submit-errata, selecting your book, clicking on the Errata Submission Form link, and entering the details.

Piracy: If you come across any illegal copies of our works in any form on the Internet, we would be grateful if you would provide us with the location address or website name. Please contact us at `copyright@packtpub.com` with a link to the material.

If you are interested in becoming an author: If there is a topic that you have expertise in and you are interested in either writing or contributing to a book, please visit `authors.packtpub.com`.

Reviews

Please leave a review. Once you have read and used this book, why not leave a review on the site that you purchased it from? Potential readers can then see and use your unbiased opinion to make purchase decisions, we at Packt can understand what you think about our products, and our authors can see your feedback on their book. Thank you!

For more information about Packt, please visit `packtpub.com`.

1
A Brief Introduction to Elixir and Phoenix

In this book, we'll walk through the process of building a functional prototype of a social web application that will rely on real-time data updates. If you've ever used any sort of live voting application out there (such as Straw Poll or Twitter Polls), then you're probably pretty comfortable with the idea already. If not, I'll summarize our application so that you know what you're going to be building throughout this book.

Our application will allow users to register for new accounts on our site. From there, they will have the option to create new polls for other users (either while logged in or anonymously) to vote on. We want to make sure that the votes for the polls are recorded and broadcast out to anyone watching the polls in real-time, so we'll take advantage of Phoenix's built-in channel support to provide this.

In addition, our application will allow users to create chat rooms that will be displayed alongside the poll. After they've voted, users will be allowed to chat and discuss the results live as the votes come in. Users will also be allowed to post images, which will be processed, and uploaded to S3.

Users who create polls will be able to decide who is allowed to vote on their polls; for example, either only logged-in users or any user. Users will be able to modify their polls until they go live.

Users who own the polls should be able to participate in real-time discussions with the people voting on and viewing their polls, including anonymous users. Being able to communicate with each other takes advantage of some of the more advanced real-time concepts that are powering Elixir behind-the-scenes and running separately from the main web portion of our Phoenix application. These concepts demonstrate how we can build larger and more performance-intensive applications!

Now, before we really dive into developing this application, we'll need to make sure we understand some of the tools that are going to help us build this application. The assumption is that you're coming into this with an existing understanding of Elixir, but if not, we will briefly cover some core Elixir concepts while also learning about a tool that will be critical for building a great application in Elixir: the IEx shell and the debugger!

To recap, in this chapter we will cover the following topics:

- Basic Elixir concepts
- The interactive Elixir shell, IEx
- Installing Phoenix
- Creating a new Phoenix project with Mix tasks
- An introduction to the Phoenix project structure

Introducing IEx and Elixir

We'll start off by talking a little bit about the Elixir programming language that Phoenix sits atop. The most important thing to note, especially if you're coming from another programming language such as Ruby, Go, PHP, JavaScript, or Java, is that there is one significant difference between Elixir and the rest: Elixir is a functional language. While this doesn't change everything dramatically, it does introduce a few gotchas that we will need to get out of the way.

 If you're already comfortable with Elixir and IEx, feel free to skip this section, as this is intended to be a quick introduction or refresher to the Elixir language and the IEx debugging tool.

Before we dive too far into those gotchas, let's first get acquainted with a tool that is going to make our development process in Elixir much simpler: IEx.

What is IEx?

The good news: Elixir includes a tool called a **Read-Evaluate-Print-Loop** (REPL), which is essentially an Elixir shell. You can think of this as being similar to an irb in Ruby or the node shell in Node.js. It is a very detailed and helpful tool that we'll be referring to quite a bit in our journey of building this full web app! To open REPL up (assuming you have Elixir installed), run the following command:

```
$> iex
```

You should see something similar to the following snippet appear on your screen:

```
$> iex
Erlang/OTP 20 [erts-9.0] [source] [64-bit] [smp:4:4] [ds:4:4:10] [async-
threads:10] [hipe] [kernel-poll:false] [dtrace]
Interactive Elixir (1.5.0) - press Ctrl+C to exit (type h() ENTER for help)
iex(1)>
```

Now we can start messing around with some sample Elixir code! Let's start off with a couple of base scenarios.

Variables in Elixir

Like most other programming languages, Elixir has a concept of variables. Variables are, simply put, just a place to store values or data. Variables in Elixir do not require any sort of type definition or declaration that they're variables, as you might see in languages such as JavaScript. We can declare a new variable as simply as follows:

```
iex(1)> greeting = "Hello There"
"Hello There"
```

 In IEx, the output of any statement entered is always the next line in the shell.

Variables point to memory locations, so when you use them in your code, the values stored in those memory locations are automatically pulled out for you, as shown in the following example:

```
iex(2)> greeting
"Hello There"
```

While variables can be reassigned in Elixir, the actual values are immutable! This brings us to our first gotcha in Elixir: immutability.

Immutability in Elixir

The first thing to note is Elixir's concept of immutability. This means that any variables used will retain their value whenever they're passed along. This is a big difference from languages such as Ruby, where the state of any data you pass on is no longer guaranteed to retain its original value. Objects are a good example of this in Ruby.

To demonstrate this concept a little bit better (don't worry about the syntax yet; we'll get to that!), let's take a look at a code snippet in Javascript, as follows:

```
function upcase_name(p) {
 p.name = p.name.toUpperCase();
}

var person = { name: "Brandon" } // Name here is still 'Brandon'
person // Output is { name: "Brandon" }
upcase_name(person)
person // Oh no! Output is now { name: "BRANDON" }
```

Oh no! We've just introduced a scenario where calling a function is destructive whether we've intended it to be or not! Let's look at a similar block of code in Elixir in the following example:

```
upcase = fn p ->
 Map.put(p, :name, String.upcase(p.name))
end

person = %{ name: "Brandon" } # Name here is still 'Brandon'
upcase.(person)
person # Output for name is still 'Brandon'!
```

This is likely our intended behavior, and it prevents people from doing wacky things while programming, such as writing functions that end in? (typically used to denote a function that answers a question about the arguments in a Boolean). (Sadly, I've seen this more times than I'd care to admit).

Of course, none of these examples are without their own respective gotchas (and honestly, which programming language nowadays doesn't have its fair share?). For example, the following snippet is considered completely legitimate code in Elixir:

```
person = %{ name: "Brandon" }
person = %{ name: "Richey" }
```

But, wait! I hear you cry, *I thought Elixir's variables are immutable!*Well, the answer to that is that they are immutable! Or rather, the memory locations that they point to are; therefore, every time we create a variable we're essentially creating a pointer to a location in memory. In our case, it stores our previous map into some memory location (we'll call it 0 x 01). When we reassign a person, however, we store the value of `%{ name: "Richey" }` into a different memory location (we'll call it 0 x 02). This is what is being passed along to our functions when we pass in the `person` variable; here, we're basically telling Elixir, *Hey, use the value stored in memory location 0 x 01, which is what the variable person is currently pointing at*. This means that we don't have to worry about the value in 0 x 01 being changed as long as it is still in use.

Understanding the different types in Elixir

Elixir has a number of different built-in types that we'll be working within the course of building our applications. They are the following:

- Strings (sometimes referred to as binaries)
- Integers
- Floats
- Lists
- Maps
- Keyword lists
- Tuples
- Modules
- Functions (functions themselves break into two separate types: module functions and anonymous functions)

Let's take a look at the various representations of these types and use some of the tools in IEx to understand more about what we're working with.

Getting more information with the i helper

IEx has a really handy helper function available to us: i. This function comes in two separate arities, i/0 and i/1 (arities, in this case, being the number of arguments that we have to supply to each version of the function). i/0 displays information about the last value output in IEx, whereas i/1 displays information about a particular value or variable. Let's take a look at a few examples:

```
iex(3)> x = 5
5
iex(4)> i
Term
5
Data type
Integer
Reference modules
Integer
Implemented protocols
IEx.Info, Inspect, List.Chars, String.Chars
```

Let's talk about what the preceding example is giving us. First, it tells us the Term, which almost literally means the value itself. Next, we have the Data type, which tells us what Elixir is classifying this particular value as (in the example, it's an integer). Next, it tells us the Reference modules, which is a fancy way of telling us what modules we should use to be able to interact with this particular data type. Finally, it gives us a list of implemented protocols. These are additional modules that provide some sort of behavior that we expect that data type to adhere to if it implements a particular behavior. You can think of them as being similar in concept to interfaces in other programming languages.

Getting more information with the h helper

IEx also provides us with another incredibly helpful built-in function: h. Similar to i, h has two arities available for us to use: h/0, which displays the help page for IEx, and h/1, which displays the help for a particular module. So, while the following example won't work:

```
iex(5)> h 5
Invalid arguments for h helper: 5
```

This following example will:

```
iex(6)> h Integer
Integer

Functions for working with integers.
```

Using i and h effectively will go a long way towards helping us understand more of Elixir as we go along!

Using IEx and helpers to understand types

Going back to our integer example, we saw that there were a few different protocols that integers implement that we can take advantage of, but they may not make immediate sense to us. Let's use String.Chars as an example, where we'll call the h helper on String.Chars to learn more about the module from its documentation:

```
iex(7)> h String.Chars
String.Chars
The String.Chars protocol is responsible for converting a structure to a
binary
(only if applicable).
The only function required to be implemented is to_string/1, which does the
conversion.
The to_string/1 function automatically imported by Kernel invokes this
protocol. String interpolation also invokes to_string/1 in its arguments.
For
example, "foo#{bar}" is the same as "foo" <> to_string(bar).
```

Neat! It's like having a language guide built into our programming environment. It's difficult to stress just how useful this ends up being in practice, especially if you're like me and like doing programming where there's little access to the internet and you need to figure out how to use something like String.Chars. Reading the previous example, we see one particular snippet:

The only function required to be implemented is to_string/1, which does the conversion.

Let's dive into that further, again using h/1, as shown in the following example:

```
iex(8)> h String.Chars.to_string/1
def to_string(term)
Converts term to a string.
```

The preceding snippet tells us a huge amount about that particular module and function. Based on the description and provided function signature, we can infer that the `Integer` module implements a `String.Chars` protocol, which that means it needs to implement a `to_string/1` function that matches the preceding function signature. Therefore, we can further infer that the way to convert an integer to a string is with the following method:

```
iex(9)> Integer.to_string(5)
"5"
```

Et voila! We've followed the chain of using i/1 and h/1 to figure out exactly how to perform an operation on a particular data set, as well as what assumptions we can make about the protocols implemented for that particular data type, and so on. Given this particular revelation, let's start expanding on this a little bit more and take a look at some of the other data types that exist in Elixir and a sample of the other operations that we can perform on them:

```
iex(10)> i 1.0
Term
1.0
Data type
Float
Reference modules
Float
Implemented protocols
IEx.Info, Inspect, List.Chars, String.Chars
```

So, if we wanted to represent something with decimal places, we'd use a float. Types in Elixir are inferred, so you don't have to explicitly specify the type for each variable. In addition, you can store any type in the same variable when you reassign it, so something like the following snippet is a perfectly valid operation (despite being very bad practice):

```
iex(11)> x = 5
5
iex(12)> x = "Hello"
"Hello"
```

If you're coming from a language such as Ruby or JavaScript none of this will be very surprising, but if you're coming from a language that is strongly-typed, this might be a little more off-putting. There are stricter ways to enforce types using tools such as Dialyzer, but in my experience, I've found those to be used relatively rarely. Let's now try using the information helper on a string of data to see what information we get back from IEx. Take a look at the following example:

```
iex(13)> i "Hello There"
Term
"Hello There"
Data type
BitString
Byte size
11
Description
This is a string: a UTF-8 encoded binary. It's printed surrounded by
"double quotes" because all UTF-8 encoded codepoints in it are printable.
Raw representation
<<72, 101, 108, 108, 111, 32, 84, 104, 101, 114, 101>>
Reference modules
String, :binary
Implemented protocols
IEx.Info, Collectable, Inspect, List.Chars, String.Chars
```

Here, we see that we have a standard string and that there are a lot of the same implemented protocols that we saw on floats and integers as well. We see the same few protocols (as well as a new one, `Collectable`). Now, if we want to see the operations provided by one of the reference modules (string in our case), IEx provides another awesome way to get that information out. In our IEx console, we can simply type in `String.` (notice the period!) and then hit *Tab* on our keyboard, for example:

```
iex(14)> String.
Break                    Casing              Chars
Normalizer               Tokenizer           Unicode
at/2                     capitalize/1        chunk/2
codepoints/1             contains?/2         downcase/1
duplicate/2              ends_with?/2        equivalent?/2
first/1                  graphemes/1         jaro_distance/2
last/1                   length/1            match?/2
myers_difference/2       next_codepoint/1    next_grapheme/1
next_grapheme_size/1     normalize/2         pad_leading/2
pad_leading/3            pad_trailing/2      pad_trailing/3
```

```
printable?/1           printable?/2           replace/3
replace/4              replace_leading/3      replace_prefix/3
replace_suffix/3       replace_trailing/3     reverse/1
slice/2                slice/3                split/1
split/2                split/3                split_at/2
splitter/2             splitter/3             starts_with?/2
to_atom/1              to_charlist/1          to_existing_atom/1
to_float/1             to_integer/1           to_integer/2
trim/1                 trim/2                 trim_leading/1
trim_leading/2         trim_trailing/1        trim_trailing/2
upcase/1               valid?/1
```

Let's use `h/1` again to get a little more information about a particular string and the operations we can perform on it, as shown in the following snippet:

```
iex(15)> h String.replace/4
def replace(subject, pattern, replacement, options \\ [])
Returns a new string created by replacing occurrences of pattern in subject
with replacement.
The pattern may be a string or a regular expression.
By default it replaces all occurrences but this behaviour can be controlled
through the :global option; see the "Options" section below.

## Options
• :global — (boolean) if true, all occurrences of pattern are replaced with
replacement, otherwise only the first occurrence is replaced. Defaults to
true
• :insert_replaced — (integer or list of integers) specifies the position
where to insert the replaced part inside the replacement. If any position
given in the :insert_replaced option is larger than the replacement string,
or is negative, an ArgumentError is raised.

# ...
```

That's a lot of information, yes, but it's also all incredibly useful. Let's start with a very simple operation and replace the e in our greeting variable to an x. We see that the signature for `String.replace/4` is `replace(subject, pattern, replacement, options \\ [])`. Given that, let's quickly create a greeting variable and change every e to an x:

```
iex(1)> greeting = "Hello"
iex(2)> String.replace(greeting, "e" ,"x", global: true)
"Hxllo"
```

Your objects have no power here

Another thing that might be a little more difficult to contend with, especially if you're coming from a language where object-oriented programming is treated as a first-class citizen, is that objects are not a thing you can use in Elixir to organize your code or group data and functionality together. Again, let's use JavaScript as an example, as follows:

```
var greeting = "Hello There"
greeting.toUpperCase() # Convert a string to upper case by calling a
function on the "greeting" string object
# End result: "HELLO THERE"
```

Here, you'll instead want to get used to the concept of using modules and functions to accomplish the same things. You can think of modules as a collection of related functions that operate on particular sets or types of data, or are otherwise grouped together by some sort of common element. So, the preceding block of code would instead be written as the following in Elixir:

```
greeting = "Hello There"
String.upcase(greeting) # Results in the same "HELLO THERE" message as the
Javascript example
```

This is going to be a very common pattern that you should familiarize yourself, as you will frequently see function called as [Module Name].[Function Name]([Arguments]). Try to shy away from calling functions on objects and data and instead get used to calling functions with the module name.

> You're not required to do this; there are actually ways to shorten this even further through the use of the **alias** and **import** statements!

Introduction to Phoenix

Phoenix is a web framework that sits on top of the Elixir programming language, much in the same way that Rails sits atop Ruby or Express sits atop Node and JavaScript. There are a few areas where Phoenix shares a lot of the same core ideas and beliefs of other frameworks and areas where Phoenix differs pretty heavily.

Phoenix is very much designed to be a standard Elixir application and thus abides by the same rules and the same principles, but also encompasses all of the same things that make Elixir so great to work with! In my mind, the first and biggest thing that Phoenix gets via Elixir is first-class and dead-simple concurrency support. Writing code that performs and scales well on multiple core machines (that is, basically every single computer out there nowadays) is a breeze, and when you're just starting out building your Phoenix application, you won't even have to think about it. It isn't until you start diving more heavily into the more advanced topics, such as OTP, GenServers, and Async Tasks, where you really need to start thinking deeply about your concurrency models and how everything fits together.

Phoenix also benefits very heavily from being based on a functional immutable language. Large codebases remain very simple to reason with, and the fear of introducing significant breaking changes because of a mutation deeply-nested in your code is now a thing of the past! If you're coming from a language where you've built a complex application and a simple change ends up breaking everything, this should be a breath of fresh air to you. I referenced this in one of my earlier examples, but when you actually see it in action and understand why it works the way it does, trust me, you won't want to go back to the old ways of building applications!

Before we do anything else, let's talk briefly about how to actually install Phoenix so that you can get started on working with it as soon as possible. The best (and most up-to-date) instructions can be found on the Phoenix framework website (`https://phoenixframework. org`), but just in case, here you are. Please note that the following instructions assume you already have Elixir installed.

Installing Phoenix 1.3

For best results, you'll want to make sure you have the most recent version of Hex installed on your local machine. Again, the assumption here is that you already have Elixir installed on your computer:

```
$ mix local.hex
Found existing entry: /Users/brandon.richey/.mix/archives/hex-0.16.1
Are you sure you want to replace it with
"https://repo.hex.pm/installs/1.5.0/hex-0.17.1.ez"? [Yn] y
* creating /Users/brandon.richey/.mix/archives/hex-0.17.1
```

Now we'll move on to installing Phoenix itself. Installing Phoenix is a little bit different from just installing something via a `hex` package on an existing Elixir project. You'll want to use Phoenix's project generators to get your project up and running, as there is a lot of additional setups required compared to a small, standard Elixir project. This is why you need to go through a separate process to install Phoenix.

To install the Phoenix framework and get access to the Mix tasks needed to create new Phoenix projects, you'll want to run the following code:

```
$ mix archive.install
https://github.com/phoenixframework/archives/raw/master/phx_new.ez
* creating /Users/brandon.richey/.mix/archives/phx_new
```

Creating a new Phoenix project

Now that we have something in place to help us understand Elixir and Phoenix and we've installed everything necessary, we can start to discuss how to actually begin implementing our first project in Phoenix. To get started on a project and generate the Phoenix application skeleton we'll need to start developing, we'll run a special command using the installed Mix application that came with Elixir. We also added the Phoenix Hex archive to our local Hex installation, so we should have access to a few new Phoenix-specific Mix tasks, such as `mix phx.new`!

Running the Phoenix Mix Task

Phoenix has gone through a few iterations of general architecture and project structures, but as of version 1.3, they've stuck on a design that is incredibly elegant and easy to use. Instead of the sometimes clumsy system they previously had, where you had your models, your controllers, your views, and your templates and nothing in between, you can now design things around controllers, views, templates, contexts, and schemas. Before we start diving into what those differences are and why they're so important, let's talk about the general project structure of a Phoenix application.

The first major thing is that Phoenix applications are considered first-class Elixir projects, so as such follow the same major rules. Generally, Elixir projects should have a test directory and a `lib` directory. Your test directory is where any new tests you write and any tests you run will live out of `lib`, on the other hand, is where the actual code for any actual work should go. Let's explore how these directories will get filled out by creating a small sample throwaway Phoenix application.

To create a new Phoenix application, we'll start off by running the `mix task phx.new`:

```
$ mix phx.new sampler
* creating sampler/config/config.exs
* creating sampler/config/dev.exs
* creating sampler/config/prod.exs
* creating sampler/config/prod.secret.exs
* creating sampler/config/test.exs
* creating sampler/lib/sampler/application.ex
* creating sampler/lib/sampler.ex
* creating sampler/lib/sampler_web/channels/user_socket.ex
* creating sampler/lib/sampler_web/views/error_helpers.ex
* creating sampler/lib/sampler_web/views/error_view.ex
* creating sampler/lib/sampler_web/endpoint.ex
* creating sampler/lib/sampler_web/router.ex
* creating sampler/lib/sampler_web.ex
* creating sampler/mix.exs
* creating sampler/README.md
* creating sampler/test/support/channel_case.ex
* creating sampler/test/support/conn_case.ex
* creating sampler/test/test_helper.exs
* creating sampler/test/sampler_web/views/error_view_test.exs
* creating sampler/lib/sampler_web/gettext.ex
* creating sampler/priv/gettext/en/LC_MESSAGES/errors.po
* creating sampler/priv/gettext/errors.pot
* creating sampler/lib/sampler/repo.ex
* creating sampler/priv/repo/seeds.exs
* creating sampler/test/support/data_case.ex
* creating sampler/lib/sampler_web/controllers/page_controller.ex
* creating sampler/lib/sampler_web/templates/layout/app.html.eex
* creating sampler/lib/sampler_web/templates/page/index.html.eex
* creating sampler/lib/sampler_web/views/layout_view.ex
* creating sampler/lib/sampler_web/views/page_view.ex
* creating sampler/test/sampler_web/controllers/page_controller_test.exs
* creating sampler/test/sampler_web/views/layout_view_test.exs
* creating sampler/test/sampler_web/views/page_view_test.exs
* creating sampler/.gitignore
```

```
* creating sampler/assets/brunch-config.js
* creating sampler/assets/css/app.css
* creating sampler/assets/css/phoenix.css
* creating sampler/assets/js/app.js
* creating sampler/assets/js/socket.js
* creating sampler/assets/package.json
* creating sampler/assets/static/robots.txt
* creating sampler/assets/static/images/phoenix.png
* creating sampler/assets/static/favicon.ico

Fetch and install dependencies? [Yn]
```

We'll now be asked if we want to fetch and install dependencies. If we say yes, a few things will happen:

1. First off, all of the standard Elixir dependencies that exist for all Phoenix applications will be downloaded from hex and compiled.
2. Next, all of the Node/JavaScript dependencies that Phoenix applications depend on (assuming you did not use the --no-brunch flag when you created your new Phoenix application) will be downloaded from npm and compiled.
3. Assets will be built and set up appropriately via Brunch.

If we say yes, we should see something akin to the following output:

```
* running mix deps.get
* running mix deps.compile
* running cd assets npm instal node node_modules/brunch/bin/brunch build

We are all set! Go into your application by running:

    $ cd sampler

Then configure your database in config/dev.exs and run:

    $ mix ecto.create

Start your Phoenix app with:

    $ mix phx.server

You can also run your app inside IEx (Interactive Elixir) as:

    $ iex -S mix phx.server
```

When everything is done, we can enter our new project directory, create our database, and start up our Phoenix server!

```
$ cd sampler && mix ecto.create
Compiling 13 files (.ex)
Generated sampler app
The database for Sampler.Repo has been created
```

To create a database, you will need to have a username and password set up for your database server of choice that has the correct permissions or roles assigned that allow you to create databases. If you are working with a role or user that does not have that permission, you can also create the database manually and instead run `mix ecto.reset`.

Running the Phoenix server for the first time

There are two ways to start up the Phoenix server, and now that the application is set up and the database is there to support our application, we can move on to actually running it! The two different ways to run your application are either via Mix `phx.server` or in the IEx console. In the context of your application requiring debugging support via IEx, you need -S Mix `phx.server`. As a general rule, I only run my application in a local development environment through IEx. This allows you to get interactive debugging via `IEx.pry`, as well as the ability to perform things like Ecto queries or test calling public functions in modules.

Remember when we talked about the interactive help functions that are built-in to Elixir and can be accessed via IEx? Well, you can do the same thing with Phoenix functions, too! For example, let's say we want to know a little more information about how we send out JSON content directly from a controller, as shown in the following example:

```
iex(4)> h Phoenix.Controller.json

  def json(conn, data)

Sends JSON response.

It uses the configured :format_encoders under the :phoenix application for
:json to pick up the encoder module.

## Examples

  iex> json conn, %{id: 123}
```

Okay, so we now have our application and we have things up and running. If we visit our browser window, we should see the Phoenix startup page, as follows:

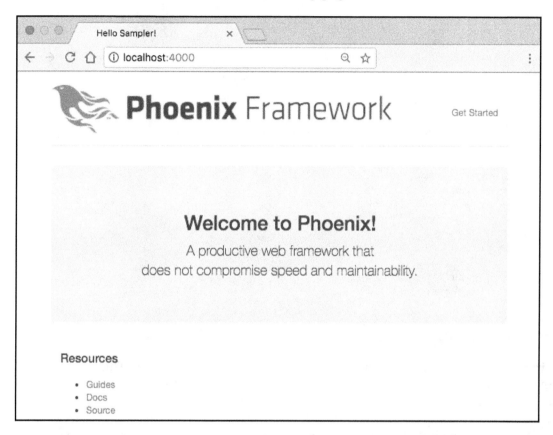

Phoenix's default application structure

As mentioned previously, Phoenix is itself a full-featured Elixir application, and as a result, tends to follow a lot of the same conventions and rules that other Elixir applications follow. We've briefly touched on the topic previously, but now it's time to get into it and take a look at how Phoenix projects are structured so that we can understand how to build on top of Phoenix. The starting directory structure looks a little something like the following:

```
├── README.md
├── assets
│   ├── brunch-config.js
│   ├── css
```

```
|       ├──── js
|       ├──── package.json
|       ├──── static
|       └──── vendor
├──── config
|       ├──── config.exs
|       ├──── dev.exs
|       ├──── prod.exs
|       ├──── prod.secret.exs
|       └──── test.exs
├──── lib
|       ├──── testapp
|       ├──── testapp.ex
|       ├──── testapp_web
|       └──── testapp_web.ex
├──── mix.exs
├──── priv
|       ├──── gettext
|       └──── repo
└──── test
        ├──── support
        ├──── test_helper.exs
        └──── testapp_web
```

Configuration files

First, we have a config directory in the root of our Phoenix application. This is where all of the application and web service configuration files will live. We typically have the config.exs, dev.exs, test.exs, prod.secret.exs, and prod.exs files by default with our Phoenix application. The first file, config.exs, is a file that stores generic configuration details that should be the same across all run-time environments for your application, whether they're testing, development, or production environments. The next few (dev.exs, test.exs, and prod.exs) are your environment-specific configuration files. Finally, we have our prod.secret.exs, which is auto-generated by Phoenix but not checked into source control by default. This file should never be checked into the source control for your application, as this is where sensitive information should live, such as API keys, secret keys, and database passwords. If this is ever checked into source control then it would be in the history of your application, which would be a pretty significant security concern for anyone having to maintain your Phoenix application!

Assets files

Next, we have our assets directory. This is where all of the front-end assets (images, CSS, JavaScript, and so on) live, as well as Brunch and NPM. (Your `node_modules` directory, for example, is found here.) The idea here is that by divorcing your front-end code and files from the rest of the work that Phoenix needs to do, Phoenix's developers can instead focus on making Phoenix great and leave the front-end and asset compilation problems to better solutions such as Brunch or Webpack, as well make asset compilation tool choices separately from those that created the framework. Even though Phoenix comes with Brunch by default, it's still straightforward to replace it with Webpack if that's more suited to your speed.

Private files

There is also a `priv` directory, which is a little trickier to explain. `Priv` contains a lot of the helper and application setup code that is required. This contains your Repo's seeds file and migrations that need to be run (which we'll cover later), translations to your application via `gettext`, and finally, your static asset files (which have been `built/compiled/transpiled/etc` from your assets directory).

Tests

Your test directory contains all of the ExUnit tests for your application, which itself is broken up into two starting directories: `(application name)_web` and `support` (plus a `test_helper` Elixir script that contains some initialization code). `(app)_web` is used to contain the web application tests that cover controllers, contexts, views, templates, and so on, so you can think of this as the container for all of your Phoenix application tests. Support is instead used to bolster the functionality of your tests and make it easier to write new tests and share common logic or helpers. For the most part, we won't be modifying the code inside here very often. Most of the changes that we're going to make will instead be in the `test/(app)_web` directory and sub-directories.

Other directories

We also have a few miscellaneous directories that you won't really be interacting with at all. `_build` and `deps`, for example, contain various build artifacts and Elixir application dependencies (these won't actually get created until you build your application).

The most important directory: lib

Now we'll move on to the real meat of our Phoenix application: `lib`. Lib is where our application lives. By default, our Phoenix application is broken into two separate ideas. Using the application name of Sampler as an example, we will see two directories: `lib/sampler` and `lib/sampler_web`. The idea behind this is that every web application in Phoenix has at least two separate applications that work together to get the job done. The first is divorced from the idea of anything web-related, so there are no controllers or templates, JSON, or anything similar. One of the most common patterns that you'll see here is all of your database-specific Ecto logic through contexts and schemas.

A context is a collection or boundary of domain-specific logic. For example, if you have users and organizations in your project, you may have a unifying context to those separate schemas called something like **Accounts**.

A Schema, on the other hand, is the one-to-one mapping of a database table to an application concept. Schemas need to be separated from the functionality of your code and used strictly to describe the shape of the data; this keeps your code pure from side-effects and helps make your code significantly easier to test in the long run.

Finally, we have `lib/sampler_web`. This is where all of the Phoenix-specific work gets done, so everything related to controller logic, templates, or views goes here in the appropriate sub-directory. Channel logic also falls underneath this particular design pattern. This is also where the `endpoint.ex` file lives, which defines how Plug constructs the Phoenix response to `browser/API consumer/etc`. It also determines how requests are parsed and how information is passed along to the Phoenix router.

Speaking of the router, our Phoenix `router.ex` file also lives here (again, because this is Phoenix-specific logic rather than the overarching common application functionality). This is where we will set up all of the rules to describe how to communicate between the browser and Phoenix's controllers.

A note about how data flows in Phoenix

If you're coming from the world of another web framework you might already be familiar with languages such as routers, controllers, templates, and views, but if you're not, let's talk a little bit about what those are, what they mean, and how the data flows in a Phoenix request all the way back out to the browser response. If you're already familiar with these topics, feel free to skip ahead to the next chapter.

When a request is received to a Phoenix application, the first thing that happens is that it gets handled by the endpoint. The endpoint's job is to take a look at the requests and to determine if there are any special functions or handlers that need to deal with the request. The request will flow through a series of plugs. A plug is a set of functionalities that takes in the connection data structure and performs a series of transformations and queries against the incoming request (for example, determining if the originator of the request is an approved server or making sure that the content types make sense). A plug must always take in a connection data structure (typically referred to as conn) and return out a conn, either modified or not. It can also additionally take in a set of options to determine how to modify the conn.

From there, the conn gets moved into the router via the endpoint. The router figures out where the information is coming from and where it is trying to get to. This is done via a combination of the URL hit, the content type, and so on. From here, if a valid route is found, the router will pass the conn on to the controller. A controller's job in a Phoenix application is to provide a means of determining what further transformations need to occur on the conn (which will eventually become our response from the server), as well as doing additional application logic such as running database queries, putting together templates, setting HTTP status codes, and much more. We can think of this as the glue for the different parts of our application that will help us construct our server's response.

The controllers then tell the view how to put together the data in the response and pass along the information it needs to determine the overall shape and feel of the response. It might be a JSON data structure if we're working with an API, or it may be a particular HTML template that we're sending back to the user with further information that is then sent along to the template. We can think of it as if the router answers where the controller answers what, and the view answers how. If we're not working with something simple, such as a JSON API, then there is an additional step that we have to work through called the **template**. The template helps Phoenix understand how, given a connection object, to build a response and what response to build, and a set of data to pass along to the consumer to build the logic that provides the nice look and feel we'd expect of a modern web app sending back HTML with layouts, partial pieces of content, and an overall structure.

Summary

We should now have a fine working knowledge of a standard Phoenix application. We should now understand how the application's structure, what the different pieces of the Phoenix application are, and how they're all used in conjunction to send something back to the browser when we, for example, send a request to `http://localhost:4000/`.

In the following chapters, we'll dive more into each of the functional areas of a Phoenix application and understand them at an even deeper level than this. Given that we have a strong foundation, we now need to move on to the real way to learn Phoenix: by building a new Phoenix application from start to finish!

Building Controllers, Views, and Templates

2

This chapter is focused on the building blocks of any Phoenix application. By understanding what controllers, views, and templates are (and how they interact), it becomes much easier to build out our web application. We'll tackle this through the perspective of building the first major component of our Live Voting application, and by writing tests to cover the new functionality introduced.

The reader will become proficient in a lot of the basic tenets of using controllers, views, and templates. In addition, the reader will learn how the three pieces fit together via functional composition. Finally, they'll begin diving into writing their first tests covering controllers and views to start enforcing a strong and real-world **systems development life cycle (SDLC)**. This will be from the perspective of building an actual application, so we'll start laying the framework for our voting app.

We've stepped through the very basics of creating a sample application and learned a little bit about the base structure of Elixir and how to use a few of the helper tools such as IEx, and also talked about what the structure of a Phoenix application will be, but now we actually need to start diving into the code itself and start understanding each of the pieces of our application. In my mind, the controllers are one of the most important pieces of a Phoenix application, as they provide that all-important bridge between what your database holds, what your schemas interpret, and what the user actually sees on their screen (whether it's via API calls or browser requests).

Understanding the flow of Phoenix connections

When the request comes in, the router takes a look at the incoming connection (referred to in the future as the conn) and determines where this request needs to get routed to. It could be something that needs to be handled in a way appropriate to the browser, a way appropriate for an API to handle, or it could also just plain and simply be a **404** error that needs to get served out (depending on what the router says exists for that particular web application).

From there, the connection is passed along through the router and into a pipeline of plugs. Plugs are constructs that can be reduced down to functions that take in the connection structure and optionally some options, and then apply some form of transformation (if appropriate) and return out a modified connection structure. The beauty of this idea is in its simplicity; each plug our connection passes through is just a function at the end of the day, and all it is doing is making modifications to the connection if appropriate, or just returning out the connection it was passed in originally. Plugs are a concept that sometimes seems extremely complicated when you're first learning Phoenix, but if you can reduce them down to their core concept (and as a result, see what they really are without any abstractions), it becomes very simple to reason about what they are, when to use them, and how to build new ones to make your own development life simpler. We can think about the flow of data with the following diagram:

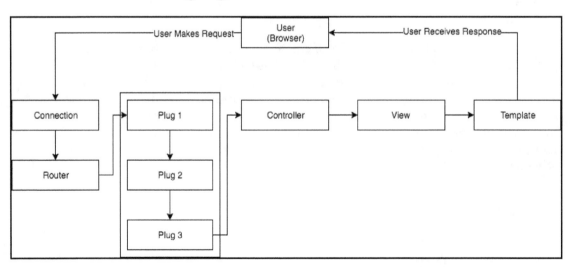

Now that we have our connection, and that connection has passed through our plug pipeline, the connection will flow into our controller (as shown preceding). The controller's job is to take in the connection, put together any data that is required from any source and any transformations that need to apply before we can serialize the data, and then determine which view and template everything should be flowing into. A lot of the calls to our Contexts and miscellaneous code/libraries will be happening here or get called from here!

Next, the data flows into our view, which is responsible for serializing the data in such a way that either the templates or an API context can use it. This could be turning the sets of data into JSON for an API or it could be creating variables accessible to the templates.

Finally, if we're working with something closer to a browser workflow, the data will flow into our templates, where we will be able to access the variables to display through our .eex templates (more on this later)! This is kind of the end result of our request workflow, and the results of this final piece of work are what gets sent back to the browser. We'll be doing a good bit of work here since our application will largely be a browser-based application and not an API.

Okay, so now we understand the flow of a request that is going to come into Phoenix, and we can start to reason about how we're going to start building things!

Creating our Social Voting project

What we haven't done yet is actually create our Phoenix project, so let's do that! I'm going to call this application "Vocial" ("Social Voting" because I am incredibly creative)! We'll start off by running our mix task to create a Phoenix application:

```
$ mix phx.new vocial
* creating vocial/config/config.exs
* creating vocial/config/dev.exs
* creating vocial/config/prod.exs
* creating vocial/config/prod.secret.exs
* creating vocial/config/test.exs
* creating vocial/lib/vocial/application.ex
* creating vocial/lib/vocial.ex
* creating vocial/lib/vocial_web/channels/user_socket.ex
* creating vocial/lib/vocial_web/views/error_helpers.ex
* creating vocial/lib/vocial_web/views/error_view.ex
* creating vocial/lib/vocial_web/endpoint.ex
* creating vocial/lib/vocial_web/router.ex
* creating vocial/lib/vocial_web.ex
* creating vocial/mix.exs
* creating vocial/README.md
```

```
* creating vocial/test/support/channel_case.ex
* creating vocial/test/support/conn_case.ex
* creating vocial/test/test_helper.exs
* creating vocial/test/vocial_web/views/error_view_test.exs
* creating vocial/lib/vocial_web/gettext.ex
* creating vocial/priv/gettext/en/LC_MESSAGES/errors.po
* creating vocial/priv/gettext/errors.pot
* creating vocial/lib/vocial/repo.ex
* creating vocial/priv/repo/seeds.exs
* creating vocial/test/support/data_case.ex
* creating vocial/lib/vocial_web/controllers/page_controller.ex
* creating vocial/lib/vocial_web/templates/layout/app.html.eex
* creating vocial/lib/vocial_web/templates/page/index.html.eex
* creating vocial/lib/vocial_web/views/layout_view.ex
* creating vocial/lib/vocial_web/views/page_view.ex
* creating vocial/test/vocial_web/controllers/page_controller_test.exs
* creating vocial/test/vocial_web/views/layout_view_test.exs
* creating vocial/test/vocial_web/views/page_view_test.exs
* creating vocial/.gitignore
* creating vocial/assets/brunch-config.js
* creating vocial/assets/css/app.css
* creating vocial/assets/css/phoenix.css
* creating vocial/assets/js/app.js
* creating vocial/assets/js/socket.js
* creating vocial/assets/package.json
* creating vocial/assets/static/robots.txt
* creating vocial/assets/static/images/phoenix.png
* creating vocial/assets/static/favicon.ico

Fetch and install dependencies? [Yn] y
* running mix deps.get
* running mix deps.compile
* running cd assets && npm install && node node_modules/brunch/bin/brunch
build
```

We are all set! Go into your application by running:

```
$ cd vocial
```

Then configure your database in `config/dev.exs` and run:

```
$ mix ecto.create
```

Start your Phoenix app with:

```
$ mix phx.server
```

You can also run your app inside IEx (Interactive Elixir) as:

```
$ iex -S mix phx.server
```

We want to answer Y to the question about fetching and installing dependencies since we will be building the HTML/JS/CSS components required for our application. This gives us a good baseline for our application. We'll want to follow the instructions to create our database and then start up our server just to make sure everything is good and has been created as expected:

```
$ cd vocial
$ mix ecto.create
Compiling 13 files (.ex)
Generated vocial app
The database for Vocial.Repo has been created

$ iex -S mix phx.server
Erlang/OTP 20 [erts-9.0] [source] [64-bit] [smp:8:8] [ds:8:8:10] [async-
threads:10] [hipe] [kernel-poll:false] [dtrace]

[info] Running VocialWeb.Endpoint with Cowboy using http://0.0.0.0:4000
Interactive Elixir (1.5.1) - press Ctrl+C to exit (type h() ENTER for help)
iex(1)> 13:27:13 - info: compiled 6 files into 2 files, copied 3 in 3.4 sec
```

Assuming all went well, we should see the default Phoenix start page (the same one that we saw in Chapter 1, *A brief Introduction to Elixir and Phoenix*). Now, one option we have for putting a lot of this together is to run Phoenix's generators to create our controllers, views, templates, and contexts/schemas all automatically for us. Generally speaking, you should avoid using these for anything other than learning purposes, since they tend to come with a lot of boilerplate code and functionality that you're probably not going to need in the long run! Sometimes they can be nice for *I need a website 30 minutes ago* situations or base prototyping, but again, you tend to end up with a lot of extra cruft in your project that you may not need or use, but will have open and available regardless of your intentions! This is also the sort of thing that can lead to unintended security vulnerabilities down the road!

Creating a poll controller

If we want to start building out our web application, we'll need to start with some of the base structures that are used to receive our incoming connection, make decisions, pull in new data, and reformat/structure out the response to the user. We'll start with the most fundamental of these: the controllers. Our controllers act as the glue between our templates, our database, and the incoming/outgoing connections; they put everything together in a way that the end user's browser or client can understand. To understand how to effectively use controllers, however, we'll need to ensure we understand how controllers are structured and how best to use them!

Understanding the controller's structure

We have a lot of work that we need to do to be able to start putting this all together and it would be very easy to get lost in the weeds, so we're going to focus down a little bit on the work that we need to do and start very small. In fact, we're not even going to build out our database schema or anything yet; instead, we'll prototype with simple data structures and, over time, build on top of those to turn them into something more usable and production-ready! We'll start by creating a brand new file in our project.

If you take a look at the /lib/vocial_web/ controllers you'll see that we start off with a page_controller.ex file first. This is the default controller that gets created for every Phoenix project created. While there is not anything significantly important or helpful in this file, it is a good basis to use to learn a controller's structure and requirements, so let's open it up and take a look:

```
defmodule VocialWeb.PageController do
  use VocialWeb, :controller

  def index(conn, _params) do
    render conn, "index.html"
  end
end
```

Remember that at the end of the day, Phoenix applications are still just Elixir applications and subject to a lot of the same design patterns and rules that govern any other Elixir application. Following in that same pattern, we see that our controllers start off with a module declaration. In this case, we see that we're namespacing our PageController module inside VocialWeb.

Remember that when creating a new Phoenix application in v1.3, we essentially have two separate applications that work together to service requests; [ApplicationName] and [ApplicationNameWeb]. ApplicationName in our case would be Vocial and thus our web side of the application would be VocialWeb! Based on that, we can see that what we're really doing here is declaring a module called PageController that lives under our VocialWeb namespace.

Next, we see our use statement. This is a Phoenix-specific macro that provides a bit of convenience to avoid us having to type in the bunch of extra imports and aliases that we need for pretty much every controller we'll write. It's important to understand exactly what this statement does, though, so we're going to look for the declaration of our VocialWeb module, which we can find at /lib/vocial_web.ex. This will also be our first little introduction to Elixir metaprogramming, which, while we won't be spending a huge amount of time learning about it, will still be worth stepping through, as it will help us understand the general flow and structure of our Phoenix application. So, if we open up /lib/vocial_web.ex, we'll see our defmodule VocialWeb do statement at the top. Next, if we look for the controller function, we'll see the following block of code:

```
def controller do
  quote do
    use Phoenix.Controller, namespace: VocialWeb
    import Plug.Conn
    import VocialWeb.Router.Helpers
    import VocialWeb.Gettext
  end
end
```

So, we see that any time we type in use VocialWeb, : controller we'll get whatever the Phoenix.Controller macro provides (which is quite a bit of functionality), as well as imports for Plug.Conn (which is what helps our controller interact with plugs and connections), VocialWeb.Router.Helpers (which gives us the code to be able to reference URLs and paths for anything defined in our routers through specially-named helpers), and VocialWeb.Gettext, which provides out-of-the-box support for internationalization. But how do we get from that, using the VocialWeb: controller statement, to the code you seen before?

If you scroll to the very bottom of the file, you'll see the following chunk of code:

```
@doc """
When used, dispatch to the appropriate controller/view/etc.
"""
defmacro __using__(which) when is_atom(which) do
  apply(__MODULE__, which, [])
end
```

So, we define a macro as part of the `VocialWeb` module, this one being a special internal macro called `__using__` that takes in a single atom as its only argument. That macro then invokes the `apply` function, which takes in a module as its first argument, the `atom` argument, and then passes in a blank array (always). Also, note the guard clause on that function, so this will only be invoked when passing in an atom; anything else will result in an error. (Specifically, an error message about no function clause matching in `VocialWeb.__using__/1`. If you want to try this experiment yourself, open up `page_controller.ex` and change the *use* statement at the top's argument from `:controller` to *controller* and then reload your browser window. You'll see the error message right up at the top.) `apply` is a special Elixir built-in function that takes in a module and an atom that corresponds with the function name it will attempt to evaluate. The final argument is a list of arguments to pass along to the function that gets evaluated. We also see that the module that is referenced is `__MODULE__`, which is just a fancy Elixir way of saying *the current module that I'm in*. Based on that, we can see that what happens is when we say use `VocialWeb`, `:controller`, the macro evaluates that as "call the function controller in the current module with no arguments passed to it." This then calls our controller function (which as we can see takes no arguments) in the `VocialWeb` module, and through the quote function, evaluates the code inside that function and injects it into our controller. To verify this, you could replace that use `VocialWeb`, `:controller` line with the following lines:

```
use Phoenix.Controller, namespace: VocialWeb
  import Plug.Conn
  import VocialWeb.Router.Helpers
  import VocialWeb.Gettext
```

Reload your browser! You'll notice that instead of getting an error message like the last experiment, this time we see the exact same thing as if the use statement were still at the top of our controller!

Next, in our `PageController`, we see a function called index that takes a conn argument as the first argument and an underlined `params` as the second argument. Remember that in Elixir, we denote any arguments in functions where we don't actually care what the value is, just that the arity matches with an underline. So what we're saying here is, "I care about the conn argument, but not the `params` argument" (which makes sense in this context; we're not watching for any special query parameters or anything, so we'll throw those right out). We always have to care about the conn argument, however, since our rule is that to send back something to the browser, we have to accept and return out a connection structure.

Finally, our function makes a final call to render, passing in the connection and passing in a name of a template to render out. By default, it is assumed that the view that the controller will be calling out to has a similar name.

Side note: In your IEx terminal session, you can actually type in the following to access some documentation about this function. This function specifically lives in Phoenix.Controller, so we can learn more about the function by typing in h `Phoenix.Controller.render` in our IEx terminal!

So in our case, our controller is named `PageController` so the assumption is that our view is `PageView`. If we open up `lib/vocial_web/views/page_view.ex`, we should see the following:

```
defmodule VocialWeb.PageView do
  use VocialWeb, :view
end
```

Now, you may be concerned that there is nothing here; certainly nothing corresponding to our `index.html` argument for our render function. This is one of the few implicit vs. explicit things in Phoenix; any calls to `*.html` will instead look for that matching template in the appropriate template directory and do not require any special functions inside of our view. This means our controller makes the render call for `index.html`, which passes through the view as it has nothing special to do. Whatever is passed in, and the connection, are passed to `lib/vocial_web/templates/page/index.html.eex` (`/templates/(controller name)/(file.html).eex` generally being the accepted patterns for these). If you open up that file you'll see the same HTML that is getting displayed when you open up the root `route` / in your browser!

Building the poll controller

Okay, so now that we're rocking a very thorough understanding of the connection flow and how Phoenix is handling each step along the way, let's start building our own controllers, views, routes, and templates to display something when a user goes to /polls in the browser. We'll start off by creating a new file, lib/vocial_web/controllers/poll_controller.ex. Much like our page controller, we're going to give this file a really basic structure:

```
defmodule VocialWeb.PollController do
  use VocialWeb, :controller

  def index(conn, _params) do
    render conn, "index.html"
  end
end
```

Next, remember that every controller and function inside of a controller should have corresponding views and templates. Let's create lib/vocial_web/views/poll_view.ex and give it a base structure as well:

```
defmodule VocialWeb.PollView do
  use VocialWeb, :view
end
```

And finally, let's create our template directory (lib/vocial_web/templates/poll) and create an index.html.eex file inside of that directory:

```
<h2>Poll!</h2>
```

That should be enough for us to visit `http://localhost:4000/polls`, right?:

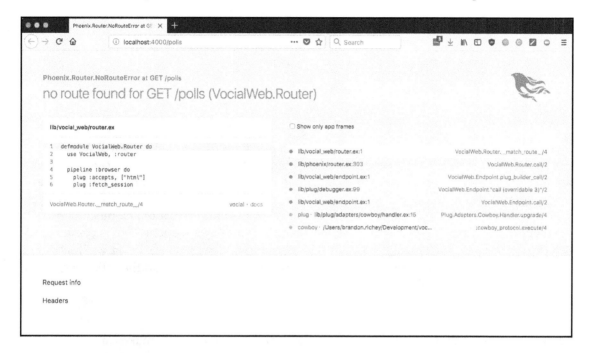

Oh no! We're still missing a critical element to our `/polls` response to the browser: the routes! Every time you create a new controller and action, these should be accompanied by route updates (assuming you want to make those public, anyway). Let's open up `lib/vocial_web/router.ex`:

```
defmodule VocialWeb.Router do
  use VocialWeb, :router

  pipeline :browser do
    plug :accepts, ["html"]
    plug :fetch_session
    plug :fetch_flash
    plug :protect_from_forgery
    plug :put_secure_browser_headers
  end

  pipeline :api do
    plug :accepts, ["json"]
  end

  scope "/", VocialWeb do
```

```
    pipe_through :browser # Use the default browser stack

    get "/", PageController, :index
  end

  # Other scopes may use custom stacks.
  # scope "/api", VocialWeb do
  #   pipe_through :api
  # end
end
```

So here, we can see the definitions of our various pipelines (one for any requests coming through the browser and one for any requests coming from the API). As you can see, these are all just plug statements where the connection passes through each step of the pipeline, top to bottom. Then, we see the scope statement. You can think of this as the namespace for your variables. Anything accessible at the top level, for example, would just be in the root (/) namespace or path. You can also see an example of an /api scope, which is commented out (this is fine; we don't have a need for API pipelines and routes yet). What we'll want to do here to make the Poll index function accessible to the browser is add the following line to our root scope:

```
    get "/polls", PollController, :index
```

What we're saying in the preceding code is that any time the browser makes an HTTP GET request to our server, asking for the /polls path, we should route that request to our PollController. Specifically, we should be targeting the index function and passing the connection and any additional params to that function. Make that change, save the routes file, and then reload your browser (which should still be pointing to http://localhost:4000/polls)/ You should see the following instead:

This is some really great progress! Except...wait, why is the Phoenix logo and giant header getting added to the top? I thought we just added a single H2 tag and nothing else! Well, every template we render also includes a template!

Understanding templates

Templates are, at a very high level, a way to include common portions of content that should be included on multiple pages. By default, any call to render that renders an HTML template will have that render happen INSIDE of a template, and that template will be under /lib/vocial_web/templates/layout/app.html.eex. If we open up that file, we can see a base HTML structure and the default file that we'll start off with:

```html
<!DOCTYPE html>
<html lang="en">
  <head>
    <meta charset="utf-8">
    <meta http-equiv="X-UA-Compatible" content="IE=edge">
    <meta name="viewport" content="width=device-width, initial-scale=1">
    <meta name="description" content="">
    <meta name="author" content="">

    <title>Hello Vocial!</title>
    <link rel="stylesheet" href="<%= static_path(@conn, "/css/app.css") %>">
  </head>

  <body>
    <div class="container">
      <header class="header">
        <nav role="navigation">
          <ul class="nav nav-pills pull-right">
            <li><a href="http://www.phoenixframework.org/docs">Get Started</a></li>
          </ul>
        </nav>
        <span class="logo"></span>
      </header>

      <p class="alert alert-info" role="alert"><%= get_flash(@conn, :info) %></p>
      <p class="alert alert-danger" role="alert"><%= get_flash(@conn, :error) %></p>

      <main role="main">
        <%= render @view_module, @view_template, assigns %>
```

```
    </main>

  </div> <!-- /container -->
  <script src="<%= static_path(@conn, "/js/app.js") %>"></script>
</body>
</html>
```

The one line you should especially pay attention to is the `render` call inside of the `<main>` tags. It's going to render the actual template that we specify inside of our controller (`lib/vocial_web/templates/poll/index.html.eex`). But, what if we want to use a special template?

Let's create a new template under `lib/vocial_web/templates/layout` called `special.html.eex`. Open the file up and give it the following contents:

```
<!DOCTYPE html>
<html lang="en">
  <head>
    <meta charset="utf-8">
    <meta http-equiv="X-UA-Compatible" content="IE=edge">
    <meta name="viewport" content="width=device-width, initial-scale=1">
    <meta name="description" content="">
    <meta name="author" content="">

    <title>Vocial - The Social Voting App!</title>
    <link rel="stylesheet" href="<%= static_path(@conn, "/css/app.css") %>">
  </head>

  <body>
    <div class="container">
      <header class="header">
        <h4>Logo</h4>
      </header>

      <p class="alert alert-info" role="alert"><%= get_flash(@conn, :info) %></p>
      <p class="alert alert-danger" role="alert"><%= get_flash(@conn, :error) %></p>

      <main role="main">
        <%= render @view_module, @view_template, assigns %>
      </main>

    </div> <!-- /container -->
    <script src="<%= static_path(@conn, "/js/app.js") %>"></script>
  </body>
</html>
```

Next, we're going to hop back to our controller code inside `poll_controller.ex`. Change the `index` function to have the following body instead:

```
def index(conn, _params) do
    conn
    |> put_layout(:special)
    |> render("index.html")
  end
```

 The `|>` operator you see in the preceding code is something called the "pipe" operator in Elixir. What this does is take the results of the previous expression and then pass that in as the first argument in the next function. That second line would, without the pipe operator, look like this: `put_layout(conn, :special)`.

Here, we're telling Phoenix that we want this connection response to instead be wrapped in a different layout. There are two ways to pass this information to Phoenix: we can either use an atom, such as in the preceding example (where it will assume that what we actually meant was `special.html`) or we can use a string to represent it via `put_layout ("special.html")`. Reload your page and you should see everything wrapped inside of your new layout!

If everything looks good, we'll move on to passing along some data to our template!

Passing data to our templates

One thing we will frequently want to do is pass some data along our controller down to the templates that are doing the display work, especially if there is any sort of conditional display logic or anything like that. If we run `h Phoenix.Controller.render` in our IEx terminal, we'll see a definition for the function that matches the following:

```
def render(conn, template, assigns)
```

Right now, we're passing along `conn` and `index.html` (remember that anything using the pipeline operator `|>` passes the result as the first argument into the next function), so let's also pass along some assigns. Specifically, we'll pass along a dummy data structure for our first `poll`. Open up `poll_controller.ex` and let's change the index function to be the following:

```
def index(conn, _params) do
    poll = %{
      title: "My First Poll",
      options: [
```

```
      {"Choice 1", 0},
      {"Choice 2", 5},
      {"Choice 3", 2}
    ]
  }

  conn
  |> put_layout(:special)
  |> render("index.html", poll: poll)
end
```

We're building a `Poll` dummy map with a simple `title` and three possible choices to vote on. We're also starting off this poll with zero votes for the first element, five for the second, and two for the third. We then modify the render statement in the controller to set the assigns with a key of `poll` and a value of `poll`. Let's take a look at the modified template now:

```
<h2>Poll: <%= @poll.title %></h2>

<%= for {option, votes} <- @poll.options do %>
 <strong><%= option %></strong>: <%= votes %> votes
 <br />
<% end %>
```

So now we have a reference to `@poll` (if you remember the assigns, we named one of the keys for the assigns as poll). Any assigns that you send from the controller will end up in the templates as @ (whatever the key for the assign was). This is just a simple shorthand syntax, but there is one major caveat to using this shortcut: if that named assign is not always set, it will throw an error when you try to load the page! The good news is that there is a simple way to get around this problem. `@conn` will be available in the top level of any template automatically (although it will need to get passed down to any partial templates that get called beyond the initial one), so you can also access the assigns via `@conn.assigns[:key]` (so, for example, `@poll` could also be accessed via `@conn.assigns[:poll]`).

Next, in our template, we have a list comprehension that, for each element in the list of options for the poll, we'll pattern match the tuple into separate option and votes values and render a small template of the name in bold and the current score for each. This is a very simple idea of a poll but it's helpful to understand in the long run. Now that we have a little bit of an interaction going between our controller and our templates, let's write a few tests to cover our code.

Writing controller tests

We'll want to have some good tests covering all of the code that we will be writing in the course of this application, since we're all good software engineers and should follow good software engineering processes! We'll start off with our controller tests, which include a few cool tools to simulate making connection requests to various controller actions and inspecting the output of the controller functions.

Understanding the code behind tests

When we start off creating our own `controllers/views/etc`, if we're not using a generator, we won't have any new logic or functionality to cover tests for the new code we're writing. Due to this, if we just run mix test without any modifications, we'll see a few passing tests but nothing that actually covers our poll controller. The best place to start is right there, so we'll start off by implementing some tests to cover our dummy data poll response first. We'll create a new file under `test/vocial_web/controllers/poll_controller_test.exs`. We'll start off by creating our skeleton structure for a controller:

```
defmodule VocialWeb.PollControllerTest do
  use VocialWeb.ConnCase
end
```

Okay, the skeleton is there, but how do we start writing tests for controllers? Or how do we start writing tests in general?

First, any tests that we write (for any Elixir code, actually) will follow this template:

```
test "Test description as a string", arguments do ... end
```

Where `arguments` is a variable that contains anything special we want passed along to our test. Let's open up the tests for `PageController` and see what that is doing:

```
defmodule VocialWeb.PageControllerTest do
  use VocialWeb.ConnCase

  test "GET /", %{conn: conn} do
    conn = get conn, "/"
    assert html_response(conn, 200) =~ "Welcome to Phoenix!"
  end
end
```

Okay, so we see the description as `"GET /"` (which makes sense: it's simulating a `GET` request to the base route). In the next part, the arguments for the test, we see it as a pattern-matched map that is looking for a key of conn (similar to what we'd be working with and passing along in our controller). But...wait, where is that map getting its data from? What is the origin of this mysterious conn assignment? To figure that out (and learn a little more about writing tests), let's open up `ConnCase` (`test/support/conn_case.ex`) and take a look at a snippet of code from it:

```
defmodule VocialWeb.ConnCase do
  # ...
  setup tags do
    :ok = Ecto.Adapters.SQL.Sandbox.checkout(Vocial.Repo)
    unless tags[:async] do
      Ecto.Adapters.SQL.Sandbox.mode(Vocial.Repo, {:shared, self()})
    end
    {:ok, conn: Phoenix.ConnTest.build_conn()}
  end
  # ...
end
```

This is a neat little bit of code. `setup` blocks are special functions that are executed before your tests run, and if they return out a tuple of `{:ok, keyword_list}`, that information is then forwarded on to your tests! So, in the example preceding, we have conn being built from the `Phoenix.ConnTest.build_conn()` function call! Based on this, we can infer that our mysterious conn object is being created as a dummy connection from this setup block that is called anywhere use `VocialWeb.ConnCase` appears!

Okay, that's all well and good and everything, but let's continue analyzing the test. On the next line (the first line of our test function), we see this:

```
conn = get conn, "/"
```

`get` is a special function for our Controller tests that simulates a `GET` request - so it would go against our router, finding a matching path and method (`GET` and `/`, which would route to `PageController.index`), and then take our dummy connection and pass that into the controller's index function! This means that our connection (the conn data structure) will contain the RESULT of running through the route, the plugs and pipeline, the controller, the view, and the templates, and our end result should be a parseable block of text that represents what we'd send out to the browser. This helps us understand what the next line of code does:

```
assert html_response(conn, 200) =~ "Welcome to Phoenix!"
```

`assert` is an ExUnit-provided function that just means, "Hey, make sure this next statement is true". Conversely, if we wanted to verify something WASN'T true, we could use `refute` instead of `assert`. Then, we see another function call, `html_response` that takes in the transformed conn and an additional argument, `200`. If you're comfortable with HTML, you probably can infer what the `200` is, but let's take this as an opportunity to reinforce the fact that you have a very, very nice library of offline documentation you can use inside of your IEx terminal. In your app's IEx console, run the following command and take a look at what the documentation says:

```
iex(3)> h Phoenix.ConnTest.html_response

                    def html_response(conn, status)

Asserts the given status code, that we have an html response and returns
the
response body if one was set or sent.

## Examples

    assert html_response(conn, 200) =~ "<html>"
```

The `200` is indeed the status of the request! We're now able to use this information to verify that this test is checking the overall HTML response from the complete transformation of the connection! If we were expecting bad data to cause the endpoint to instead throw something like a 422, this is where we'd put that value to verify the resulting HTTP status code!

The last part of this is the `=~ "Welcome to Phoenix"`, which is just a shortcut around "verify the string I'm passing on the left side contains the value on the right side of the `=~` operator". Since the default page `index.html.eex` contains the `"Welcome to Phoenix"` text inside the template, we can see that this test should indeed pass if everything is good with our application!

Writing the poll controller test

Since we're now experts on controller tests, let's start writing our poll controller test. Open up our `test/vocial_web/controllers/poll_controller_test.exs` file and let's write our first major test:

```
test "GET /polls", %{conn: conn} do
  conn = get conn, "/polls"
  assert html_response(conn, 200) =~ "My First Poll"
end
```

Then we'll run `mix test` and verify that our new test passes:

```
$ mix test
.....


Finished in 0.2 seconds
5 tests, 0 failures

Randomized with seed 169967
```

Fantastic! Remember that in our dummy object, we gave the poll a title of `"My First Poll"`, so that's why that test is structured the way it is! One habit you'll want to get into, especially as you're starting out, is slightly changing tests to make sure that they fail when the assumptions change. In our case, let's change the text that we're looking for to be something like `"My Last Poll"` and run that instead:

```
$ mix test
....

  1) test GET /polls (VocialWeb.PollControllerTest)
     test/vocial_web/controllers/poll_controller_test.exs:4
     Assertion with =~ failed
     code:  assert html_response(conn, 200) =~ "My Last Poll"
     left:  "<!DOCTYPE html>\n<html lang=\"en\">\n  <head>\n    <meta
charset=\"utf-8\">\n    <meta http-equiv=\"X-UA-Compatible\"
content=\"IE=edge\">\n    <meta name=\"viewport\" content=\"width=device-
width, initial-scale=1\">\n    <meta name=\"description\" content=\"\">\n
<meta name=\"author\" content=\"\">\n\n    <title>Vocial - The Social
Voting App!</title>\n    <link rel=\"stylesheet\" href=\"/css/app.css\">\n
</head>\n\n  <body>\n    <div class=\"container\">\n      <header
class=\"header\">\n        <h4>Logo</h4>\n      </header>\n\n        <p
class=\"alert alert-info\" role=\"alert\"></p>\n        <p class=\"alert
alert-danger\" role=\"alert\"></p>\n\n      <main role=\"main\">\n<h2>Poll:
My First Poll</h2>\n\n  <strong>Choice 1</strong>: 0 votes\n  <br />\n
<strong>Choice 2</strong>: 5 votes\n  <br />\n  <strong>Choice 3</strong>:
```

```
2 votes\n   <br />\n        </main>\n\n      </div> <!-- /container -->\n
<script src=\"/js/app.js\"></script>\n    </body>\n</html>\n"
      right: "My Last Poll"
      stacktrace:
        test/vocial_web/controllers/poll_controller_test.exs:6: (test)



Finished in 0.1 seconds
5 tests, 1 failure

Randomized with seed 477119
```

Exactly as expected! Change it back and then we'll clean up the structure of our test a little bit more:

```
test "GET /polls", %{conn: conn} do
  poll = %{
    title: "My First Poll",
    options: [
      {"Choice 1", 0},
      {"Choice 2", 5},
      {"Choice 3", 2}
    ]
  }

  conn = get conn, "/polls"
  assert html_response(conn, 200) =~ poll.title
  Enum.each(poll.options, fn {option, votes} ->
    assert html_response(conn, 200) =~ option
    assert html_response(conn, 200) =~ "#{votes} votes"
  end)
end
```

This runs assertions against the expected title from our dummy poll's title and each of its options! Rerun our tests again and we should see a fully green test suite. Congratulations, you've just written your first successful controller test! The good news is that since we really didn't write any custom code for our Poll View, there's nothing for us to write to add test coverage there.

Summary

We're now at a point where we have a good baseline to work from for our Poll Controller, which means we're also at a point where we can start transitioning from here into the work for our data side of things. In the next chapter, we'll start diving into Contexts and Schemas and try to get a good working understanding of integrating a data model into our Phoenix application (and a lot of the design decisions that influence the current structure and why those decisions were made)!

So, now that we know how to glue together the different parts of our application and we understand a few of the pieces that are getting assembled, we need to explore what is arguably one of the largest and more complex pieces of the request/response puzzle: the database! We'll take a deep dive into Ecto and, of course, write good tests to cover any new code we write!

3
Storing and Retrieving Vote Data with Ecto Pages

When we left off last, we had sat down and gained a thorough knowledge of controllers and the entire connection model. We began with the internal request, going through the router, hitting the glue of the controller, and finally wiring up data and displaying it back to the user via our views and templates. All of this is great by itself, but if we don't have somewhere to store and retrieve data, our application is largely decorative and not terribly functional. We're going to change that by implementing a means of getting our data and putting it back into a database.

Before we can dive too far into storing our data, however, we need to understand the model behind how Ecto takes the information from the database and presents it to the application at large. Ecto, the database library that we'll be using in our project, relies on the concepts of Schemas and Contexts. Through the combination of these techniques, we can safely separate out the side effects of working with a database that may be changing constantly due to interactions with our application. Let's take a few minutes first, however, to understand how contexts and schemas interact with each other and what roles they take in the data interaction layer of our application.

In this chapter, we'll take a deep dive into the topics most directly facing the backend of our application. Specifically, we'll be taking on:

- What the roles of schemas are in our application
- Creating new migrations
- How to write migrations
- Understanding the roles of contexts
- Hooking a context up to a controller
- Writing some basic unit tests to cover functionality

These are all necessary to really understand how the database side of things glues the rest of our application together over time. By the end of the chapter, you should have a thorough working knowledge of all of the database-specific parts of your application and how they all fit together!

Understanding the role of schemas

The first thing to start understanding is where and how schemas define the shape of the data in your database. Schemas help describe what tables your application uses behind the scenes and what fields exist to Ecto; the Schemas themselves do not define the overall structure to the database itself.

This helps describe the columns and define what types each of the columns are (for example, a string, an integer, or a reference to another table). The important thing to note about schemas in Ecto is what they are intended to do: separate the ideas of data from operations. By keeping our schemas very specific to understanding, describing, and translating the data, we can keep our applications largely side-effect-free when interacting with the database!

Before we can take a really deep dive into schemas, we should start by talking about what our initial voting data model should look like! Let's take a look at the code we introduced for our data model in the controller that we wrote in the last chapter:

```
poll = %{
  title: "My First Poll",
  options: [
    {"Option 1", 0},
    {"Option 2", 5},
    {"Option 3", 1}
  ]
}
```

Based on this, we can probably decide that our model for our Vote concept in the database can be a pretty simple thing. We have the Vote itself, which has a title attached to it, and then the options that people can decide between. We're going to make an assumption here that you're using the default database choice for Phoenix applications, Postgres (but it shouldn't change much regardless of your database choice!). So, a very simple database table model would be:

Poll	Title Options (reference to another table
Option	Poll ID (reference to the poll this option is attached to) Title Votes

This creates two separate tables: Polls and Options. The Polls table will store all of the Polls themselves and then the options table will store the possible vote choices and their current scores. The Options table will store a reference back to the original poll (we'll get into this later when we start talking about associations). This is typically referred to as a "one to many" relationship between the two tables; a Poll can have many Options, but an Option can only have one Poll. This also means that the referencing of different tables only needs to take place on the Option, not on the Poll.

Creating a new migration

Given our newfound understanding of our complex object, we need to create our database table. Now, there are a few ways to do this. For example, we can use Phoenix and Ecto's built-in generators to give us a skeleton for this, but since we're trying to learn and understand the underlying systems that are needed for our application, we'll start by NOT using generators to build our initial skeletons; later on, we'll dive a little bit into using the generators and how to use them.

We'll get into a habit of learning what we can from the various help commands that exist in mix and IEx, so let's do the same. We can search for any of the Ecto commands that exist for mix with the following:

```
$ mix help | grep ecto
mix ecto                 # Prints Ecto help information
mix ecto.create          # Creates the repository storage
mix ecto.drop            # Drops the repository storage
mix ecto.dump            # Dumps the repository database structure
mix ecto.gen.migration   # Generates a new migration for the repo
```

```
mix ecto.gen.repo      # Generates a new repository
mix ecto.load          # Loads previously dumped database structure
mix ecto.migrate       # Runs the repository migrations
mix ecto.migrations    # Displays the repository migration status
mix ecto.rollback      # Rolls back the repository migrations
mix phx.new.ecto       # Creates a new Ecto project within an umbrella
project
```

Typically any generator will have a `.gen` as part of the command itself. We've already run `mix ecto.create` to create our database, and we don't need more `help` information, nor do we want to drop or dump anything from our database. We don't need to load, and we have nothing to migrate yet, so that also crosses `mix ecto.migrate` and `mix ecto.migrations` off our list. Finally, we see `mix phx.new.ecto`, which talks about creating a new Ecto project within an umbrella project, which also doesn't fit into what we're trying to accomplish here, so that leaves us with our two generator commands.

`mix ecto.gen.repo` creates a new repository for our application, which we don't need, so we're going to work with `mix ecto.gen.migration` to create a migration for our application! One of my favorite parts of working with Elixir and Phoenix is how entirely fantastic the documentation that is built-in to almost every single command is, so let's take a look at the documentation for the migration generator and learn how to use it. To get help for anything in mix remember that we can prefix `help` to any of the commands; let's run `mix help ecto.gen.migration`:

```
$ mix help ecto.gen.migration

                    mix ecto.gen.migration

Generates a migration.

The repository must be set under :ecto_repos in the current app
configuration
or given via the -r option.

## Examples

    mix ecto.gen.migration add_posts_table
    mix ecto.gen.migration add_posts_table -r Custom.Repo

The generated migration filename will be prefixed with the current
timestamp in
UTC which is used for versioning and ordering.

By default, the migration will be generated to the
"priv/YOUR_REPO/migrations"
```

```
directory of the current application but it can be configured to be any
subdirectory of priv by specifying the :priv key under the repository
configuration.

This generator will automatically open the generated file if you have
ECTO_EDITOR set in your environment variable.

## Command line options

• -r, --repo – the repo to generate migration for

Location: _build/dev/lib/ecto/ebin
```

Okay, this is a pretty simple command! Based on the help documentation, we can see that what we want to do is create a migration that creates a new table, which we've referred to previously as Polls.

Creating the Polls table migration

Based on that, let's create our new migration, `add_polls_table`:

```
$ mix ecto.gen.migration add_polls_table
* creating priv/repo/migrations
* creating priv/repo/migrations/20171005161434_add_polls_table.exs
```

By default, that will give us a mostly blank file consisting of:

```
defmodule Vocial.Repo.Migrations.AddPollsTable do
  use Ecto.Migration

  def change do

  end
end
```

This allows us to start putting together the definitions for our table! Let's take a look at what this file does:

First, we define a new module under `Vocial.Repo.Migrations` called `AddPollsTable` (remember that the `gen.migration` command we had used previously took `add_polls_table` as the only argument).

Next, we tell Ecto that this module should be using the macros and functions defined in the `Ecto.Migration`. In our IEx session, we can run `h Ecto.Migration` to learn more about the module and what it provides. The actual output is super-long so we won't include the whole thing, but it does provide a very handy example that we can use to piece together our migration:

```
defmodule MyRepo.Migrations.AddWeatherTable do
  use Ecto.Migration

  def change do
    create table("weather") do
      add :city,    :string, size: 40
      add :temp_lo, :integer
      add :temp_hi, :integer
      add :prcp,    :float

      timestamps()
    end
  end
end
```

This is pretty close to our initial skeleton, so let's take a look at what this file provides so that we can figure out how to properly write our migration files. The first thing in our migrations file is that a `create table` statement, where `table` is a function that takes in a string as the argument. That string is the name of the table that we want to create, so we'll start creating our change statement in our `add_polls_table` migration:

```
def change do
  create table("polls") do
  end
end
```

Next, we need the statements that actually create the columns in our table. Looking at the example again, we see a bunch of `add` statements that take in two atoms as their arguments. The first argument is the name of the column that we want to add, and the second argument is the type of the column we want to add! There is also an additional optional third argument, which is a keyword list of options to the type (such as size, default, null, and so on). But what types are available to us? By default, Ecto supports the following types out of the box:

- `:integer` - A representation of any non-decimal numbers (like 3)
- `:string` - A representation of any types of string data (like banana)

- :text - A representation of larger blocks of strings (where, string may be the right choice for something simple like a title, :text might be the right choice for a big, long block of text, such as the content of a page; I'll skip the example of this one!)
- :float - A representation of decimal numbers (like *3.14*)
- :datetime - A date and time representation of time
- :json - A representation of a JSON data structure (only available in some databases!)

You can also specify references as a part of types, but we'll get back into this later!

Okay, so, looking back at our original design for the Polls table, all that we need to specify is the title column, which should just be a string. There's also a helper to handle creation/insertion of the inserted_at and updated_at columns, which are timestamps that tell us when the Polls are created or updated. This helper is called timestamps()! That's everything we need to know, so let's finally create our migration:

```
defmodule Vocial.Repo.Migrations.AddPollsTable do
  use Ecto.Migration

  def change do
    create table("polls") do
      add :title, :string

      timestamps()
    end
  end
end
```

Now that we've filled out our file, let's run our actual migration! From our terminal, we'll run mix ecto.migrate:

```
$ mix ecto.migrate
[info] == Running Vocial.Repo.Migrations.AddPollsTable.change/0 forward
[info] create table polls
[info] == Migrated in 0.0s
```

We should have a table that looks something like this:

Creating our Options table migration

Hooray! We've created our migrations, and run them successfully! Now, we have our representation of the first table in our models. We'll continue on with creating another migration for our Options since our data model will be woefully incomplete without it! Let's begin:

```
$ mix ecto.gen.migration add_options_table
* creating priv/repo/migrations
* creating priv/repo/migrations/20171005185040_add_options_table.exs
```

If we open up the file, we'll see the same skeleton we started within our last file. The new things we'll be using here are default values, and references as well! If you remember the design of our Options table, we have a title (which is a string), the votes (which is an integer counter of the number of votes (which we should start off at zero)), and the `poll_id`, which is a reference back to the polls table. And, of course, we'll want to add our timestamps for audit information! Let's take a look at the finished file:

```
defmodule Vocial.Repo.Migrations.AddOptionsTable do
  use Ecto.Migration

  def change do
    create table("options") do
      add :title, :string
      add :votes, :integer, default: 0
      add :poll_id, references(:polls)

      timestamps()
    end
  end
end
```

If all went well when we run mix `ecto.migrate` we should expect to see no errors:

```
$ mix ecto.migrate
[info] == Running Vocial.Repo.Migrations.AddOptionsTable.change/0 forward
[info] create table options
[info] == Migrated in 0.0s
```

We've done it! We've created a database representation that matches our initial design and we can now start moving forward with the actual coding of our schemas! Let's take a look at the structure of this table that we've created to make sure what's in the database is what we're expecting to see overall:

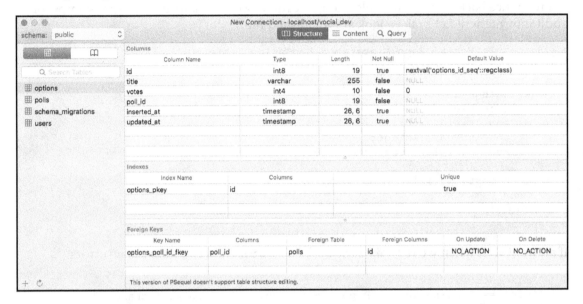

One thing that we'll need to do is create a directory that will map all of the related concepts together (this is commonly referred to as a Context, but we're going to gloss over that for now). So, in our `lib/vocial` directory, we'll create a new directory called votes. Let's create our first schema in that directory: `poll.ex`.

Creating our Poll schema

A schema in Ecto needs one `use` statement and one `import` statement by default. In addition, we want to namespace the modules that we define for our new schema with the name of the app (but not the web app!) and the name of the context. We created votes as the subdirectory under the app "Vocial", so we'll create our module as `Vocial.Votes.Poll`. Next, we need to tell Ecto that this file will be using all of the Ecto functions and helpers that are available to us.

The schema will also be in charge of telling Ecto how to build changesets to modify data in our database, so we'll need to include that functionality via an import statement. We'll also want to make our lives easier by including an alias for our full module definition so that we can just say `%Poll{}` instead of `%Vocial.Votes.Poll{}`. So we'll start off building our file like this:

```
defmodule Vocial.Votes.Poll do
  use Ecto.Schema
  import Ecto.Changeset
  alias Vocial.Votes.Poll
end
```

Next, we need to tell Ecto how to read rows from our database and our polls table as Elixir data structures, so we need to define a `Schema`. Let's add the following block to our file:

```
schema "polls" do
  field :title, :string

  timestamps()
end
```

Now we've told Ecto how to define our data and how to pull information out of the database. The final piece that's required for any schema file in Ecto is defining the changeset. Let's add a `changeset` function that will tell Ecto how to make modifications and insert or update those rows in our database. Typically, a changeset takes in the Struct representing the data structure you want to modify and the attributes you want to give to that data structure. You can think of it this way: a changeset **always** performs modifications, so if you're creating a new row in the database, you'd start with a blank object and roll your changes on top of that. If you're modifying an existing row, you'd take the Ecto representation of that existing row and perform modifications on top of that!

Next, your changeset has to take that initial representation and determine what columns are allowed to be modified (this is because we may have something like virtual fields, which are columns that don't actually exist in the database). This helps prevent against issues like mass assignment, where maybe you don't want the application to be able to set certain columns as modifiable.

Finally, your changeset should validate whichever columns are required for this to be valid. This will make sure that in the final representation that goes into the database, all of the columns marked as required have values in them. This means that `update` statements do not have to include updates for columns that already have data in them, so you don't have to worry about validations being performed on columns that already have data in them! All of this talk is great and all, but let's take a look at what the code for that actually should be:

```
def changeset(%Poll{}=poll, attrs) do
  poll
  |> cast(attrs, [:title])
  |> validate_required([:title])
end
```

We now have a fully-built and fully-functional representation of our Poll object in Ecto! Hooray!

Testing our Poll schema

While it's great that we have written some code that describes our Poll object in the database, it's no good if we can't actually validate that the code does what we need it to. A good way for us to test this, since we haven't hooked anything up to our controllers yet, is to run our tests in IEx instead!

We'll need to alias a few modules first, to make our lives a little easier when we're writing our code. We'll start off with aliasing `Vocial.Votes.Poll` and `Vocial.Repo`. The first alias gives us access to our changeset and Poll struct, whereas the second gives us access to the `Repo.insert()` function, which we'll use to actually get the data into the database. Next, we need to create the actual changeset, since that tells Ecto how to actually get that `insert` statement into the database. We'll do this through the `Poll.changeset()` function, and pass it in a blank `Poll` struct as our starting point (remember our earlier conversation about how changesets are always modifications on top of some starting structure?). Finally, we'll pass the resulting finished changeset into the `Repo.insert()` function, and we'll see an `insert` SQL statement appear in our IEx window:

```
iex(1)> alias Vocial.Votes.Poll
Vocial.Votes.Poll
iex(2)> alias Vocial.Repo
Vocial.Repo
iex(3)> changeset = Poll.changeset(%Poll{}, %{title: "Sample Poll"})
#Ecto.Changeset<action: nil, changes: %{title: "Sample Poll"}, errors: [],
data: #Vocial.Votes.Poll<>, valid?: true>
iex(4)> Repo.insert(changeset)
[debug] QUERY OK db=51.9ms queue=0.1ms
```

```
INSERT INTO "polls" ("title","inserted_at","updated_at") VALUES ($1,$2,$3)
RETURNING "id" ["Sample Poll", {{2017, 10, 5}, {20, 18, 8, 931657}},
{{2017, 10, 5}, {20, 18, 8, 933798}}]
{:ok,
%Vocial.Votes.Poll{__meta__: #Ecto.Schema.Metadata<:loaded, "polls">, id:
1,
  inserted_at: ~N[2017-10-05 20:18:08.931657], title: "Sample Poll",
  updated_at: ~N[2017-10-05 20:18:08.933798]}}
```

Sure enough, if we take a look at the database, we'll see that the data from our `insert` statement was successfully inserted into the database:

id	title	inserted_at	updated_at
1	Sample Poll	2017-10-05 20:18:08.931657	2017-10-05 20:18:08.933798

This is a pretty great bit of progress! Let's continue our momentum by creating our (admittedly trickier) option schema!

Creating our Option schema

We'll need to create an Option schema, just like we have the Poll schema, but we'll need to do some additional legwork to make sure our representation makes sense. We'll also need to go back and fix up one thing we omitted from our Poll schema! First, we want to name our module `Vocial.Votes.Option` instead of `Vocial.Votes.Poll` (for obvious reasons). Next, we'll need to alias both `Vocial.Votes.Poll` and `Vocial.Votes.Option`. This is because we need the sanity helper for referencing the struct of our Option schema, and also because we'll need to reference the Poll schema as well to define our relationship to that table. We'll also need to create a `:votes` column on the schema; this one should be an integer with a default value of `0`. Let's take a look at the finished file with all of those bells and whistles:

```
defmodule Vocial.Votes.Option do
  use Ecto.Schema
  import Ecto.Changeset
  alias Vocial.Votes.Option
  alias Vocial.Votes.Poll

  schema "options" do
    field :title, :string
    field :votes, :integer, default: 0

    belongs_to :poll, Poll
```

```
    timestamps()
  end

  def changeset(%Option{}=option, attrs) do
    option
    |> cast(attrs, [:title, :votes, :poll_id])
    |> validate_required([:title, :votes, :poll_id])
  end
end
```

We have our first example here of specifying options for the definitions of our fields via the votes field definition. Here, we're saying that the default value for any Option that gets created is a 0 in the votes column; this will make writing our insert statements a little easier and save us from wacky scenarios where an Option has nil votes or something like that. In addition, notice that we have a new statement here, the `belongs_to` statement. As mentioned earlier, we designed this as a `has_many` relationship between Polls and Options. Specifically, here we're saying that an Option `belongs_to` a Poll, so one thing we quickly need to do is return to our Poll schema and add a `has_many` statement to tell Ecto that there is another side to the association. We'll add the following line to the top, near our other alias statement:

```
alias Vocial.Votes.Option
```

And we'll add the `has_many` statement inside of our schema block in the Poll schema:

```
has_many :options, Option
```

Let's go back to the IEx session that we tested our Poll schema in and try out our Options schema! First, we'll make sure we get a Poll back from our database by running `Repo.all(Poll)`:

```
iex(4)> Repo.all(Poll)
[debug] QUERY OK source="polls" db=3.5ms decode=4.7ms
SELECT p0."id", p0."title", p0."inserted_at", p0."updated_at" FROM "polls"
AS p0 []
[%Vocial.Votes.Poll{__meta__: #Ecto.Schema.Metadata<:loaded, "polls">, id:
1,
  inserted_at: ~N[2017-10-05 20:18:08.931657], title: "Sample Poll",
  updated_at: ~N[2017-10-05 20:18:08.933798]}]
```

We have a Poll with an ID of 1, so let's use that to create our options! We'll create two simple options, `yes` and `no`, so let's start by adding the alias for our Option schema:

```
iex(5)> alias Vocial.Votes.Option
Vocial.Votes.Option
```

And finally, let's insert changesets for our two new options using a `poll_id` of 1:

```
iex(6)> Option.changeset(%Option{}, %{title: "Yes", poll_id: 1}) |>
Repo.insert()
[debug] QUERY OK db=0.2ms
begin []
[debug] QUERY OK db=5.6ms
INSERT INTO "options"
("poll_id","title","votes","inserted_at","updated_at") VALUES
($1,$2,$3,$4,$5) RETURNING "id" [1, "Yes", 0, {{2017, 10, 5}, {21, 14, 32,
58102}}, {{2017, 10, 5}, {21, 14, 32, 59711}}]
[debug] QUERY OK db=19.4ms
commit []
{:ok,
%Vocial.Votes.Option{__meta__: #Ecto.Schema.Metadata<:loaded, "options">,
 id: 1, inserted_at: ~N[2017-10-05 21:14:32.058102],
 poll: #Ecto.Association.NotLoaded<association :poll is not loaded>,
 poll_id: 1, title: "Yes", updated_at: ~N[2017-10-05 21:14:32.059711],
 votes: 0}}
iex(7)> Option.changeset(%Option{}, %{title: "No", poll_id: 1}) |>
Repo.insert()
[debug] QUERY OK db=0.3ms
begin []
[debug] QUERY OK db=7.1ms
INSERT INTO "options"
("poll_id","title","votes","inserted_at","updated_at") VALUES
($1,$2,$3,$4,$5) RETURNING "id" [1, "No", 0, {{2017, 10, 5}, {21, 15, 3,
797493}}, {{2017, 10, 5}, {21, 15, 3, 797517}}]
[debug] QUERY OK db=6.2ms
commit []
{:ok,
%Vocial.Votes.Option{__meta__: #Ecto.Schema.Metadata<:loaded, "options">,
 id: 2, inserted_at: ~N[2017-10-05 21:15:03.797493],
 poll: #Ecto.Association.NotLoaded<association :poll is not loaded>,
 poll_id: 1, title: "No", updated_at: ~N[2017-10-05 21:15:03.797517],
 votes: 0}}
```

This time we took a slightly different route and piped the results of the changeset call directly into the `Repo.insert()` function via the pipeline operator! We need to verify that this added the options to our Poll object, so let's fetch our Poll out of the database:

```
iex(11)> poll = Repo.get!(Poll, 1)
[debug] QUERY OK source="polls" db=3.2ms
SELECT p0."id", p0."title", p0."inserted_at", p0."updated_at" FROM "polls"
AS p0 WHERE (p0."id" = $1) [1]
%Vocial.Votes.Poll{__meta__: #Ecto.Schema.Metadata<:loaded, "polls">, id:
1,
```

```
inserted_at: ~N[2017-10-05 20:18:08.931657],
options: #Ecto.Association.NotLoaded<association :options is not loaded>,
title: "Sample Poll", updated_at: ~N[2017-10-05 20:18:08.933798]}
```

Understanding the gotchas of associations

Cool! We now have our Poll, representing a row in the database with an ID of 1. Let's try to access the options on that poll:

```
iex(12)> poll.options
#Ecto.Association.NotLoaded<association :options is not loaded>
```

This seems strange. We queried for the Poll and got that back, so why didn't it load our `Options` association with it? Well, this is actually intentional behavior for Ecto; it's designed to not lazy-load data from the database. Anyone who has ever worked with a lazy loading relational model can tell you just what sorts of problems it tends to introduce over time concerning the performance and maintenance of an application, so to avoid that problem Ecto just straight up doesn't lazy load any associations. Instead, you'll need to tell Ecto that you want to include those associations directly, either via a join statement or via `Repo.preload`. So let's try our statement again, but this time with a `Repo.preload` instead:

It is a common scenario to see your tests fail or see Controllers throw error messages in development mode. Any time you get an error message about a changeset not matching the expected value or something going wrong in the display of a changeset, make sure you're not missing a preload statement!

```
iex(13)> poll = Repo.get!(Poll, 1) |> Repo.preload(:options)
[debug] QUERY OK source="polls" db=4.3ms
SELECT p0."id", p0."title", p0."inserted_at", p0."updated_at" FROM "polls"
AS p0 WHERE (p0."id" = $1) [1]
[debug] QUERY OK source="options" db=3.7ms
SELECT o0."id", o0."title", o0."votes", o0."poll_id", o0."inserted_at",
o0."updated_at", o0."poll_id" FROM "options" AS o0 WHERE (o0."poll_id" =
$1) ORDER BY o0."poll_id" [1]
%Vocial.Votes.Poll{__meta__: #Ecto.Schema.Metadata<:loaded, "polls">, id:
1,
inserted_at: ~N[2017-10-05 20:18:08.931657],
options: [%Vocial.Votes.Option{__meta__: #Ecto.Schema.Metadata<:loaded,
"options">,
  id: 1, inserted_at: ~N[2017-10-05 21:14:32.058102],
  poll: #Ecto.Association.NotLoaded<association :poll is not loaded>,
  poll_id: 1, title: "Yes", updated_at: ~N[2017-10-05 21:14:32.059711],
```

```
    votes: 0},
 %Vocial.Votes.Option{__meta__: #Ecto.Schema.Metadata<:loaded, "options">,
   id: 2, inserted_at: ~N[2017-10-05 21:15:03.797493],
   poll: #Ecto.Association.NotLoaded<association :poll is not loaded>,
   poll_id: 1, title: "No", updated_at: ~N[2017-10-05 21:15:03.797517],
   votes: 0}], title: "Sample Poll", updated_at: ~N[2017-10-05
20:18:08.933798]}
iex(14)> poll.options
[%Vocial.Votes.Option{__meta__: #Ecto.Schema.Metadata<:loaded, "options">,
  id: 1, inserted_at: ~N[2017-10-05 21:14:32.058102],
  poll: #Ecto.Association.NotLoaded<association :poll is not loaded>,
  poll_id: 1, title: "Yes", updated_at: ~N[2017-10-05 21:14:32.059711],
  votes: 0},
 %Vocial.Votes.Option{__meta__: #Ecto.Schema.Metadata<:loaded, "options">,
  id: 2, inserted_at: ~N[2017-10-05 21:15:03.797493],
  poll: #Ecto.Association.NotLoaded<association :poll is not loaded>,
  poll_id: 1, title: "No", updated_at: ~N[2017-10-05 21:15:03.797517],
  votes: 0}]
```

Huzzah! We're now getting our poll object out of the database and including the options as part of our preload statement! We have our way of getting the data in and out, we have our way of accessing the data via Elixir data structures, and we understand how to tell Ecto to relate our two separate schemas to each other! Now, imagine that you're writing code in your application and every single time you want to do something with Polls and Options you have to alias both schemas, include appropriate references and changesets for both, link everything together in the right way, include code to handle preloads and joins…

…and then imagine you have to do that every single time. Yikes! That's a ton of extra boilerplate code that we do not want to have to deal with! In addition, that code becomes incredibly brittle, because what if you change those changesets? New columns could get added pretty frequently and, if you have to search and find for the nine separate places you referenced those schemas could get incredibly tricky far too quickly! What's worse, you're even more likely to miss a spot where you needed to go through and change something, so you'd also have a broken application in a way that would be painstakingly difficult to diagnose and repair! We want to avoid that situation, so instead, let's use another recent Ecto concept to tackle this problem: Contexts.

Understanding the role of contexts

We talked a little bit about the sorts of issues that would lead us to want to control how our code is used and written since we don't want maintenance to become a giant hassle for us in the future. Therefore, let's instead simplify our lives by providing a single interface for related schemas and database operations.

Contexts fill that void by providing that unified interface, typically providing human-readable functions that allow the fetching, inserting, updating, and deleting of data. It can also do other database-specific operations that may be difficult to figure out ownership of (for example, should adding a new option to a poll live on the Poll or live on the schema? The correct answer is: neither!).

Overall, the end goal is that when someone else is working on our codebase (or, when we're working on this same codebase six months later and can't remember any of the decisions or code structure rules we originally laid out), we have a very simple way to interact with some of the more complicated parts of most applications. We provide simple and human-readable function names and control usage/interfaces for modifying or otherwise dealing with that data. This code used to just get shoved into helper modules scattered throughout your codebase or, even worse, littered your controller files with tons of non-controller-specific code. This code was hard to test, hard to track, and if you were working with a tight deadline on something, there was a good chance that you'd end up duplicating that code frequently instead of making sure the code was testable, maintainable, and otherwise useful.

Every context should have some helpers imported into it and aliased, but there's no special macro magic going on here. It's basically just a handy module that the application can use! It should also follow a simple naming definition. Since we created our context directory as `lib/vocial/votes`, we'll create `lib/vocial/votes/votes.ex` as our context!

Creating a Votes context

Our module definition will be `Vocial.Votes` (not `Vocial.Votes.Votes`), and in it we'll want to import `Ecto.Query` so we can build out any special queries that may be required. We'll also want to alias in our Repo, Poll, and Option modules, just like we did in our IEx window. So, our starting skeleton should look like this:

```
defmodule Vocial.Votes do
  import Ecto.Query, warn: false

  alias Vocial.Repo
```

```
alias Vocial.Votes.Poll
alias Vocial.Votes.Option
end
```

 The warn: false option on the import and alias statements tells Elixir not to give warnings when we import or alias something and then don't use it. It's a good thing to use important functionality imports such as Ecto.Query in a Context, but you should generally try to avoid using warn: false whenever you can, as it can hurt the readability and maintainability of your code long-term!

Okay, so now that we have a nice, handy, single interface to grab data out of the database, we should start by writing something that does precisely that. Let's grab a list of all of the Polls out of the database (and make sure we include our Options with it).

Grabbing a list of data

We'll build a function that can provide a simple interface to get the data out of the system and to our controllers. So what do we want here? We want a simple function that is going to return an array of data (in our case, Polls). Of course, we'll also want to preload the Options for those Polls as well. The good news is that writing functions for our interfaces is just as simple as writing functions in Elixir! Let's take a look at our first example:

```
def list_polls do
  Repo.all(Poll) |> Repo.preload(:options)
end
```

All we've done here is written a single line of code, and yet this is also the code that will give us access to our Poll and Option data! Now, when we want a list of Polls, we don't need to think about having multiple schemas to interact with or multiple files to deal with; it's just one simple interface!

Okay, so we're talking a lot about how great it is that we've made this simple interface; let's actually put it into action! Before we move on any further, though, we should likely spend a few minutes talking about how to actually write queries in Ecto, as you may be doing quite a bit of that and it will be very important to understand exactly how to get data out of the database and into data structures that Elixir can properly interpret.

Understanding Ecto query writing

If we go back and look at the `list_poll()` function that we just wrote, you can see that we have the `Repo.all/1` query and that it gets passed into a `Repo.preload/1` statement. Without really understanding what's going on here, this is all just going to feel a bit like magic. Nothing in Elixir should ever just be reduced to magic, so let's take a peek behind the curtains, so to speak.

In this case, when we call `Repo.all`, we're just passing it the name of the schema. If we run `h Vocial.Repo.all` in our IEx terminal, we'll see something like the following:

```
iex(2)> h Vocial.Repo.all

@callback all(queryable :: Ecto.Query.t(), opts :: Keyword.t()) ::
[Ecto.Schema.t()] | no_return()

Fetches all entries from the data store matching the given query.

May raise Ecto.QueryError if query validation fails.

## Options

    • :prefix - The prefix to run the query on (such as the schema path in
      Postgres or the database in MySQL). This overrides the prefix set in
the
      query.

See the "Shared options" section at the module documentation.

## Example

    # Fetch all post titles
    query = from p in Post,
        select: p.title
    MyRepo.all(query)
```

Based on the documentation, we can see that the first argument that we pass in is something that is `queryable`. In our case, the schema name is `queryable`, so Ecto will convert `Repo.all(Poll)` into:

```
Repo.all(from p in Poll)
```

Returning back to our IEx terminal, let's verify the behavior here:

```
iex(5)> Repo.all(Poll)
[debug] QUERY OK source="polls" db=12.3ms
SELECT p0."id", p0."title", p0."user_id", p0."inserted_at", p0."updated_at"
FROM "polls" AS p0 []
[]
```

We expect this to be the same as the longer form of writing out this query. If you've ever seen anything like LINQ syntax before, this is pretty similar:

```
iex(7)> Repo.all(from p in Poll)
[debug] QUERY OK source="polls" db=10.3ms
SELECT p0."id", p0."title", p0."user_id", p0."inserted_at", p0."updated_at"
FROM "polls" AS p0 []
[]
```

You can see here that we get an identical query when we write out the query itself. We write it out as "from (alias) in (schema)". We could expand on this, as well. For example, let's say we want to include a where clause in our query:

```
iex(8)> Repo.all(from p in Poll, where: p.title == "Hello")
[debug] QUERY OK source="polls" db=34.9ms
SELECT p0."id", p0."title", p0."user_id", p0."inserted_at", p0."updated_at"
FROM "polls" AS p0 WHERE (p0."title" = 'Hello') []
[]
```

If you want to learn more about Ecto query construction, you can type in `h Ecto.Query` at any point in your IEx shell to learn a lot about query construction!

Hooking up the context to our controller

If we go back to our controller (`lib/vocial_web/controllers/poll_controller.ex`), we'll see that our index function is currently only set up to display a single Poll, not multiple Polls! We need to figure this out first before we move on. The first thing we'll need to do is get rid of the garbage data that we originally created since we don't need placeholder data anymore! The next thing we'll need to do is use `polls` as our variable name instead of `poll` since we're working with multiple sets of data. Finally, we'll need to change what we're passing on to the views and templates from `poll: poll` to `polls: polls`.

It may seem like a little thing to do but it's important to make sure that our code is readable and simple to maintain! This is the sort of thing that influences decisions made throughout the lifetime of your project (and they also tend to be problems that quickly balloon into massive headaches later on). Let's take a look at our new modified controller:

```
defmodule VocialWeb.PollController do
  use VocialWeb, :controller

  def index(conn, _params) do
    polls = Vocial.Votes.list_polls()

    conn
    |> put_layout(:special)
    |> render "index.html", polls: polls
  end
end
```

Note the inclusion of our nice new Votes context and the `list_polls()` function that we just created! We'll also need to quickly modify the templates to display this new set of data:

```
<%= for poll <- @polls do %>
  <h2>Poll: <%= poll.title %></h2>

  <%= for option <- poll.options do %>
    <strong><%= option.title %></strong>: <%= option.votes %>
    <br />
  <% end %>
<% end %>
```

The first change here is that we have a list comprehension on the outside going through each of our polls, now referencing the `@polls` variable instead of the `@poll` that was referenced in this file previously. The next change is that since the list of options is no longer a simple tuple of `{option, votes}` and is instead another struct, we need to treat that data that way and reference it via normal struct accessors.

 A list comprehension is a way of defining operations on each item inside of a list with a function (in our case, an anonymous function). You can think of it as "for every item in the list, the item should be described by this function".

Other than that, this file is basically identical to what we had before, and the good news is that we also don't have to make any modifications to the View since this was already solid, so we're done with this transformation work! Let's take a look at the finished product:

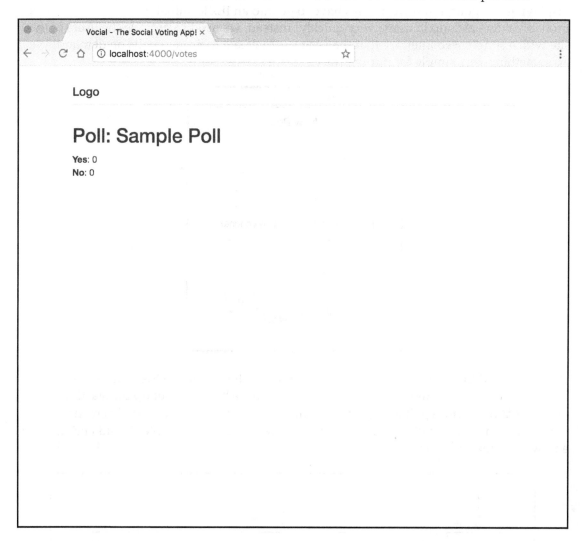

This is not too bad at all! We have a good solid foundation to build the rest of our Vote Controller operations on, and we have our handy Context to make building all of that simple! Let's move on to providing a way for people to create new Polls from the interface!

Creating a new poll

We have a nice new (well, okay, it's not that nice, but it is functional at least) interface for displaying our polls, but if we always have to go into an IEx terminal to create new polls it probably won't pick up in usage very quickly! Instead, we need to provide the users of the site with a simple web interface that they can use to create their own polls on demand! We'll do something very simple for our interface:

We'll also need to create two new actions in our controller to dictate the flow of new data into our database: new and create. The job of the new action is to set up the starting point of data that our form is going to work with, and create will handle actually creating the data and send some result of posting the form back to the end user! We should end up with a flow that looks like this:

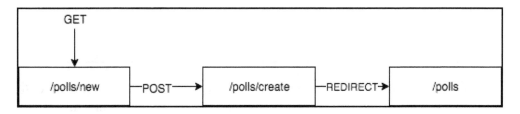

We'll need to understand a little more about how the data needs to be set up for each request as well; the simplest way for us to do that is to actually go in and start mocking all of the code up! We'll start at the router level since we can't do anything or verify our results if we don't have a way for our web browser to actually get to that point! Open up lib/vocial_web/router.ex and let's get to work! We'll need to add in routes for new and create, the former of which will be a GET request and the latter of which will be a POST request. We'll add the following two lines to our router file:

```
get "/polls/new", PollController, :new
post "/polls", PollController, :create
```

Creating the new action in the controller

Right now, those routes won't work, because they don't yet have a controller action associated with them. Let's hop into our poll_controller.ex file and create the new action:

```
def new(conn, _params) do
   poll = Vocial.Votes.new_poll()
   conn
   |> put_layout("special.html")
   |> render "new.html", poll: poll
end
```

First, we start off by creating a new blank poll object. We'll use a function in our context that doesn't actually exist yet. We want to keep our context as the main method of interaction between our controller and our database, so we'll just pick a function name and use that later. Next, we'll basically just copy our index function over from the controller and use that code.

One thing you might notice is that we actually already have a lot of duplication in our code. We should start off by just replacing the default layout that comes with Phoenix with our special.html layout, so let's delete lib/vocial_web/templates/layout/app.html.eex and rename lib/vocial_web/templates/layout/special.html.eex to app.html.eex. Then, we can delete the put_layout ("special.html") lines from our code. At the top of the PollController, we should also add an alias Vocial.Votes line to make that code a little cleaner. Our new controller should look like this:

```
defmodule VocialWeb.PollController do
  use VocialWeb, :controller
  alias Vocial.Votes
```

```
def index(conn, _params) do
  polls = Votes.list_polls()
  render conn, "index.html", polls: polls
end

def new(conn, _params) do
  poll = Votes.new_poll()
  render conn, "new.html", poll: poll
end
end
```

We also need to build out the new function in our Context. We need it to create a blank changeset for us to start working with, so let's open up `lib/vocial/votes/votes.ex` and add the following function:

```
def new_poll do
  Poll.changeset(%Poll{}, %{})
end
```

Now let's create the `new.html` template that our app is using. Create `lib/vocial_web/templates/poll/new.html.eex` and just give it a quick "hello" line. Now, if we pull up `/polls/new` in our browser, we should see everything that we created!

We can now start building up our forms and start using them! We will use some of Phoenix's built-in HTML helpers to help us put our poll form together. So in our new template, we have a quick header and we'll wrap everything inside of a `div` to be a good web developer citizen. Now we need to create a form that we can use to post our changes to the create route. Next, we'll use another helper to help us build a text box for our title attribute. The options portion is going to be a little bit trickier. We'll pick the simplest implementation path to start by just saying that each poll choice should be separated by a comma. This means we'll expect the data to come into our controller in the format "One, Two, Three". Finally, we'll need a submit button to bring it all back together at the end:

```
<div class="poll-form">
 <h2>New Poll</h2>
 <%= form_for @poll, poll_path(@conn, :create), fn f -> %>
   <label>
     Title:<br />
     <%= text_input f, :title %>
   </label>
   <br />
   <label>
     Options (separated by commas):<br />
     <input type="text" name="options" />
   </label>
   <br />
```

```
    <%= submit "Create" %>
  <% end %>
</div>
```

If we go back to our browser, we should see our nice new created form! Perfect! Now, we need to verify that it actually works, as writing all of this code isn't really worth much if we cannot demonstrate that it is all functional.

 A workflow that you'll eventually settle into when you're building up your UI is keeping your controller and templates open at the same time. This is a good way to keep your code flowing logically from point A to point B

Let's go back into our poll controller and piece together our `create` function!

Creating our create function

We have a new form that is sending data along to our create controller action, but nothing to actually handle that. We'll jump back into `lib/vocial_web/controllers/poll_controller.ex` and add a new `create` function and pattern match on the following:

```
def create(conn, %{"poll" => poll_params, "options" => options}) do
  split_options = String.split(options, ",")
  with {:ok, poll} <- Votes.create_poll_with_options(poll_params,
split_options) do
    conn
    |> put_flash(:info, "Poll created successfully!")
    |> redirect(to: poll_path(conn, :index))
  end
end
```

We're expecting to see both a `poll` and an `options` parameter be passed in. We know that our options should be a comma joined list of poll options, as well. We're going to make assumptions about how our `create` function is going to work in our context (at this point, the importance of working with our context to keep the rest of our code will become very, very clear). We'll assume that we'll create a handy `create_poll_with_options` function that will take in the poll parameters and a list of options to add to that poll.

We'll then use the Elixir `with` statement to make sure the results we get from that function make sense. If all is good, we'll send a flash message out and redirect back to the list of polls! Let's take a look at our context next. In `lib/vocial/votes/votes.ex` let's add our `create_poll_with_options` function, taking in the Poll attributes and list of Options:

```
def create_poll_with_options(poll_attrs, options) do
  Repo.transaction(fn ->
    with {:ok, poll} <- create_poll(poll_attrs),
         {:ok, _options} <- create_options(options, poll)
    do
      poll
    else
      _ -> Repo.rollback("Failed to create poll")
    end
  end)
end
```

We'll wrap the entire thing inside of a transaction first. The Repo.transaction statement takes in a function as its only argument and expects either the operation to complete or a rollback to be issued (via the `Repo.rollback()` function). So we have another `with` statement after that, wherein the first check is a call to an arbitrary `create_poll` function, and the second check is a `create_options` function that takes in the list of options and the database-created poll (we'll need that to link the option back to the appropriate `poll_id`). We'll throw out the resulting options since we don't need those options (they'll be attached to the Repo anyways). If all goes well, we'll return the resulting poll; otherwise, we'll roll back the entire transaction!

Next, we'll write up our `create_poll` function, which is a pretty simple function. It just starts with a blank Poll struct, passes that into the changeset function on the Poll schema, and then finally inserts the whole thing to `Repo.Repo.insert()`. If it is successful, it will return data in the format `{:ok, returned_struct_from_db}`:

```
def create_poll(attrs) do
  %Poll{}
  |> Poll.changeset(attrs)
  |> Repo.insert()
end
```

Next, we need to create a `create_options` function, which will iterate over a list of options, add the `poll_id` to each poll title, and create each poll. If any fail, the whole thing should fail and rollback the transaction. If all went well, we should return back the created options:

```
def create_options(options, poll) do
  results = Enum.map(options, fn option ->
    create_option(%{title: option, poll_id: poll.id})
  end)

  if Enum.any?(results, fn {status, _} -> status == :error end) do
    {:error, "Failed to create an option"}
  else
    {:ok, results}
  end
end
```

And finally, the last piece of this puzzle; we need the singular `create_option` function, which is basically a copy-paste of the `create_poll` function:

```
def create_option(attrs) do
  %Option{}
  |> Option.changeset(attrs)
  |> Repo.insert()
end
```

Now, if we return back to `/votes/new` in our browser, we should be able to create a new Poll with Options (each option separated by a comma), and everything should work just fine! Let's build a little bit of extra assurance into our app by writing up some unit tests to cover this functionality so we don't get too trusting of our manual QA process.

Writing our unit tests

If we really want to be able to mark this code as complete, we need to start testing our code, to get a better picture of if it is working as expected and performing all of the necessary functions we need. We'll create a couple of new folders and a new file, `test/vocial/votes/votes_test.ex`, which will be in charge of testing our Context code.

Like most Phoenix code that we write, we'll start off by defining a test module. We'll also need some helper macros defined in our app's `DataCase` module and a few `alias` statements to make our lives easier. So we'll start out with:

```
defmodule Vocial.VotesTest do
  use Vocial.DataCase

  alias Vocial.Votes
end
```

This will be the beginning of our test code. Next we're going to write some code to tackle our simplest test cases, and we'll start by tackling the case for Polls. We'll use ExUnit's `describe` function to block this off, and then we'll start off with a beginning set of valid attributes to create a poll with.

 ExUnit is the built-in unit testing framework provided as part of every standard Elixir project!

Another thing we'll need to be able to get our tests moving at a decent pace are fixtures. Fixtures, in the case of an Ecto application, are just helper functions that create rows in our database that we can use to verify functionality like the `list_poll()` function! Based on the starting set of valid attributes we can specify to create a fixture, we then create a poll and return the poll that we created out as the return value of that function.

Finally, we'll write our first test, which should create a single starting poll and verify that `list_polls` returns a list of just that poll. This will be enough for us to have a good starting point for our tests and be able to write tests that cover some of the more complicated bits of functionality later:

```
describe "polls" do
  @valid_attrs %{ title: "Hello" }

  def poll_fixture(attrs \\ %{}) do
    with create_attrs <- Enum.into(attrs, @valid_attrs),
         {:ok, poll} <- Votes.create_poll(create_attrs),
         poll <- Repo.preload(poll, :options)
    do
      poll
    end
  end

  test "list_polls/0 returns all polls" do
    poll = poll_fixture()
```

```
        assert Votes.list_polls() == [poll]
    end
end
```

We're creating a single poll and verifying that the single (and only) poll is what gets returned to us in our `list_poll()` function, inside of our Votes context! We have a few other functions that we've defined as public, so let's also make sure that those new functions are appropriately covered!

The next test that we'll tackle is the `new_poll()` function. This just returns us a blank changeset, so this should be incredibly easy to test out:

```
test "new_poll/0 returns a new blank changeset" do
    changeset = Votes.new_poll()
    assert changeset.__struct__ == Ecto.Changeset
end
```

`__struct__` is a special property built into Elixir structs that tell you which module they map to, so since we're just verifying that it creates a new changeset, this gives us everything we need!

Let's move on to a slightly more complicated example (which we've already sort of tested, but it's always nice to be explicit with our tests), testing `create_poll()`:

```
test "create_poll/1 returns a new poll" do
    {:ok, poll} = Votes.create_poll(@valid_attrs)
    assert Enum.any?(Votes.list_polls(), fn p -> p.id == poll.id end)
end
```

This just says "Hey, make sure that when you just create a poll it gets added to the list of polls returned." Simple! Next, we'll test out `create_poll_with_options`, which should create our poll and all three options as well! This should also be a pretty simple test: we'll verify that the created poll matches the title we supply, and that it has the same number of options as we specify in the `create` function:

```
test "create_poll_with_options/2 returns a new poll with options" do
    title = "Poll With Options"
    options = ["Choice 1", "Choice 2", "Choice 3"]
    {:ok, poll} = Votes.create_poll_with_options(%{title: title}, options)
    assert poll.title == title
    assert Enum.count(poll.options) == 3
end
```

This should go off without a hitch, right? Let's run it to make sure:

```
$ mix test
......


  1) test polls create_poll_with_options/2 returns a new poll with options
(Vocial.VotesTest)
     test/vocial/votes/votes_test.exs:32
     ** (Protocol.UndefinedError) protocol Enumerable not implemented for
#Ecto.Association.NotLoaded<association :options is not loaded>. This
protocol is implemented for: DBConnection.PrepareStream,
DBConnection.Stream, Date.Range, Ecto.Adapters.SQL.Stream, File.Stream,
Function, GenEvent.Stream, HashDict, HashSet, IO.Stream, List, Map, MapSet,
Postgrex.Stream, Range, Stream
     code: assert Enum.count(poll.options) == 3
     stacktrace:
       (elixir)
/private/tmp/elixir-20180130-3962-102gd1x/elixir-1.6.1/lib/elixir/lib/enum.
ex:1: Enumerable.impl_for!/1
       (elixir)
/private/tmp/elixir-20180130-3962-102gd1x/elixir-1.6.1/lib/elixir/lib/enum.
ex:153: Enumerable.count/1
       (elixir) lib/enum.ex:554: Enum.count/1
       test/vocial/votes/votes_test.exs:37: (test)



  2) test GET /polls (VocialWeb.PollControllerTest)
     test/vocial_web/controllers/poll_controller_test.exs:4
     Assertion with =~ failed
     code:  assert html_response(conn, 200) =~ poll.title()
     left:  "<!DOCTYPE html>\n<html lang=\"en\">\n  <head>\n    <meta
charset=\"utf-8\">\n    <meta http-equiv=\"X-UA-Compatible\"
content=\"IE=edge\">\n    <meta name=\"viewport\" content=\"width=device-
width, initial-scale=1\">\n    <meta name=\"description\" content=\"\">\n
<meta name=\"author\" content=\"\">\n\n    <title>Hello Vocial!</title>\n
<link rel=\"stylesheet\" href=\"/css/app.css\">\n  </head>\n\n  <body>\n
<div class=\"container\">\n      <header class=\"header\">\n        <nav
role=\"navigation\">\n          <ul class=\"nav nav-pills pull-right\">\n
<li><a href=\"http://www.phoenixframework.org/docs\">Get Started</a></li>\n
</ul>\n        </nav>\n        <span class=\"logo\"></span>\n
</header>\n\n      <p class=\"alert alert-info\" role=\"alert\"></p>\n
<p class=\"alert alert-danger\" role=\"alert\"></p>\n\n        <main
role=\"main\">\n        </main>\n\n      </div> <!-- /container -->\n
<script src=\"/js/app.js\"></script>\n  </body>\n</html>\n"
     right: "My First Poll"
     stacktrace:
       test/vocial_web/controllers/poll_controller_test.exs:17: (test)
```

This is also an exercise that you'll want to repeat every time you're thinking about adding something. When you think you just need to add a table to something, it's very easy to just do it and forget about it. This is one of the most common ways that web applications tend to bloat over time; the mentality of *just do it and forget it* tends to lead to duplicate tables or duplicate information, legacy portions of the code base, and other maintenance nightmares and headaches that will compound very quickly over the course of your engineering career!

Designing our user schema

Let's start with one of the most important introductory steps for adding a new table and schema into our application—designing the database table. This isn't just about designing the table, because you don't want to just think about the database impacts of creating/adding a new table and shaping the data model for this table; you also want to give a lot of thought to how the data model will impact your application's design and structure over time.

We'll start by figuring out what questions our application is trying to answer in regards to our new users schema. First off, we ask **WHAT** information we want to store:

```
Users
-----
-* id
- username
- email
- encrypted_password
- active
-* inserted_at
-* updated_at

(* means it is a default column created as part of the Ecto migration
process)
```

This design gives us the minimal amount of user information that we can comfortably store without asking for too much storing too little. To start, we'll separate the idea of the user's username and email from each other to provide a way for a user to change their email address in the system without affecting their login information.

Next, we'll store the email address for the user, because maybe someday we'll want to add support for emailing a user a link to reset their password or send them information about the polls they created. Maybe there will be some other thing we'll need down the line, like the ability to send them marketing emails to get them to use the site more or upsell some sort of premium memberships! The sky is the limit for us!

Then we have our `encrypted_password` field. This will not store a human-readable (usually referred to as the *plaintext*) representation of our password, but rather one that has been encrypted through an algorithm using some sort of internal secret key. We'll later introduce the concept of **virtual** fields later that we can use for things like the password and password confirmation values that won't actually get stored anywhere in the database but still need to be tracked in some temporary way by the application.

 For now, we're going to be faking the encryption of the user's passwords into the system until a later section where we will discuss in much greater detail how to properly secure our system.

`active` will be used to determine if a user has been logically deleted (but not actually deleted) from the database. If we only logically delete a user, it will prevent weird scenarios later on in the life of our application where old polls and votes are attributed to some user that no longer exists with any sort of representation in our system anymore!

`inserted_at` and `updated_at` are timestamp columns that Ecto adds to most migrations and tables by default. These help keep track of when information in the database is either added or changed so that we can keep track of at least some form of basic audit information.

Creating our user schema

We're pretty comfortable with how our design for our user schema currently looks, so let's start working with this a little bit more and actually create the initial migration for our application! As per Chapter 3, *Storing and Retrieving Vote Data with Ecto Pages*, we'll be working through all of this manually to make sure we get the design and creation of everything set exactly as we're expecting; sometimes working with generators will give you a lot of extra cruft and code that you may not necessarily want as part of the baseline for your application. Let's call our first migration `create_users_table` and run the Ecto migration generator `mix` command:

```
$ mix ecto.gen.migration create_users_table
* creating priv/repo/migrations
* creating priv/repo/migrations/20171017173615_create_users_table.exs
```

This will give us our default blank starting point for our migration:

```
defmodule Vocial.Repo.Migrations.CreateUsersTable do
  use Ecto.Migration

  def change do

  end
end
```

Remember that id will always be created by default with any table creation and that we should include timestamps via the built-in timestamps() helper, leaving us needing to create username, email, and active. We should also set active to have a default value of true, since we don't want to be accidentally creating everyone's user account as inactive by default. Finally, we'll want to store the encrypted_password for the user (although we'll dive into how to implement that later).

 That's actually not to say you couldn't set the default to false. You may have a scenario where you don't want user accounts to be active until they finish some portion of the registration process. For example, maybe they need to click a link to verify their supplied email address before they're made a fullyactive account!

This should leave us with a migration file that looks something like this:

```
defmodule Vocial.Repo.Migrations.CreateUsersTable do
  use Ecto.Migration

  def change do
    create table(:users) do
      add :username, :string
      add :email, :string
      add :active, :boolean, default: true
      add :encrypted_password, :string
      timestamps()
    end
  end
end
```

If we're satisfied with the results, we can start the process of actually running our migration. Returning to our terminal, we'll run the following command:

```
$ mix ecto.migrate
[info] == Running Vocial.Repo.Migrations.CreateUsersTable.change/0 forward
[info] create table users
[info] == Migrated in 0.1s
```

Success! We now have the users table created in our application. We can verify this through any database application that allows you to view the structure of your tables, such as **Psequel** for OS X:

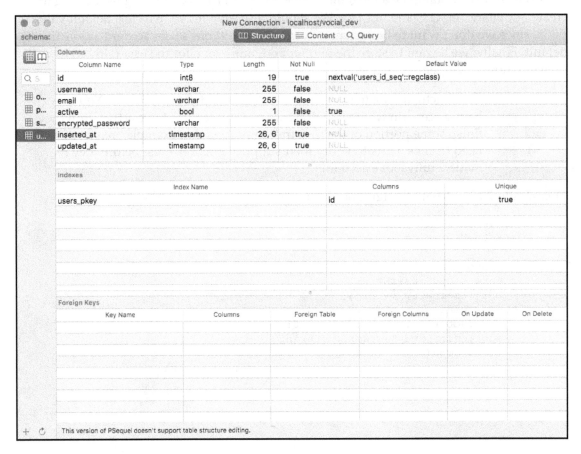

Great, it's all there! We can now move on to creating the actual schema file in our application! Remember that, by default, we'll be starting with no file or anything, as we're doing everything ourselves instead of using generators to accomplish those tasks, so let's dive into things! We'll start off by briefly mentioning that we'll be creating an **accounts** context for our user schema, since this directly informs the directory and file structure that we'll need to create for our application. Under `lib/vocial`, create an `accounts` directory that just has one file in it: `user.ex`. We'll start off with a baseline for our user schema, similar to both the migration and previous schemas that we have created for polls and votes:

```
defmodule Vocial.Accounts.User do
  use Ecto.Schema
  import Ecto.Changeset

  alias Vocial.Accounts.User

  schema "users" do
    field :username, :string
    field :email, :string
    field :active, :boolean, default: true
    field :encrypted_password, :string

    timestamps()
  end

  def changeset(%User{}=user, attrs) do
    user
    |> cast(attrs, [:username, :email, :active])
    |> validate_required([:username, :email, :active])
  end
end
```

Okay, we have a good baseline and have introduced the User Schema into our application. We've set it up with the initial columns that we designed and handled our standard imports, aliases, and macros to make this all fit nicely into Ecto's world. Let's move on to our context so we can start making sense of our schema!

 We haven't added `encrypted_password` to our list of fields in either `cast` or `validate_required` yet on purpose! We're going to be dealing with this column specifically later on when we deal with password encryption!

Creating our accounts context

We'll need to start off by creating the actual file that will be used as the primary interface for our context. We already created our `lib/vocial/accounts` directory, so it will be pretty easy for us to next create our context file. Let's create `lib/vocial/accounts/accounts.ex` and give it a basic structure:

```
defmodule Vocial.Accounts do
  import Ecto.Query, warn: false

  alias Vocial.Repo
  alias Vocial.Accounts.User
end
```

Next, we'll need to give it some sort of starting function so that we can actually start to test that we've successfully hooked up the user schema to the accounts context and then to our application at large. We'll start simply, by creating a `list_users()` function that will just return a list of every user in our system:

```
def list_users, do: Repo.all(User)
```

To make sure this works before we start hooking everything up, we should probably go to the open IEx shell that's running our application and try this out. We'll first run `recompile` to rebuild our application and then we'll try actually calling this new function:

```
iex(1)> recompile
Compiling 2 files (.ex)
Generated vocial app
:ok
iex(2)> Vocial.Accounts.list_users()
[]
[debug] QUERY OK source="users" db=16.6ms queue=0.1ms
SELECT u0."id", u0."username", u0."email", u0."active", u0."inserted_at",
u0."updated_at" FROM "users" AS u0 []
```

No errors, so that's a good start! We also don't have any data in here yet, so that's going to make things harder for us. Let's add a function to our context that will create a user, and a function that will just give us back a blank changeset that we can utilize later on:

```
def new_user, do: User.changeset(%User{}, %{})

def create_user(attrs \\ %{}) do
  %User{}
  |> User.changeset(attrs)
  |> Repo.insert()
end
```

Now return back to your iex shell, recompile, and run the following command to create a new user:

```
iex(5)> Vocial.Accounts.new_user()
#Ecto.Changeset<action: nil, changes: %{},
 errors: [username: {"can't be blank", [validation: :required]},
   email: {"can't be blank", [validation: :required]}],
 data: #Vocial.Accounts.User<>, valid?: false>
iex(6)> Vocial.Accounts.create_user(%{username: "test", email:
"test@test.com", encrypted_password: "abc123"})
[debug] QUERY OK db=31.6ms
INSERT INTO "users"
("active","email","username","inserted_at","updated_at") VALUES
($1,$2,$3,$4,$5) RETURNING "id" [true, "test@test.com", "test", {{2017, 10,
17}, {18, 29, 43, 812187}}, {{2017, 10, 17}, {18, 29, 43, 814326}}]
{:ok,
 %Vocial.Accounts.User{__meta__: #Ecto.Schema.Metadata<:loaded, "users">,
   active: true, email: "test@test.com", id: 1,
   inserted_at: ~N[2017-10-17 18:29:43.812187],
   updated_at: ~N[2017-10-17 18:29:43.814326], username: "test"}}
```

Great! We were able to insert a user into our database using our context's helper function, so we should also be able to use the `list_users()` helper function to get at least one user back from the database!

```
iex(7)> Vocial.Accounts.list_users()
[debug] QUERY OK source="users" db=6.7ms
SELECT u0."id", u0."username", u0."email", u0."active", u0."inserted_at",
u0."updated_at" FROM "users" AS u0 []
[%Vocial.Accounts.User{__meta__: #Ecto.Schema.Metadata<:loaded, "users">,
   active: true, email: "test@test.com", id: 1,
   inserted_at: ~N[2017-10-17 18:29:43.812187],
   updated_at: ~N[2017-10-17 18:29:43.814326], username: "test"}]
```

 The keys you get back in the map may not match the order that they're queried, and that's okay! A map has no dependencies on the ordering of its keys so there's nothing here that will cause you grief down the line!

We will also likely need to be able to select a single user out of the table by its primary key, so we'll quickly add a `get` function as well:

```
def get_user(id), do: Repo.get(User, id)
```

For the final piece, we'll test this out in our iex shell as well to make sure that we've done everything we need to make this (at least minimally) useful for now! As per the previous bits of code that we added, we should very quickly test this out in an iex shell:

```
iex(9)> Vocial.Accounts.get_user(1)
[debug] QUERY OK source="users" db=8.8ms
SELECT u0."id", u0."username", u0."email", u0."active", u0."inserted_at",
u0."updated_at" FROM "users" AS u0 WHERE (u0."id" = $1) [1]
%Vocial.Accounts.User{__meta__: #Ecto.Schema.Metadata<:loaded, "users">,
 active: true, email: "test@test.com", id: 1,
 inserted_at: ~N[2017-10-17 18:29:43.812187],
 updated_at: ~N[2017-10-17 18:29:43.814326], username: "test"}
```

Great! The few helper functions that we wrote for our context are working exactly as expected! This is a very strong start to getting the rest of our application up and running, so let's dive right into writing some unit tests to make sure the baseline behavior for our Context is covered. Tackling this now will make writing the code connecting our controller to our context significantly simpler, so that's why we're specifically interrupting our workflow to write some tests now!

Writing our user unit tests

Before you ever start to add new tests to your application, you should always take a quick step back to verify that your test suite is currently green, so let's do that very quickly before we do anything else:

```
$ mix test
Compiling 3 files (.ex)
Generated vocial app
. . . . . . . . . .

Finished in 0.2 seconds
11 tests, 0 failures

Randomized with seed 742658
```

Seeing that our test suite is currently green, we can confidently move on and start writing more of our test suite. We'll need to create a new directory and file, similar to what we did previously with adding the new context to our application. Generally speaking, writing tests for your context is enough since it should cover the functionality of your schemas nearly 100%, so we'll only need to create the one test file. Create `test/vocial/accounts/accounts_test.exs` and we'll start building up our file.

We'll want to define this as a module, use the DataCase macros, and alias the relevant other modules in our code base (accounts and repo). Next, we'll build up a describe block for the user-related functionality in our context. We'll need to create a simple user fixture that we can reuse to quickly create a new user (this uses our context's `create_user/1` function!), and finally we'll write a simple test for `list_users/0`:

```
defmodule Vocial.AccountsTest do
  use Vocial.DataCase

  alias Vocial.Accounts

  describe "users" do
    @valid_attrs %{ username: "test", email: "test@test.com", active: true
}

    def user_fixture(attrs \\ %{}) do
      with create_attrs <- Map.merge(@valid_attrs, attrs),
           {:ok, user} <- Accounts.create_user(create_attrs)
      do
        user
      end
    end

    test "list_users/0 returns all users" do
      user = user_fixture()
      assert Accounts.list_users() == [user]
    end
  end
end
```

We'll run our tests; we should have 11 passing tests now instead of 10, and still 0 failures! Next, we'll write tests for `get_user/1` (which should just return the user that we specify the ID for), `new_user/0` (which should get the returned value from `new_user` and verify it is a changeset), and `create_user/1` (which should grab a before and after of the `list_users/0` function output and verify the user doesn't exist in the list before it's created but does exist in the list after it is created):

```
test "get_user/1 returns the user with the id" do
  user = user_fixture()
  assert Accounts.get_user(user.id) == user
end

test "new_user/0 returns a blank changeset" do
  changeset = Accounts.new_user()
  assert changeset.__struct__ == Ecto.Changeset
end
```

```
test "create_user/1 creates the user in the db and returns it" do
  before = Accounts.list_users()
  user = user_fixture()
  updated = Accounts.list_users()
  assert !(Enum.any?(before, fn u -> user == u end))
  assert Enum.any?(updated, fn u -> user ==u end)
end
```

After rerunning our test suite, we should see all green tests (15 tests in total so far) with no failures! This is a wonderful place to start building up the rest of our application, so let's move on to actually creating something tangible in our application: a user signup page!

Creating a user signup page

Okay, we have our tests, we have our context, we have our database set up and ready to go, so we don't really have any further barriers to entry into us creating our interface for people to sign up and start creating their user accounts! We'll need to go through a lot of the same processes and steps to accomplish all of this that we've needed to do in the past. We'll need to:

- Create the route that will tell the browser how to get to the right pages
- Create the controller and the functions in the controller that will tell Phoenix how to handle the routes
- Create the templates that will represent the actual interface that the user sees
- Hook the context up to each of the functions
- Write tests that actually cover all of this new functionality that we're adding over time

Creating the routes

We're starting off by just providing the user a simple way to sign up; we will essentially just be displaying a new users page with a form and then showing some sort of profile page for the user. The flow of information in the browser may look something like this:

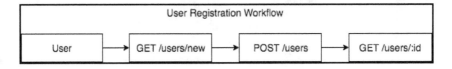

This will help us figure out how to create the routes for our application. If we're following a strictly RESTful design methodology, then the signup page should be a *new* route on the user's resource. Creating the user (clicking `Submit` on our form) would be a `POST` to the user's resource, with the body being the user we're trying to create. Finally, if successful, we'll show the created user (something like a user profile, essentially) back out to the user. If we were thinking about this strictly from the perspective of our Phoenix routes definition, we would expect it to look something like this:

```
get "/users/new", UserController, :new
get "/users/:id", UserController, :show
post "/users", UserController, :create
```

We'll need a `UserController` to route these requests and three new functions: `new`, `show`, and `create`. We can create `lib/vocial_web/controllers/user_controller.ex` and start it off with a pretty basic skeleton.

Creating the controller code (with tests)

Next, following the example of other bits of functionality we've been adding along the way in this chapter, we'll also simultaneously write some tests as we go along to make the general process of testing all of this significantly easier. The controller code will start off like this:

```
defmodule VocialWeb.UserController do
  use VocialWeb, :controller

  def new(conn, _) do
    conn
  end

  def create(conn, _) do
    conn
  end

  def show(conn, _) do
    conn
  end
end
```

The test code (located at
`test/vocial_web/controllers/user_controller_test.exs`) will start off like this:

```
defmodule VocialWeb.UserControllerTest do
  use VocialWeb.ConnCase

  test "GET /users/new", %{conn: conn} do
    conn = get conn, "/users/new"
    assert html_response(conn, 200)
  end

  test "GET /users/:id", %{conn: conn} do
    conn = get conn, "/users/1"
    assert html_response(conn, 200)
  end

  test "POST /users", %{conn: conn} do
    conn = post conn, "/users"
    assert html_response(conn, 200)
  end
end
```

Now, if you try to run any of these yet, they absolutely WILL fail! That's okay, though! We're doing a little bit of red/green/refactor (where we expect the tests to fail on the first run, then figure out what we need to do to make them pass on the next run, and then finally clean-up/refactor some of the code to start adding additional logic). We'll go through this cycle a few times as we start iterating on this functionality by addressing the things that are broken to start.

Maybe we'll start off by saying *our user signup page should at least say User Signup somewhere on it.* We'll go back to the /users/new test and modify it to test for that behavior:

```
test "GET /users/new", %{conn: conn} do
  conn = get conn, "/users/new"
  assert html_response(conn, 200) =~ "User Signup"
end
```

Now we'll start building up the functionality of our controller, view, and template so that this test passes. Returning back to our user controller, we should tell the controller function to take the connection object and render a `new.html` template with it. Remember that we want to pass along a change set any time we display a form to the user, so we'll also need to incorporate the `new_user` call into our controller code:

```
alias Vocial.Accounts

def new(conn, _) do
  user = Accounts.new_user()
  render(conn, "new.html", user: user)
end
```

This will also require us to create a view file, since you cannot render anything out to the browser without macros unless you have one, so create `lib/vocial_web/views/user_view.ex`:

```
defmodule VocialWeb.UserView do
  use VocialWeb, :view
end
```

If we rerun our tests, we should be down to only two failing tests! Next we'll move on to the *create* call in our user controller. If you remember from the work that we did to create our `create` function in the poll controller, we're essentially going to be doing the same thing, except with user information here instead of vote information:

```
def create(conn, %{"user" => user_params}) do
  with {:ok, user} <- Accounts.create_user(user_params) do
    conn
    |> put_flash(:info, "User created!")
    |> redirect(to: user_path(conn, :show, user))
  end
end
```

Swap back over to the test, where we will assert that when attempting to create a user with valid data, we are redirected off to the user path:

```
test "POST /users", %{conn: conn} do
  user_params = %{"username" => "test", "email" => "test@test.com"}
  conn = post conn, "/users", %{"user" => user_params}
  assert redirected_to(conn) =~ "/users/"
end
```

Finally, we need to make our last test a little more cohesive. We'll start by creating a show template for the user, so create `lib/vocial_web/templates/user/show.html.eex` and give it this content:

```
<h2><%= @user.username %>'s Profile</h2>
```

Additionally, return back to `lib/vocial_web/controllers/user_controller.ex` and update the `show` function to pull a user from the database and pass it into the template:

```
def show(conn, %{"id" => id}) do
  with user <- Accounts.get_user(id), do: render(conn, "show.html",
  user: user)
end
```

We'll modify the test itself to test for the appearance of the user's username on the page, which is probably a good initial template to start with:

```
test "GET /users/:id", %{conn: conn} do
  with {:ok, user} <- Vocial.Accounts.create_user(%{"username" =>
  "test", "email" => "test@test.com"}) do
    conn = get conn, "/users/#{user.id}"
    assert html_response(conn, 200) =~ user.username
  else
    _ -> assert false
  end
end
```

We're using a `with` block here to make sure we get back a valid created user and then we're fetching the user page for that created user. From there, we're verifying that the user's username does indeed appear on that page, as we expect!

Finally, we should probably go back and add to our `new.html.eex` form a little more. It should actually be a form, to start, and it should have all of the fields we'd need to be able to create a new user. Create `lib/vocial_web/templates/user/new.html.eex` and give it this body (you'll have to create the `templates/user` directory):

```
<h2>User Signup</h2>
<hr />
<div>
  <%= form_for @user, user_path(@conn, :create), fn f -> %>
    <%= label f, :username, "Username:" %>
    <br />
    <%= text_input f, :username %>
    <br />
    <%= label f, :email, "Email:" %>
    <br />
```

```
      <%= text_input f, :email %>
      <br />
      <%= submit "Sign Up" %>
   <% end %>
</div>
```

If we rerun our tests now, everything should succeed! Let's make sure our test checks for two things:

- That we've set the user value on the conn to be a changeset
- That we have a form on the page

To test these, we'll modify our test and make it a little more in-depth:

```
test "GET /users/new", %{conn: conn} do
  conn = get conn, "/users/new"
  response = html_response(conn, 200)
  assert response =~ "User Signup"
  assert conn.assigns.user.__struct__ == Ecto.Changeset
  assert response =~ "action=\"/users\" method=\"post\""
end
```

Run your tests after adding those changes and we should be back to a fully-green test suite; we've managed to write a good chunk of our code without even opening up our web browser! Our code is in a pretty good spot, so now it's time to clean up and refactor a few things!

First, we have the user form on the *new* template, but what if we want to be able to reuse that for an *edit* profile page? There's no clean way for us to do that as-is, so let's create a new file in the *user* template directory called `form.html.eex` and give it the following contents:

```
<div>
  <%= form_for @user, user_path(@conn, :create), fn f -> %>
    <%= label f, :username, "Username:" %>
    <br />
    <%= text_input f, :username %>
    <br />
    <%= label f, :email, "Email:" %>
    <br />
    <%= text_input f, :email %>
    <br />
    <%= submit "Sign Up" %>
  <% end %>
</div>
```

Then, we'll hop over to the `new.html.eex` file in the same directory and tell it to instead use the new template to display the user form:

```
<h2>User Signup</h2>
<hr />
<%= render("form.html", %{ user: @user, conn: @conn }) %>
```

That's it! Now, we are set up in a good way to be able to allow the user to edit their profile later on (when we get to that step in our project), so let's re-run our tests:

```
$ mix test
Compiling 1 file (.ex)
.................

Finished in 0.3 seconds
18 tests, 0 failures

Randomized with seed 57047
```

If you've followed along, you should see a user form that looks something like this:

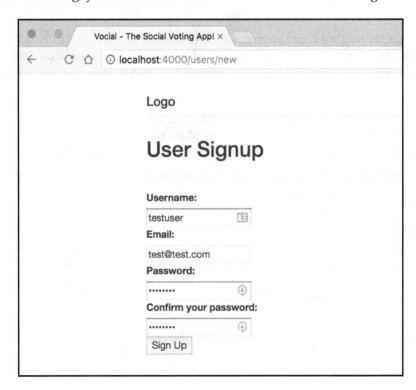

The last bit of housekeeping is that we can change our routes to instead use a separate helper to help clean that file up as well. Instead of manually specifying each route with its appropriate method, we can instead just use the `resources` helper to describe our routes. Going back to `lib/vocial_web/router.ex`, we can rewrite our root scope to instead be:

```
scope "/", VocialWeb do
  pipe_through :browser # Use the default browser stack

  get "/", PageController, :index

  resources "/votes", VoteController, only: [:index, :new, :create]
  resources "/users", UserController, only: [:new, :show, :create]
end
```

Now, for one final time, we'll go back and re-run our tests, verify that the test suite is green, and be ready to move on to adding the *password* portion of our signup page!

Setting up the password functionality

We have our controller, our context, our schema, and everything in between! Our code is supported by a well-tested foundation and at least a baseline level of functionality, so let's move on to making the user signup portion better-protected by dealing with passwords and encryption! The first thing we'll want to do before we do anything else is install a library that will help us handle the encryption portion of building our user account system. For us to be able to do that, we will want to use a handy library called *Comeonin*. This library provides a number of different password encryption schemes, but we'll stick to just using bcrypt, an incredibly common and reliable password encryption algorithm!

Installing Comeonin

First we'll need to install `comeonin` into our Phoenix application through the `mix.exs` file. We'll also need to include the `bcrypt_elixir` hex package into our project to provide the hooks into the bcrypt encryption protocol for our password. First, we'll need to modify the `mix.exs` file in the root of our Vocial application. If you look for the `deps` function in the file, you'll find a list of tuples that specify the dependencies of our project by their hex package name and the version. Modify that function to include the two new libraries:

```
defp deps do
  [
    {:phoenix, "~> 1.3.0"},
    {:phoenix_pubsub, "~> 1.0"},
    {:phoenix_ecto, "~> 3.2"},
```

```
        {:postgrex, ">= 0.0.0"},
        {:phoenix_html, "~> 2.10"},
        {:phoenix_live_reload, "~> 1.0", only: :dev},
        {:gettext, "~> 0.11"},
        {:cowboy, "~> 1.0"},
        {:comeonin, "~> 4.0.3"},
        {:bcrypt_elixir, "~> 1.0.4"}
    ]
  end
```

Next, return back to your IEx terminal and terminate the running session, and then run the command:

```
$ mix do deps.get, compile
Resolving Hex dependencies...
Dependency resolution completed:
  bcrypt_elixir 1.0.6
  comeonin 4.0.3
  ...

Generated vocial app
```

You've now successfully added new dependencies to your Phoenix application! We can now take advantage of the encryption libraries that already exist instead of trying to create our own, which means we're ready to start modifying the incoming change sets for users to encrypt the incoming password!

 While we will be generally avoiding including too many third-party libraries in the course of this book, this is one of the few exceptions that I'll be making, as the functionality is core enough and difficult enough to write ourselves that it wouldn't pay off for us to make our own!

Adding Comeonin to the user schema file

Now that we have Comeonin and the libraries to support bcrypting passwords in place, we need to actually hook it up to the rest of our application. This entails a few steps for us:

1. We need to have Comeonin interact with our changesets to insert the encrypted password.
2. We need to have the Controller check our password against the hash rather than the plaintext password.

It's pretty easy for us to implement this first step, so we'll start with this. Generally speaking, you should avoid adding any new code to your schemas unless it's something that is very specific to the shape of the data that is entering/leaving your database. Since this is taking information at the final step (just before inserting into the database), modifying it, and then inserting the modified value into the database, this is a great candidate for code that should live in the schema.

Right now, there's no easy way for a password and a password confirmation to enter our schema at all. That means that if we just straight up tried to implement password encryption we would fail rather quickly, because there would never be anything for our code to encrypt in the first place! The easiest way for us to tackle this to take it head-on and introduce two new fields to our schema: `password` and `password_confirmation`. The confirmation field is needed as well, because we want Phoenix and Ecto to be able to make sure that the user entered the same password twice; we don't want them to accidentally set the password to something strange or something with a typo in it and then not remember how to log in!

Unfortunately, if you remember from our schema, we also have absolutely no representation of either of those fields in our database table. All we have right now is the final representation of the password: our `encrypted_password` column. The good news is that Ecto supports a concept of *virtual fields*, which are fields that may need to exist in the code and in the changeset but are not supported by physical representations in the database table itself. Let's hop up to our schema definition in `lib/vocial/accounts/user.ex` and add our two virtual fields:

```elixir
schema "users" do
  field :username, :string
  field :email, :string
  field :active, :boolean, default: true
  field :encrypted_password, :string

  field :password, :string, virtual: true
  field :password_confirmation, :string, virtual: true

  timestamps()
end
```

Next, we'll hop over to our changeset function, since we'll need to modify the casts and required fields. We'll need to add our two new virtual fields to our cast list, since they are both valid fields to try to assign values to and should not get stripped out. We'll also introduce a new step into our changeset pipeline to encrypt the password based on the `password` and `password_confirmation`. We'll also want to add a quick validation to ensure that the `password` value is the same as the `password_confirmation` value! Let's take a look at the new changeset function:

```
def changeset(%User{}=user, attrs) do
  user
  |> cast(attrs, [:username, :email, :active, :password,
  :password_confirmation])
  |> validate_confirmation(:password, message: "does not match
  password!")
  |> encrypt_password()
  |> validate_required([:username, :email, :active,
  :encrypted_password])
end
```

The next step is to write out our `encrypt_password/1` function itself. We'll take the changeset that is being sent in through our pipeline, use `get_change/2` to pull the password value out of it, and then encrypt it and put it back into the changeset via `put_change/3`. Let's write that `encrypt_password` function now:

```
def encrypt_password(changeset) do
  with password when not is_nil(password) <- get_change(changeset,
  :password) do
    put_change(changeset, :encrypted_password,
    Comeonin.Bcrypt.hashpwsalt(password))
  else
    _ -> changeset
  end
end
```

Updating our tests

This all looks good, but if we go back and write our tests, we're going to see a ton of failures! The reason for this is that when we were running around creating our fixtures for various tests, we never specified any values for `password` and `password_confirmation`, which is now a required value for us to be able to save any changeset. We'll start off by modifying `test/vocial_web/controllers/user_controller_test.exs`. The easiest thing to do to start with is setting a module attribute in `VocialWeb.UserControllerTest` that sets all of the valid creation parameters for a user now:

```
@create_params %{
  "username" => "test",
  "email" => "test@test.com",
  "password" => "test",
  "password_confirmation" => "test"
}
```

Notice the addition here of `password` and `password_confirmation` (and that they have the same value). Remember that this is the set of valid creation attributes, so we want to have them in that map and matching to avoid any errors on changeset creation. Next we'll modify the `GET /users/:id` test and the `POST /users` test to use the `create_params` map:

```
test "GET /users/:id", %{conn: conn} do
  with {:ok, user} <- Vocial.Accounts.create_user(@create_params) do
    conn = get conn, "/users/#{user.id}"
    assert html_response(conn, 200) =~ user.username
  else
    _ -> assert false
  end
end

test "POST /users", %{conn: conn} do
  conn = post conn, "/users", %{"user" => @create_params}
  assert redirected_to(conn) =~ "/users/"
end
```

Notice the use of `@create_params` as the argument to `create_user/1`! Rerun your tests now and you should have a few more successful test passing! We now have a few failing tests, in `test/vocial/accounts/accounts_test.exs`, so we'll fix those by doing essentially the same thing:

```
@valid_attrs %{
  username: "test",
  email: "test@test.com",
  active: true,
  password: "test",
  password_confirmation: "test"
}

def user_fixture(attrs \\ %{}) do
  with create_attrs <- Map.merge(@valid_attrs, attrs),
       {:ok, user} <- Accounts.create_user(create_attrs)
  do
    user |> Map.merge(%{password: nil, password_confirmation: nil})
  else
    error -> error
  end
end
```

There's a little bit of extra logic in this code: in the `user_fixture` function, we added a `Map.merge` call that sets `password` and `password_confirmation` to `nil`! We need to do this, because remember that those two fields are virtual fields; this means they will not receive a value when you select them out of the database! Without this code change, we'll get failures when comparing the users created to users pulled out of the database because they'll have mismatched fields. This should fix the few remaining failing tests for us, which is great! We'll also want to buff up our tests a little bit to include scenarios where we don't pass in passwords or where the password and password confirmation fields are mismatched:

```
test "create_user/1 fails to create the user without a password and
password_confirmation" do
    {:error, changeset} = user_fixture(%{password: nil,
password_confirmation: nil})
    assert !changeset.valid?
end

test "create_user/1 fails to create the user when the password and
the password_confirmation don't match" do
    {:error, changeset} = user_fixture(%{password: "test",
```

```
        password_confirmation: "fail"})
          assert !changeset.valid?
        end
```

Rerunning our tests now, we should see 20 tests with 0 failures! Now we can be confident about the behavior and functionality of our tests, so we should update the UI to include the password and password confirmation fields as well.

Updating the UI to include password fields

The good news is that updating our UI to include these options is actually really simple! All we need to do is add two new password inputs on the user form for each of the virtual fields. Because we were smart about things and added them as virtual fields to our changeset, we don't have to do any extra work, which is fantastic! Let's take a look at lib/vocial_web/templates/user/form.html.eex:

```
<div>
  <%= form_for @user, user_path(@conn, :create), fn f -> %>
    <%= label f, :username, "Username:" %>
    <br />
    <%= text_input f, :username %>
    <br />
    <%= label f, :email, "Email:" %>
    <br />
    <%= text_input f, :email %>
    <br />
    <%= label f, :password, "Password:" %>
    <br />
    <%= password_input f, :password %>
    <br />
    <%= label f, :password_confirmation, "Confirm your password:" %>
    <br />
    <%= password_input f, :password_confirmation %>
    <br />
    <%= submit "Sign Up" %>
  <% end %>
</div>
```

If you try that, everything should work as expected! If you pull that user from the database, you'll see a value like `$2b$12$mUmjMLEqa1I9O/Vw7wuR.eLaU.JhSy94IaZyiQYGg9xC8DTTDMUVS` in your database as the encrypted password value for that user! Unfortunately, if you add a mismatched password and password confirmation you'll instead get an error page, which is not ideal! It will complain about not returning a connection object in all cases, which is true if you look at the create function. We return a modified conn in the case where everything was good, but we don't have anything for when something goes wrong!

The good news, again, is that this is a simple fix! We just need to add an `else` case to our `with` statement that accounts for when an error is returned when attempting to create the user account:

```
def create(conn, %{"user" => user_params}) do
  with {:ok, user} <- Accounts.create_user(user_params) do
    conn
    |> put_flash(:info, "User created!")
    |> redirect(to: user_path(conn, :show, user))
  else
    {:error, user} ->
      conn
      |> put_flash(:error, "Failed to create user!")
      |> render("new.html", user: user)
  end
end
```

Try it again with bad data and we'll get a nice, clean error page and be returned back to the form where the user can re-enter the bad information but the good information remains in place! Now that we can have our users sign up, we should start giving users a means of actually logging into our system!

Creating a user login page

To create our user login experience, we'll need to start by creating a session controller that will be responsible for a few separate operations:

1. Users must be able to log in through some form.
2. Users must get logged in, set something in the user's session, and redirect out somewhere.
3. Users must be able to log out.

The best way for us to accomplish this is to create a separate sessions resource, where `create` represents the posted login that sets the user session and redirects. We'll also want a way to log in and log out (although we'll want to handle those separately). We'll start out with a few simple basics. To start, we need to modify our routes to include these new methods, and we'll also probably want to create simple URLs for login and logout, so we'll tackle both of these as well. In `lib/vocial_web/router.ex`, add the following to the root scope:

```
resources "/sessions", SessionController, only: [:create]

get "/login", SessionController, :new
get "/logout", SessionController, :delete
```

Then, create `lib/vocial_web/controllers/session_controller.ex` to start working on our session controller:

```
defmodule VocialWeb.SessionController do
  use VocialWeb, :controller

  def new(conn, _) do
    render(conn, "new.html")
  end

  def delete(conn, _) do
    conn
    |> delete_session(:user)
    |> put_flash(:info, "Logged out successfully!")
    |> redirect(to: "/")
  end

  def create(conn, _), do: conn
end
```

We're going to make a few assumptions here. First off, the new template should just be called `new.html.eex`, so we'll use the appropriate render call here for the `new` function. We don't care about what's passed in as `params`, so we can skip that. Second, our `delete` should just clear out the session (whichever key we choose to use to store the user information, which I've arbitrarily chosen as *user*). This also means that our inverse operation, `create`, should set the `:user` key in the session to something useful (generally a subset of the user's attributes). Finally, our create function will just be a dummy function for now; we'll get around to fleshing that out further a little bit later.

We'll also need to create a really quick login form under templates and a nearly empty session view. First, let's create the view at `lib/vocial_web/views/session_view.ex`:

```
defmodule VocialWeb.SessionView do
  use VocialWeb, :view
end
```

Then, let's create our login form at `lib/vocial_web/templates/session/new.html.eex`:

```
<div>
  <%= form_tag session_path(@conn, :create) do %>
    <label>
      Username:<br />
      <input type="text" name="username">
    </label>
    <br />
    <label>
      Password:<br />
      <input type="password" name="password">
    </label>
    <br />
    <%= submit "Login" %>
  <% end %>
</div>
```

We don't have a changeset that we're working with this time, so we can't just use the `form_for` function; we'll need to use `form_tag` to create the form with the appropriate CSRF protection. Then we'll just create the HTML inputs ourselves, and we should have an overall okay-looking login form:

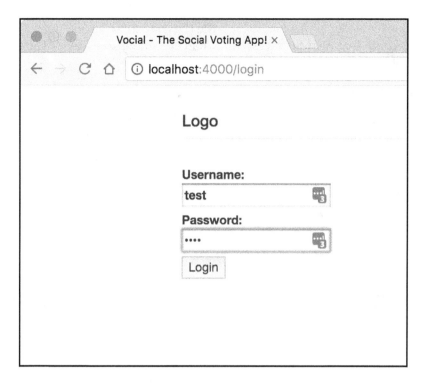

Building our create session function

Create is going to be a little trickier to write, but not by too much. One of the first gotchas is that we'll need to update the accounts context to look a user up by their username. Hop over to the accounts context (`lib/vocial/accounts/accounts.ex`) and add the following function:

```
def get_user_by_username(username) do
  Repo.get_by(User, username: username)
end
```

In the case where we don't get any users back, we'll return a nil value, but otherwise we'll assume that we got back a user that we can use to check the encrypted password of! `get_by\2` just takes the query (in our case, just any user schema) and the conditions to check by and attempts to return back the appropriate row from the table specified in the query.

Returning back over to our controller, we'll write the code to look for a user, a dummy function call to check that the user's password matches, and the session-setting logic. First, add an alias to `Vocial.Accounts` at the top:

Then, we'll build the `create` action:

```
def create(conn, %{"username" => username, "password" => password}) do
  with user <- Accounts.get_user_by_username(username),
       {:ok, login_user} <- login(user, password)
  do
    conn
    |> put_flash(:info, "Logged in successfully!")
    |> put_session(:user, %{ id: login_user.id, username:
login_user.username, email: login_user.email })
    |> redirect(to: "/")
  else
    {:error, _} ->
      conn
      |> put_flash(:error, "Invalid username/password!")
      |> render("new.html")
  end
end

defp login(user, password) do
  true
end
```

If you go back to the login page by visiting `http://localhost:4000/login` and type in a username for a user that exists in your system and any password, you should get a successful login message! This is great, but let's make it a tiny bit more secure by ACTUALLY checking the password using Comeonin. Again, good news: this is a really simple thing to do, thanks to the Comeonin developers:

```
defp login(user, password) do
  Comeonin.Bcrypt.check_pass(user, password)
end
```

`check_pass/2` verifies that the supplied struct or map has either an `encrypted_password` key or a `password_hash` key, and then verifies that encrypted value against the plaintext password that the user supplied by encrypting the plaintext password and comparing the two. In the case that a nil is passed along as the first argument of `check_pass`, it will simulate checking a password so that timing can't be used to verify if a username is valid or not! Now return back to your login form, try to log in with the right username/password, verify the results, and then try again with the wrong information! Everything should be working exactly as expected! You have now successfully implemented a user login and session system!

Writing session controller tests

As with the previous examples, we don't want to just leave our functionality here. We want to make sure that we're covering everything we write with an adequate amount of tests, so we'll need to write new tests for the session controller functions that we've added and the additional function in our accounts context. That will actually be the easiest one to write the tests for, so we'll start off with that one. Return over to `test/vocial/accounts/accounts_test.exs` and let's add a test for `get_user_by_username\1`. We'll start off with the positive case:

```
    test "get_user_by_username/1 returns the user with the matching
username" do
        user = user_fixture()
        assert Accounts.get_user_by_username(user.username)
    end
```

This is a very simple test; first create the user for purposes of this test, and use that created user to check to see if a user exists in the database with that particular username. This is a good test but hardly exhaustive; at a minimum, we should be writing a test to verify the behavior for when no user exists in our database with that particular username. Let's add a check for that now:

```
    test "get_user_by_username/1 returns nil with no matching username" do
        assert is_nil(Accounts.get_user_by_username("fail"))
    end
```

Rerun our tests and verify that we're still sitting at all green tests! Bear in mind that part of the reason that we're specifically doing a check to verify that when no user exists in the database with a failing username, it's because we've written some behavior in our controller that is specifically relying on this behavior being a given. Specifically, we need to pass in a nil value for when we cannot find the appropriate user by username to our `Comeonin.Bcrypt.check_pass\2` function, to ensure that it runs through the dummy password check function and prevents our site from being vulnerable to timing attacks.

We currently don't have any tests in place at all to verify any of the functionality of our session controller, so that's our next target to make sure we have good, working test coverage. Let's create `test/vocial_web/controllers/session_controller_test.exs`:

```
defmodule VocialWeb.SessionControllerTest do
  use VocialWeb.ConnCase

  test "GET /login", %{conn: conn} do
    conn = get conn, "/login"
    assert html_response(conn, 200) =~ "Login"
  end
end
```

We'll start off with our most simple test. It should just visit the "/login" route that we created earlier and verify that it does in fact contain the text Login somewhere in it. Because this page is so simple, we don't have to worry entirely too much about this test being very extensive. Next, we'll need a test for our login method, and this one will be significantly more complicated. We'll actually need to start by making sure there is a created user for this to work. There is actually a really nice way to handle this that I had previously glossed over: the ability to setup data for your tests in `setup` blocks! Let's see what our setup block looks like:

```
@valid_create_params %{
  username: "test",
  email: "test@test.com",
  password: "test",
  password_confirmation: "test"
}

setup do
  conn = build_conn()
  {:ok, user} = Vocial.Accounts.create_user(@valid_create_params)
  {:ok, conn: conn, user: user}
end
```

One thing that every controller needs is a starting conn object, so we'll start that off using the `build_conn\0` helper function and store the resulting conn object. Next, we'll create a set of user creation `params`, similar to what we've done previously in the tests for our Accounts Context. Finally, if we successfully create a user, we'll include that out in the return tuple with the conn object we built previously. If we fail to create a user, we want this to error out and fail all of our tests here, since that likely means that the status of all of our other tests would be potentially invalid. Now let's write up our create function test. Again, we'll want to create both a positive and negative test case to verify the behavior:

```
test "POST /sessions (with valid data)", %{conn: conn, user: user} do
  conn = post conn, "/sessions", %{ username: user.username, password:
"test"}
  assert redirected_to(conn) == "/"
  assert Plug.Conn.get_session(conn, :user)
end

test "POST /sessions (with invalid data)", %{conn: conn, user: user} do
  conn = post conn, "/sessions", %{ username: user.username, password:
"fail"}
  assert html_response(conn, 200)
  assert is_nil(Plug.Conn.get_session(conn, :user))
end
```

Notice that in both tests, we're catching the values returned out of the setup block to grab both the conn and the user objects. In the positive case, we verify that we were redirected and that the user value in the session was set to some non-nil value. Similarly, in the negative case, we verify that we're not getting a redirection and instead getting a rendered view, and we also verify that the user value does not exist anywhere in the session through the `Plug.Conn` module! Finally, we'll tackle the new `delete` function by sending an HTTP DELETE to the `/logout` URL. First we'll want to log in, verify that we've logged in, and then log out and verify that the user is missing from the session:

```
test "DELETE /sessions", %{conn: conn, user: user} do
  conn = post conn, "/sessions", %{ username: user.username, password:
"test"}
  assert Plug.Conn.get_session(conn, :user)
  conn = delete conn, "/logout"
  assert is_nil(Plug.Conn.get_session(conn, :user))
end
```

Run your test suite and we should see the results below:

```
$ mix test
.........................

Finished in 4.5 seconds
26 tests, 0 failures

Randomized with seed 580981
```

Summary

Now we have our functionality in place to have users be able to create accounts, and also be able to log in to the system and log out appropriately. We've tackled some more in-depth form building and we've covered everything we've written in this chapter with a significant amount of tests. We can feel confident whenever we have to make any further changes to our code base that no insidious bugs have been introduced into our system!

Our work is not quite complete yet, however! We still haven't actually tied our polls to real users, nor have we locked any functionality behind our user's session or provided a visual way for the user to log out. In the next chapter, we'll dive more heavily into these topics and also spend a little bit of time talking more about handling different types of validations in Ecto and display error messages in our forms!

5
Validations, Errors, and Tying Loose Ends

In the previous chapter, we worked on how to add user accounts to our web app, as well as how to add a new Hex package to our project to help us deal with password encryption.

In this chapter, we're going to spend some time putting the rest of everything together, filling the gaps we left in the previous chapter and then building on top of our application a little more. We'll work on cleaning up the interconnectivity of the different schemas and contexts and doing a better job of making sure our tests are sufficiently cover the majority of our application.

Finally, we'll do a deep dive into the different validation methods provided to us by Ecto out of the box (validation, in this case, meaning the validation of data before it is inserted into the database). We'll also work on improving user experience by displaying error messages on each field when a user signs up for a new account. These are all of the fundamental elements that we need to be able to build a web application that visibly reflects functionality in the majority of user-friendly web applications, so working with Ecto is a great skill to have under your belt!

In this chapter, we'll cover the following topics:

- The different validation methods available in Ecto
- Building more migrations
- Working with Ecto associations
- Fixing tests
- Sending information from Ecto to our controllers and views

Connecting polls to users

As mentioned previously, we did a lot of work when setting up user accounts in our system but nothing to actually connect, or even restrict access to, polls and user accounts. Thinking back to how we've set up other associations, there are a couple of steps that we have to implement before all of our polls are correctly linked to users. They are as follows:

1. We need to link our tables by creating a migration that adds `user_id` to our `polls` table.
2. We then need to modify the code in our schemas to represent the addition of the association.
3. We need to modify all of the creation code in the context to set the poll's `user_id` to the appropriate user.
4. Finally, we need to modify all of the `delete` and `update` code to only allow those functions to happen if the current user is the owner of that poll.

Creating the migration

We'll begin by creating the migration, as that's the foundation that will allow us to build and complete the rest of the code. Let's create a new migration as follows:

```
$ mix ecto.gen.migration add_user_id_to_polls
* creating priv/repo/migrations
* creating priv/repo/migrations/20171030030840_add_user_id_to_polls.exs
```

We'll need to do two things here: add the user ID column (which is a reference to the user's table) and create an index on `user_id`, shown as follows:

```
defmodule Vocial.Repo.Migrations.AddUserIdToPolls do
  use Ecto.Migration

  def change do
    alter table(:polls) do
      add :user_id, references(:users)
    end
    create index(:polls, [:user_id])
  end
end
```

Running the migration after this should result in no error messages, as shown in the following snippet:

```
$ mix ecto.migrate
[info] == Running Vocial.Repo.Migrations.AddUserIdToPolls.change/0 forward
[info] alter table polls
[info] create index polls_user_id_index
[info] == Migrated in 0.0s
```

Modifying the schemas

Now that we've gone back and added `user_id` to the actual database table, we'll need to mirror those changes in our codebase as well. So, let's open up the schema file for the polls table first. In here, inside the `schema` block, we need to add a reference to the user in the form of a `belongs_to` relationship. We'll also need to add an `import` statement for the `Vocial.Accounts.User` module, since that lives in a different context and code file as well. Open up `lib/vocial/votes/poll.ex` to change the schema definition as follows:

```
defmodule Vocial.Votes.Poll do
  # ...
  alias Vocial.Accounts.User

  schema "polls" do
    field :title, :string

    has_many :options, Option
    belongs_to :user, User

    timestamps()
  end
  # ...
end
```

As a quick sanity check here, we'll re-run our tests to make sure that we haven't broken anything. When running tests, a full green suite of tests means things are doing well. Next, we'll add the reverse association to our `Users` schema, as we'll want to know both when a poll is associated with a user and vice versa. Open up `lib/vocial/accounts/user.ex` and add a `has_many` reference to the schema pointing to `Polls`. You should also add an alias for `Vocial.Votes.Poll` at the top of the module, adding the `has_many` line to the schema definition, as follows:

```
defmodule Vocial.Accounts.User
  # ...
```

```
alias Vocial.Votes.Poll

schema "users" do
  field :username, :string
  field :email, :string
  field :active, :boolean, default: true
  field :encrypted_password, :string

  field :password, :string, virtual: true
  field :password_confirmation, :string, virtual: true

  has_many :polls, Poll

  timestamps()
end

# ...
end
```

Again, let's run a quick `mix test` to verify that we haven't broken anything. The process of going back and adding everything to our controllers, models, and tests is going to be a little difficult, so to avoid getting into any difficult situations that are hard to recover from, we'll run through a few steps first. You should start by modifying the tests to work with the new idea of associating polls with users, verifying the functionality on the backend side of the code, and then, once everything is verified, modifying the templates to work with the new world you've constructed.

The simplest set of tests will be those regarding polls. Note that we'll be writing code and modifying and adding tests as we go along, so everything should make sense over time. One of the first things we need to do is modify our `Polls` schema to allow the code to pass in `user_id` with the rest of the creation struct. This will properly associate that poll with a user, but in doing so will also cause a number of tests to fail. If you go into the `changeset\2` function in `lib/vocial/votes/poll.ex`, you can add `:user_id` to the call to `cast` and `validate_required`, as follows:

```
defmodule Vocial.Votes.Poll do
  # ...
  def changeset(%Poll{}=poll, attrs) do
    poll
    |> cast(attrs, [:title, :user_id])
    |> validate_required([:title, :user_id])
  end
  # ...
end
```

Fixing broken poll tests

If we run the `mix` test as it is it will fail, but that's okay as it's actually our expected behavior. As we have just added a new requirement of `user_id` for the creation of all polls, we should expect all of our previous poll creation logic to fail without a user ID as part of the changeset. We'll tackle the failing tests in `test/vocial/votes/votes_test.exs`, which will involve a lot of code-but not a lot of complicated code.

First, we need to add some code to the top of our `Vocial.VotesTest` module, which creates a user that we can use as the user ID value for all future polls. As mentioned in the last chapter, ExUnit provides a very simple way for us to set those features up, via the `setup` function. So, we'll now create a `setup` function that will return out `:ok` and a pre-created user for us to use:

```
setup do
  {:ok, user} = Vocial.Accounts.create_user(%{
    username: "test",
    email: "test@test.com",
    password: "test",
    password_confirmation: "test"
  })
  {:ok, user: user}
end
```

Remember that every `setup` function that we write into our tests needs to send out `:ok` as part of the tuple as well as anything we want to be returned as part of the second value. In our case, we'll use a keyword list where the only initial key in it is `:user`, which will store the newly-created user from the account's context. Next, we start modifying each of the tests, starting at the top; `list_polls()` needs to account for the new user and user ID values before the user is created in order to verify the results:

```
test "list_polls/0 returns all polls", %{user: user} do
  poll = poll_fixture(%{user_id: user.id})
  assert Votes.list_polls() == [poll]
end
```

After adding a description of the test, we add a pattern match statement to catch the user key returned as part of the `setup` function. Then, in our `poll_fixture` function call, we add an additional set of parameters that includes `user_id`. This will pass `user_id` to the changeset and will verify that a poll has been associated with the right user on creation. Next, we'll need to scroll down to our creation tests and make those pass, following essentially the same patterns as previously:

```
test "create_poll/1 returns a new poll", %{user: user} do
    {:ok, poll} = Votes.create_poll(Map.put(@valid_attrs, :user_id,
user.id))
        assert Enum.any?(Votes.list_polls(), fn p -> p.id == poll.id end)
    end
```

Again, we catch the user. As we're not using the fixture in this particular function (because we want to specifically test the `create` function in isolation), we're just going to call `Map.put\3` to return a modified version of the creation hash that includes both the values from `@valid_attrs` and `user_id`. Now we need to modify the next few `create_poll_with_options` tests, as follows:

```
test "create_poll_with_options/2 returns a new poll with options",
%{user: user} do
        title = "Poll With Options"
        options = ["Choice 1", "Choice 2", "Choice 3"]
        {:ok, poll} = Votes.create_poll_with_options(%{title: title, user_id:
user.id}, options)
        assert poll.title == title
        assert Enum.count(poll.options) == 3
    end
```

We'll also need to modify the next test, even if it's currently passing. We do this to keep the semantics of the test clear, as shown in the following snippet:

```
test "create_poll_with_options/2 does not create the poll or options
with bad data", %{user: user} do
        title = "Bad Poll"
        options = ["Choice 1", nil, "Choice 3"]
        {status, _} = Votes.create_poll_with_options(%{title: title, user_id:
user.id}, options)
        assert status == :error
        assert !Enum.any?(Votes.list_polls(), fn p -> p.title == "Bad Poll"
end)
    end
```

Finally, we need to pop over into the `describe` block for `options`, as there is a `create` test there that can also fail without modifications:

```
describe "options" do
  test "create_option/1 creates an option on a poll", %{user: user} do
    with {:ok, poll} = Votes.create_poll(%{ title: "Sample Poll",
user_id: user.id }),
         {:ok, option} = Votes.create_option(%{ title: "Sample Choice",
votes: 0, poll_id: poll.id }),
         option <- Repo.preload(option, :poll)
    do
      assert Votes.list_options() == [option]
    end
  end
end
```

As I said, we've covered a lot of code, but not a lot of complicated code. This will be a pretty common feature as we continue to run through and implement Elixir projects. But don't worry, the simplicity of Elixir allows you to spend more time actually designing the system you want instead of considering every potential failure in it.

Since the test suite is passing (although not the entire test), we now need to hook up the controllers to be able to use the logic as well. Let's move on now that our foundation is secure!

Sending a user ID through the controller

Now we need to devise a way to send the user ID of a logged-in user through the controller to the template and back again; this way, a user can be properly associated with every poll they create. To do this, we need to work with Phoenix's built-in session handling code. The good news is that getting data out of the session is just as easy as putting data into the session; essentially, the only difference is that we'll be calling `get_session/2` instead of `put_session/3`.

Retrieving data from sessions

Let's start by taking a look at some of the session code that we wrote in the previous chapter to get a better sense of the shape of the data we're currently storing in the session. This will help us understand how to pull the data back out of the session and use it appropriately, shown as follows:

```
conn
|> put_flash(:info, "Logged in successfully!")
|> put_session(:user, %{ id: login_user.id, username:
login_user.username, email: login_user.email })
|> redirect(to: "/")
```

The preceding code places a key into the session storage called `:user`, so that's what we'll use to get the user ID back out of the session. Let's dive into our poll controller code to properly set the user ID inside of our creation `with` statement, as shown in the following snippet:

```
with user <- get_session(conn, :user),
     poll_params <- Map.put(poll_params, "user_id", user.id),
     {:ok, _poll} <- Votes.create_poll_with_options(poll_params,
split_options)
  do
    # ...
  end
```

There are a few more prerequisites to take note of before getting to the success clause of our `with` statement. Being able to add more conditions, criteria, and operations as part of a single statement is one of the bonuses of the `with` statement in Elixir. Not only is it a simple statement, but it requires a lot less fiddling with and refactoring in general. Let's now analyze the preceding code line-by-line:

```
with user <- get_session(conn, :user),
```

In this first line, we're pulling the user out of the session using the `get_session\2` function. It takes in `conn` as the first argument and then the key we want to pull the data out of (in our case, "user"). We have to use "user" and `0:user` because any `params` that are passed to our controller from a form will be string-based keys rather than atom-based keys.

This is a security measure, as every atom occupies memory and using atoms for everything could open the web application up to certain types of flooding attacks! As a general rule, never create atoms from user-supplied input!

```
poll_params <- Map.put(poll_params, "user_id", user.id),
```

Next, we are updating the original `poll_params` variable to also include the session's user ID. Notice that this statement is less of a check (we're not verifying that the result is `{:ok, something}` like we have previously), but more of a statement of work (*modify the existing map by adding a new value and key to it, and return the modified map*), which then gets used in the next line.

 You don't have to reuse the `poll_params` variable name here. This is called variable reassignment and people generally have mixed opinions about its impacts in a codebase. You can use a different name if you wanted to clarify you were modifying the passed-in params.

```
{:ok, _poll} <- Votes.create_poll_with_options(poll_params, split_options)
```

The preceding code is the same line of code that existed in our `with` statement (previously as the only statement). Again, this highlights the powerful tools that Elixir gives us to work with our code. We haven't changed this line at all; all we've done is change how the `poll_params` map is built as well as ensure it is passed to the function in the same way as before. If we test out our code by going to `/login`, logging in as a sample user, and then going to `/votes/new` and creating a new poll, we should see everything work as expected!

Unfortunately, one of the gaps that we have in our codebase is that we never wrote the original controller tests for the Poll Controller, so let's now take a little time to do that. Get into the habit of doing periodic spot-checks of your codebase to find gaps in test coverage (whether through manually checking your codebase or using code coverage tools) and correcting them when you see them because this will save you a lot of time and frustration later on.

Writing our Poll Controller's tests

We need to start off by creating a new file to handle the tests for our Poll Controller. Open up `test/vocial_web/controllers/poll_controller_test.exs` and begin to update the tests in it. Its contents should be as follows:

```
defmodule VocialWeb.PollControllerTest do
  use VocialWeb.ConnCase

  test "GET /polls", %{conn: conn} do
    {:ok, poll} =
      Vocial.Votes.create_poll_with_options(%{title: "Poll 1"}, [
        "Choice 1",
        "Choice 2",
        "Choice 3"
      ])

    conn = get(conn, "/polls")
    assert html_response(conn, 200) =~ poll.title

    Enum.each(poll.options, fn option ->
      assert html_response(conn, 200) =~ "#{option.title}"
      assert html_response(conn, 200) =~ ": #{option.votes}"
    end)
  end
end
```

We should already have a user created and ready to go for our tests, so let's now create a setup block that will create a new user account. Remember that the syntax for creating helper syntax blocks requires a block that returns a tuple with `:ok` as the first value and whatever data we want to expose to each of our tests as the second value. This should be added to the `poll_controller_test.exs` file that we were working within the preceding snippet.

```
setup do
  conn = build_conn()
  {:ok, user} = Vocial.Accounts.create_user(%{
    username: "test",
    email: "test@test.com",
    password: "test",
    password_confirmation: "test"
  })
  {:ok, conn: conn, user: user}
end
```

In the previous snippet, we created a valid sample user that we can use as part of our association process when creating new polls. This will give us a pretty good test of the logic in our controller by making sure that there is at least one valid user in the system. We should now create our starting `conn` object, as that is a necessary part of every controller test. Another thing we'll need is a way to simulate a logged-in user; the creation of the user account itself isn't enough to produce adequate results on our testing codebase. For this, we'll create a new private login function that will take in the `conn` and the existing user, shown as follows:

```
defp login(conn, user) do
   conn |> post("/sessions", %{username: user.username, password:
user.password})
   end
```

In this, we take the `connection` object and run it through the session creation action. We do this to make it a real test of our login and session logic since this will simulate a longer-lasting user workflow that involves logging in as well as creating and visiting new user polls. We have already developed a good initial test for our `Polls` index in the file, but we still need to add the user from the `setup` block and the `create` call for it to work as follows:

```
test "GET /polls", %{conn: conn, user: user} do
   {:ok, poll} =
      Vocial.Votes.create_poll_with_options(%{title: "Poll 1", user_id:
user.id}, [
         "Choice 1",
         "Choice 2",
         "Choice 3"
      ])

   conn = get(conn, "/polls")
   assert html_response(conn, 200) =~ poll.title

   Enum.each(poll.options, fn option ->
      assert html_response(conn, 200) =~ "#{option.title}"
      assert html_response(conn, 200) =~ ": #{option.votes}"
   end)
   end
```

As you can see, this is a pretty simple test. It's not using our login function yet, so don't worry if you see a `function login/2 is unused` warning if you run `mix test`. The important part is that our test suite is still green! Now we need to move on to writing a test for the new poll page, which will essentially be a simple *make sure it works* test.

```
test "GET /polls/new with a logged in user", %{conn: conn, user: user} do
    conn = login(conn, user) |> get("/polls/new")
    assert html_response(conn, 200) =~ "New Poll"
end
```

Next, we use our shiny new private login function. To do this, we take in the starting `conn`, pass it to our `login` function, and then pass the resulting logged-in connection to the `/polls/new` path. Right now, as we haven't written any code to restrict access to poll creation, this test would pass with or without the call to log in, but we want to think ahead about how our tests will be created. Next, we're going to move on to the two tests needed to create polls (one with valid data and one with invalid data). We'll start with the valid data test, as shown in the following snippet:

```
test "POST /polls (with valid data)", %{conn: conn, user: user} do
    conn = login(conn, user)
        |> post("/polls", %{"poll" => %{ "title" => "Test Poll" }, "options"
=> "One,Two,Three" })
    assert redirected_to(conn) == "/polls"
end
```

If we now rerun the `mix test`, we should still be in the clear! Note that here we're expecting two top-level keys as part of the `POST` body: `"poll"` and `"options"`. Also, when the poll is created successfully, we are redirected to the index, so we need to account for that. Finally, we need to handle what happens when we try to post a new poll with invalid data, shown as follows:

```
test "POST /polls (with invalid data)", %{conn: conn, user: user} do
    conn = login(conn, user)
        |> post("/polls", %{"poll" => %{ title: nil }, "options" =>
"One,Two,Three" })
    assert html_response(conn, 200)
end
```

When we try to run the preceding code, our test will fail, even though everything looks like it should result in a green test. This is actually a case where writing tests for our code helped us catch bad code that could have resulted in a frustrating and unhelpful error message for the user. The error message is as follows:

```
 2) test POST /polls (with invalid data) (VocialWeb.PollControllerTest)
    test/vocial_web/controllers/poll_controller_test.exs:40
    ** (RuntimeError) expected action/2 to return a Plug.Conn, all plugs
must receive a connection (conn) and return a connection
    code: conn = login(conn, user) |> post("/polls", %{"poll" => %{ title:
nil }, "options" => "One,Two,Three" })
    ...
```

The error message occurs because our controller code isn't very robust—something that our tests have now pointed out to us. If we go back to our Poll Controller, we can see that in our create function, we never accounted for what happens when we fail to create a poll. Any time you're writing with statements, you should get into the habit of deciding whether or not you need else clauses in the statement to handle any errors. What we want to happen here instead is that we are redirected to the new poll form if there are any issues, so let's write our else clause back in lib/vocial_web/controllers/poll_controller.ex create action as follows:

```
else
  {:error, poll} ->
    conn
    |> put_flash(:alert, "Error creating poll!")
    |> redirect(to: poll_path(conn, :new))
end
```

Now if we get an error when attempting to create our poll, we get a flash alert informing us of the error we are brought back to the new pool form. Note that the test itself now needs to be modified a little, too:

```
test "POST /polls (with invalid data)", %{conn: conn, user: user} do
  conn = login(conn, user)
    |> post("/polls", %{"poll" => %{ title: nil }, "options" =>
"One,Two,Three" })
  assert html_response(conn, 302)
  assert redirected_to(conn) == "/polls/new"
end
```

Run the test suite as demonstrated in the preceding snippet and you should see all green tests! We can now move on to the next important bit of functionality: restricting access to poll creation.

Restricting access via sessions

We have some tests in place to make sure that our code works well enough, but we haven't done anything to actually secure the creation of new polls in our application. We want to make sure that the user is actually logged in - and if they're not, we need to be able to redirect them to the root page with a message explaining the situation. For this, we're going to write a `Plug` module so that we can reuse this code anywhere we need it. We'll call this `VerifyUserSession`, as that is the intended use case of the plug. Let's create `lib/vocial_web/verify_user_session.ex` and give it a starting skeleton, shown as follows:

```
defmodule VocialWeb.VerifyUserSession do
  def init(opts), do: opts

  def call(conn, _opts) do
    conn
  end
end
```

We're not going to do anything too fancy with this because we want to test being able to hook it up to our controller before we start implementing the rest of the logic. Return to the Poll Controller and add the following line of code between the `alias` statement and the actions:

```
plug VocialWeb.VerifyUserSession when action in [:new, :create]
```

This will call out to our new plug every time someone goes to /polls/new or posts to /polls! Run the tests quickly to verify the results are still green, and then start writing the actual logic for the plug's `call` function. We will need to add a few `import` statements at the top to make our code a little more readable; they are as follows:

```
import Plug.Conn, only: [get_session: 2, halt: 1]
import Phoenix.Controller, only: [put_flash: 3, redirect: 2]
```

We only need these three functions to be able to write our plug, so we'll keep our import statements pretty light. Next, we need to work on the `call` function itself:

```
def call(conn, _opts) do
  case get_session(conn, :user) do
    nil ->
      conn
      |> put_flash(:error, "You must be logged in to do that!")
      |> redirect(to: "/")
      |> halt()
    _ -> conn
```

```
      end
   end
```

We should now attempt to get the user out of the `conn`'s session. If we don't get anything out of it (that is, we get a `nil` value), we'll send an error message to the user and redirect them to the root. We'll also halt the response to make sure nothing else attempts to write to the response. Otherwise, we'll let the `conn` continue unabated!

Here comes the moment of truth. So, make sure you're logged out (if you're not, just visit the `/logout` path in your browser) and then visit `/polls/new`. If all worked as expected, you should see the redirect and the **You must be logged in to do that!** message!

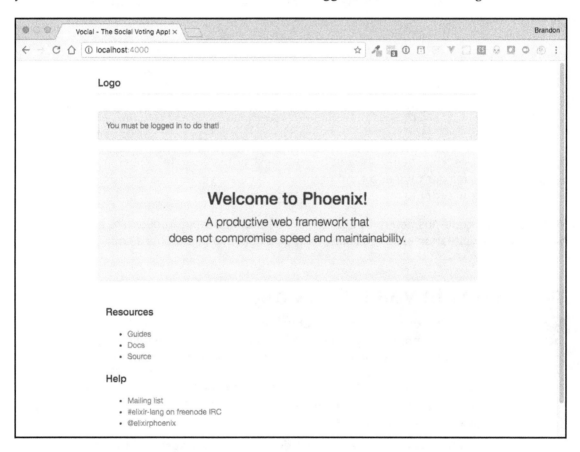

The final part we need to complete is writing the tests to make sure our `new` and `create` routes are properly protected with the plug we just created. First, we'll write the not-logged-in test for the `/polls/new` route, shown as follows:

```
test "GET /polls/new without a logged in user", %{conn: conn} do
  conn = get(conn, "/polls/new")
  assert redirected_to(conn) == "/"
  assert get_flash(conn, :error) == "You must be logged in to do that!"
end
```

Note that we're checking both that we get redirected and that we also see an error flash message. Moving forward, we'll write a similar test for the `POST /votes` endpoint too, shown as follows:

```
test "POST /polls (with valid data, without logged in user)", %{conn: conn}
do
  conn = post(conn, "/polls", %{"poll" => %{ "title" => "Test Poll" },
"options" => "One,Two,Three" })
  assert redirected_to(conn) == "/"
  assert get_flash(conn, :error) == "You must be logged in to do that!"
end
```

If you run the tests, you should see a fully-green test suite yet again! Note that as we've also written the tests for our plug as a form of integration test, we don't have to do any additional work in order to make our test suite comprehensive.

We're now in a good position to be able to dive a little bit deeper into Ecto validations and how to handle validation errors in changesets and in the codebase. Let's jump in!

Working with validations and errors

Ecto provides a number of built-in changeset validations that we can hook into to ensure the data integrity of an application. Out of the box, Ecto provides the following validations to use (note that there are more than those listed; this is just a small sample):

- `validate_change` validates the changeset against a provided function
- `validate_confirmation` validates a field and the field's confirmation match (for example, `password` and `password_confirmation`)
- `validate_format` validates that a field matches the specified format
- `validate_length` validates that the field is the expected length
- `validate_number` validates that the field has the specified numeric properties

- `validate_required` validates that the field **is present and not empty**
- `unique_constraint` validates that a DB-level unique constraint exists and is not violated for a field

As of now, we've already worked with `validate_required` and `validate_confirmation`. Remember that there are even more validations than the ones specified previously (especially in regards to checking database constraints), but these are the most common. With that in mind, a good place for us to start is to make it so that a given username can only exist once in our application (a unique constraint), so let's crack on!

Making usernames unique

At the moment, multiple people can register with the same username, something that would inevitably cause a lot of problems in a real-world situation. Ecto does not allow us to verify the username's uniqueness without there being a database-level constraint check, so let's start by creating a migration to make usernames unique in the database. First, let's generate the migration:

```
$ mix ecto.gen.migration make_usernames_unique
* creating priv/repo/migrations
* creating priv/repo/migrations/20180201223131_make_usernames_unique.exs
```

Then, we'll give the migration the following code. Note that all we're doing here is telling Ecto to add a unique index to the `users` table on the `username` column:

```
defmodule Vocial.Repo.Migrations.MakeUsernamesUnique do
  use Ecto.Migration

  def change do
    create unique_index(:users, [:username])
  end
end
```

And then we'll run our migrations as follows:

```
$ mix ecto.migrate
[info] == Running Vocial.Repo.Migrations.MakeUsernamesUnique.change/0
forward
[info] create index users_username_index
[info] == Migrated in 0.0s
```

Again, to sanity-check our work, we'll run the `mix` test and verify that we're still seeing green specs. If all is good, we can move on to writing our test to verify that creating duplicate usernames fails. Jump into `test/vocial/accounts/accounts_test.exs` and write the following new test:

```
test "create_user/1 fails to create the user when the username already
exists" do
  _user1 = user_fixture()
  {:error, user2} = user_fixture()
  assert !user2.valid?
end
```

If we run the test suite now, we'll see an error message about a constraint failure about existing data. This is correct, but kind of messy overall. Instead, let's follow the error's helpful advice and add the `unique_constraint/3` call to our `User` schema. Open up `lib/vocial/accounts/user.ex` and add the `unique_constraint` to the bottom of the `changeset` function as follows:

```
def changeset(%User{}=user, attrs) do
  user
  # ...
  |> unique_constraint(:username)
  # ...
end
```

Now, if we rerun the test that failed previously, we should see green tests! We also need to verify that our email address field looks like an email address (we're not going to go full tilt into email address validation here, so we'll stick with a basic validation), so let's also add an example for `validate_format`:

```
def changeset(%User{}=user, attrs) do
  user
  # ...
  |> validate_format(:email, ~r/@/)
  # ...
end
```

We'll then add a new test for this, as follows:

```
test "create_user/1 fails to create the user when the email is not an email
format" do
  {:error, user} = user_fixture(%{email: "testtestcom"})
  assert !user.valid?
end
```

Writing custom validations

In some scenarios, we may have custom error messages and validations that don't really match up to the provided Ecto validations out of the box. We have two ways to handle this with Ecto:

1. We write a custom validation using Ecto's built-in `validate_change` function with our own custom anonymous validator function.
2. We write a totally brand new validation using our own function and some of Ecto's other functions.

Let's explore both options. First, if we want to use `validate_change`, it's very simple. We'll start with the simplest implementation and then refactor it to get a good sense of how it all fits together:

```
def changeset(%User{}=user, attrs) do
  user
  # ...
  |> validate_change(:email, fn :email, value ->
    if value == "test@fake.com" do
      [email: "cannot be a fake email!"]
    else
      []
    end
  end)
  # ...
end
```

We'll then write a test to verify this behavior as follows:

```
test "create_user/1 fails to create the user when the email is a fake email
address" do
  {:error, user} = user_fixture(%{email: "test@fake.com"})
  assert !user.valid?
end
```

After running tests we should see that everything is green, but we're aware that this is a really messy block of code! Let's refactor that `anonymous` function to be a `module-level` function, as follows:

```
def changeset(%User{}=user, attrs) do
  user
  # ...
  |> validate_change(:email, &fake_email_address?/2)
  # ...
end
```

We now also need to create a `fake_email_address` function with an arity of 2 to catch this. We'll also lean on pattern matching by creating a catch-all version of our function that will just return an empty list, shown as follows:

```
def fake_email_address?(:email, "test@fake.com"), do: [email: "cannot be a
fake email!"]
def fake_email_address?(_, _), do: []
```

This is one way that we can implement and test out our custom validation function. If we wanted to go down a more manual route, we could also do something like the following:

```
def changeset(%User{}=user, attrs) do
  user
  # ...
  |> validate_not_fake(:email)
  # ...
end
```

To support this, we'll need a special custom function in our module to handle it, shown as follows:

```
def validate_not_fake(changeset, key) do
  case get_change(changeset, key) do
    "test@fake.com" -> add_error(changeset, key, "cannot be a fake email!")
    _ -> changeset
  end
end
```

And we're done! This is another really nice way of writing our own custom validations when we need to do something specific that Ecto won't support out of the box. We get the change out of the changeset first and pass that into a `case` statement. We then pattern match on that returned value; if it matches our idea of a *fake* email address, then we add an error, which will result in the changeset returning "`false`" for the `valid?` function. This will prevent the changeset from being saved to the database.

The last validation that's commonly used that we'll demonstrate is `validate_length`, an incredibly common validation that is used in web applications. We'll (arbitrarily) decide to limit username creation to a minimum of 3 characters and a maximum of `100`:

```
def changeset(%User{}=user, attrs) do
  user
  # ...
  |> validate_length(:username, min: 3,
 max: 100)
  # ...
end
```

We'll need to write a test to cover this example as well:

```
test "create_user/1 fails to create the user when the username is too
short" do
  {:error, user} = user_fixture(%{username: "a"})
  assert !user.valid?
end
```

And we're done! We've now explored a variety of the most common Ecto validation functions, and we've also come up with a few examples of writing our own custom validation functions as well! Based on that, you should feel pretty confident that the code you're writing is going to preserve data integrity at an in-depth level in the codebase. By the time all is said and done, you should end up with a changeset function and custom validation function that looks something like the following:

```
def changeset(%User{}=user, attrs) do
  user
  |> cast(attrs, [:username, :email, :active, :password,
:password_confirmation])
  |> validate_confirmation(:password, message: "does not match
password!")
  |> validate_format(:email, ~r/@/)
  |> validate_not_fake(:email)
  |> validate_length(:username, min: 3, max: 100)
  |> encrypt_password()
  |> validate_required([:username, :email, :active, :encrypted_password])
  |> unique_constraint(:username)
end

def validate_not_fake(changeset, key) do
  case get_change(changeset, key) do
    "test@fake.com" -> add_error(changeset, key, "cannot be a fake
email!")
    _ -> changeset
  end
end
```

Running the test suite should result in green, even though we've added a ton of new tests and functionality, as follows:

```
$ mix test
Compiling 1 file (.ex)
.................................

Finished in 14.7 seconds
35 tests, 0 failures

Randomized with seed 343891
```

Displaying validation errors in our forms

As of yet, we haven't actually hooked up any of this new shiny logic in our form, so if we try to submit anything we'll just see a generic error message that isn't very helpful. One thing that we left out of each of our forms is a per-field error message. Phoenix will helpfully wrap any errors inside of a span with a `help-block` class, so first let's open up `assets/css/app.css` and add the following code:

```
span.help-block {
  color: #f00;
}
```

Next, we'll jump into our users form and start adding `error_tag` statements to each of our fields. Open up `lib/vocial_web/templates/user/form.html.eex` and follow along with each field update as follows:

- **Username:**

  ```
  <%= label f, :username, "Username:" %>
  <br />
  <%= text_input f, :username %>
  <%= error_tag f, :username %>
  ```

- **Email:**

  ```
  <%= label f, :email, "Email:" %>
  <br />
  <%= text_input f, :email %>
  <%= error_tag f, :email %>
  ```

- **Password**:

```
<%= label f, :password, "Password:" %>
<br />
<%= password_input f, :password %>
<%= error_tag f, :password %>
```

- **Password Confirmation**:

```
<%= label f, :password_confirmation, "Confirm your password:" %>
<br />
<%= password_input f, :password_confirmation %>
<%= error_tag f, :password_confirmation %>
```

Now let's return to the user creation form and add bad data in each of the fields to verify the results, as shown in the following screenshot:

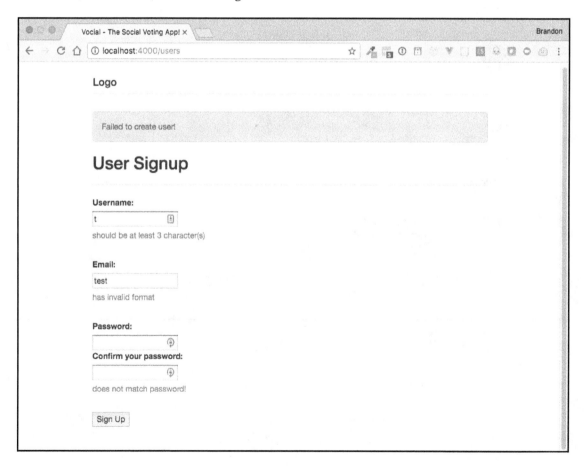

We should also verify that creating two users with the same username fails. In that scenario, we should expect to see an error message underneath the **Username** field that says something along the lines of *has already been taken*, as shown in the following screenshot:

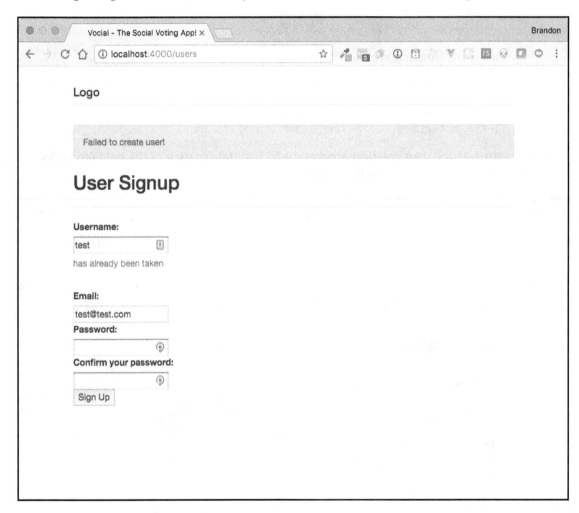

Summary

Now we've tied up all of the loose ends in our application and done everything we can to preserve the integrity of both the data and functions in it. We're now at a point where we can be confident in our web application and we've set ourselves up for success in a pretty significant way!

At this point, I think we can pat ourselves on the back. We have a good, working application with some (basic) security checks in place and a lot of the functionality that people expect from their web applications. We've also learned how to interact with more of the Phoenix and Ecto built-ins and provided modules. We're now ready to start diving into some of the more complicated parts of building an Elixir or Phoenix application (especially one including real-time channels for data), so let's start putting together what it means to build a truly real-time live application!

6
Live Voting with Phoenix

Previously, we finished all of the remaining work that we needed to get our application polished up and tested across the board. Our application is pretty solid and we're finally at a point where we can start diving into some of the truly amazing features of Phoenix: the out-of-the-box support for web sockets! Before we can dive too deep into how to start implementing these in Phoenix, we should probably take a quick sidebar to discuss what web sockets even are!

Web Sockets are means of passing data back and forth through a dedicated line (or *socket*) that allows for real-time communication back and forth between a client (your web browser) and the server (your Phoenix application). This information can either be solely limited to communication with a single client or multiple clients simultaneously (a broadcast message, similar to chat rooms). This allows the construction of real-time applications where the server is responsible for acting as the message broker by taking data in from the client, processing it, and then broadcasting the results back out to all listening parties.

It's important to note that this specifically works via constructing a client that is capable of *listening* on these sockets for changes and broadcasts, which means that in this chapter we'll also be diving into JavaScript programming. While this is primarily an Elixir/Phoenix book, it's also very important to understand how the specific JavaScript libraries for Phoenix's web socket implementation work. The Phoenix example code also deals very specifically with JavaScript's ES2015 syntax, so we'll also take a little bit of time to very explain some of the syntaxes that you'll see in a lot of code samples for channels.

By the end of this chapter, you should have a thorough understanding of:

- What channels and topics are in Phoenix
- How to build your own channels and topics
- How to write the client code to interact with Phoenix
- How to begin writing your tests to cover channels
- An introduction on how to architect real-time web applications

Building channels and topics in Phoenix

Phoenix's real-time application support relies on two major core components in Phoenix: channels and topics. The general idea is that for a real-time application to be able to accurately broadcast out every message to the right parties (and for it to be able to understand messages that are sent in as well), Phoenix needs a system for how the messages get in and out. This represents our channels. Channels themselves are the Phoenix-side of sockets; where the socket represents how the information is transferred between the client and the server, the channel represents how the information hits the server and gets translated into something useful that Phoenix can work with.

In addition to that, we also need a way for the client and the server to acknowledge which messages each of them cares about. The server needs to understand how to route messages inbound from the client, and the client needs to be able to only listen to the topics it actually needs to listen to and care about. An analogy that you may be more comfortable with at this point is thinking about these in terms of controllers and actions. The channel represents our controller; a single module dictating the shape of communication bidirectionally between the server and the client. The topic represents each individual action or function in the controller itself. When I visit `/polls/new` in my browser, I'm communicating with my Polls controller (*channel*) and telling it that I am interested in the *New* action (*topic*).

Since the most common way to implement channels and topics in Phoenix is to build a chat client, let's look at a diagram of how this communication flow between channels and topics might look. We start off with setting up a way for the clients to let the server know which topics it actually cares about, and on the server-side of things, a way for the server to verify that the person trying to subscribe to the specific topic actually has the means and ability to do so (for example, they may need to be a logged in user to be able to subscribe to a chat channel). Each client will send a message to the server saying *Hey, I'm so-and-so, and I want to subscribe to all future messages on this topic*. Typically, Phoenix topics will follow the format of `channel:topic` (and may additionally also support subtopics, which may look similar to something like `channel:topic:subtopic`).

A diagram of how channels and topics work might look something like this:

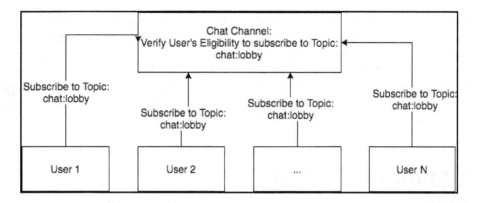

First, we start off with each of our clients announcing their intention to listen to a particular topic. In this case, we're saying that the `channel:topic` pairing is `chat:lobby`. We can think of this as something like an implementation of a very, very simple chatroom. Next, we'll want to see what it looks like when one of the users wants to send a message to the chat room and broadcast to all users in the same room:

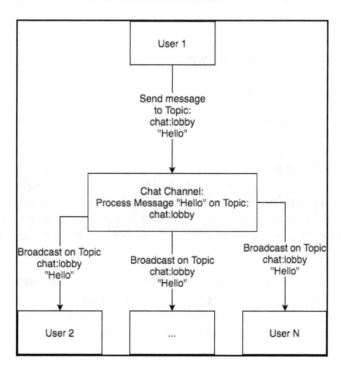

Here we get the first user sending a message to the rest of the users in the room. To do this, User 1's client (usually something written in JavaScript) will take the message from the user and send it along to the server, which will then be processed by the channel. The channel will look for the appropriate handler based on the topic and then take whatever action the handler specifies. In some cases, this may be something like broadcasting the message out to all of the listeners of that particular topic (like in the previous example). The message will then be sent across the socket to each subscriber to that topic!

Understanding sockets

The easiest way for us to start thinking about how real-time applications work in actual practice is to start building our own. Through this we can experiment and learn each of the moving pieces that are involved with implementing the real-time portion of our application. When we start off, our application we will have a `user_socket.ex` file in `/lib/vocial_web/channels`. If we open this file up we can get a good starting picture for how to start constructing our sockets and channels.

Sockets are responsible for setting up exactly how a client can connect and authenticate with the appropriate channels and topics. You can think of sockets as the actual means of connecting the client to the channel and topic (doing things like verifying the authentication information, determining how to route to specific channels and which channels are even available to the Phoenix application, and some other tasks).

The second line in `user_socket.ex` (after the module definition) is this line, use `Phoenix.Socket`

We'll use our IEx session to get a little more information about what macros and functionality this `use` statement provides to us. If we type in `h Phoenix.Socket` in our IEx session we'll get a very helpful page back out that explains a lot of what some of the boilerplate code is and what each line does. We also are provided some sample code that matches what we find in `user_socket.ex` (without the comments). Per the help documentation:

> `Phoenix.Socket` *is used as a module for establishing and maintaining the socket state via the* `Phoenix.Socket struct`*. Once connected to a socket, incoming and outgoing events are routed to channels. The incoming client data is routed to channels via transports. It is the responsibility of the socket to tie transports and channels together.*

The next line that we need to pay attention to is commented out but important nonetheless:

```
## Channels
# channel "room:*", VocialWeb.RoomChannel
```

This line is where we would start building out each of the channels and figure out how to start telling Phoenix about the existence of these channels and which modules to map specific topics to. An asterisk here means that there is a wildcard handler. This means any topic matching the pattern of `room:(something)` would get mapped to the `RoomChannel`, where we would likely have some function definitions with a pattern match something like this:

```
def join("room:" <> chat_room) do
  # ...
end
```

Let's move on to the next lines in our code. This is the section that sets up what protocol our Phoenix application is going to be using for managing/routing these long-lived sockets:

```
## Transports
transport :websocket, Phoenix.Transports.WebSocket
# transport :longpoll, Phoenix.Transports.LongPoll
```

Here you can see that we're relying on the web socket protocol for our Phoenix application. This is a pretty sound default that you'll use most of the time unless you are working with perhaps legacy browsers or clients that don't support web sockets but do support long-polling.

 Long-polling is a very simple JavaScript-based method of interacting with a client where the client essentially establishes a long-lived connection that isn't terminated until the server has a response to send back to the client. The request itself is long-lived (thus the *long-polling* moniker).

That line sitting in there allows you to very quickly change the mechanism you want to use to deliver information to the client from the server. Again, most of the time, you'll just want to stick with the web socket protocol in general (and that's what we'll be using for the purposes of our Phoenix application).

Scroll down a little bit and we'll come to the next substantial bit of our boilerplate Phoenix code. This is the actual connection code that is responsible for telling both the server and the client that the request by the client to subscribe to the topic specified is a valid request and that both the server and the client can start relying on that to send information: bidirectionally. By default, we start with this code

```
def connect(_params, socket) do
  {:ok, socket}
end
```

All this does is tell Phoenix and the client that yes, this connection and subscription request is completely valid, no matter what (whether it should be valid or not). This might seem harmful but the reality is that your web application may not actually need authentication for all parts of its real-time communication. For example, we may want users to be able to view the results of polls live without creating a user account, or maybe we want to allow anonymous connections to the discussion room for each poll that's created. Either way, we're less concerned with actually checking the validity of the connection and more concerned with establishing that connection in the first place. It's also worth noting that this does not lock you into having to allow every subscription and join that may happen in your application; you can set up separate sockets or separate channels/topics that are private when we start talking about channels and the `join` function!

If we instead wanted to deny any incoming socket connection requests for any reason, we would want to send back `:error` as the first value in the tuple with the socket. So let's say we only want to allow subscription to a particular socket when a special value is set:

```
# Allow connections to the socket when the "secret" param has the value of
"letmein"
def connect(%{"secret" => "letmein"}=_params, socket) do
  {:ok, socket}
end
# Deny all other connections
def connect(_params, socket), do: {:error, socket}
```

This pattern of `{:ok, _}` and `{:error, _}` shows up a lot and makes it easy for other developers to reason about your application very simply. This is idiomatic Elixir code; always try to write statements like this when you can!

This pattern also allows you to conditionally set particular values on the socket when certain inputs are passed in. For example, you can start keeping track of a user's individual ID or some other unique pieces of information related to them at the start of the connection. This will drastically cut down on the number of times you have to reload whatever that information was, which can be a major time saver if you're having to perform that operation every time a new channel is joined, a topic is subscribed to, or even every time a new message is sent or received!

The final bit of code in this file is something that is currently unimportant. The intent of the `id` function is to create a unique identifier that can be used to identify a particular combination of user/socket through essentially creating a new, special topic. This topic can then be used to isolate a particular user and broadcast messages to that specific user/connection. The way this function works is that if you return a string, it's assumed that string is the topic identifier you'll be using for that particular user/socket combination. If it returns `nil`, that means it will be an anonymous connection. The provided function starts off with an anonymous socket:

```
def id(_socket), do: nil
```

It also includes an example in the comments for explicitly assigning an identifier to a user:

```
def id(socket), do: "user_socket:#{socket.assigns.user_id}"
```

Right now, we're going to start off with absolutely the simplest case first, since it is always easy to build up on top of something but always incredibly difficult to tear down code once it is in place. We'll leave the code as-is for right now; we'll need to return later on to add more modifications to this boilerplate code! Let's move on to the next piece of the puzzle for real-time applications in Phoenix: channels!

Understanding channels

As mentioned previously, channels are the in-between for sockets and topics. They essentially act as the controllers of the Phoenix real-time application puzzle. The easiest way for us to really understand this is to dive right into the code and start messing around with things until they break!

Phoenix provides a set of macros for us to use with channels, much in the same way it does for controllers (via `use VocialWeb, :controller`) or with views (via `use VocialWeb, :view`). We'll create a new file at `lib/vocial_web/channels/polls_channel.ex`:

```
defmodule VocialWeb.PollsChannel do
  use VocialWeb, :channel
end
```

Notice that here we're using the `:channel` macro instead of `:controller` or `:view` or anything like that! Next, we'll need to figure out how actually to handle dealing with joining, leaving, and dealing with messages for particular topics! We'll tackle these in the order they essentially need to be handled. The first is dealing with our join code. We'll delete this code later, but right now we'll create a very simple lobby for polls that we'll be using to simulate sending our messages back and forth. The first thing we'll need to do is implement a `join/3` function:

```
def join("polls:lobby", _payload, socket) do
  {:ok, socket}
end
```

Again, we're keeping things exceedingly simple here to start. We'll just allow people to join the lobby every time! This will make our lives much easier in the long-run! Looking deeper at the preceding function, we can break it down into separate parts, starting with the arguments being passed into the `join/3` function:

```
def join(topic, additional_data, socket)
```

Where the first argument is the topic that we're joining (*subscribing to*), the second argument is whatever extra data we'll need to pass in via JavaScript to that particular socket, and finally, the third argument is the socket itself. Much like the rest of the code that we've been looking at, join should return an `{:ok, socket}` for success and `{:error, something_else}` in the case of failures!

In the previous case, we don't care about the incoming params, so we mark those with an underscore. Our socket and the pattern-matching clause on the topic are critical, so we include those, and just return out our `{:ok, socket}` return statement. This allows us to just allow all connections to the Polls Lobby and not worry about implementing any sort of authentication or anything else tricky yet!

The next step for us to be able to start actually joining this lobby is to add a single line to our User Socket since that is the main socket we'll be passing everything through. If you remember back to some of the sample code we were looking at earlier, there was a default commented-out line that included a topic and which channel to route that particular topic to. We'll need to do the same for our newly-created topic and channel. In `lib/vocial_web/channels/user_socket.ex`, add the following:

```
channel "polls:lobby", VocialWeb.PollsChannel
```

This by itself won't be quite enough, so we'll need to jump into writing some actual JavaScript code to connect to our channels! First, we'll need to jump into our `assets/js/app.js` file and uncomment the line referencing the socket JavaScript code. You can also delete the starter comments that are in the file, leaving you with something like this:

```
// Import the default Phoenix HTML libraries
import 'phoenix_html';

// Import the User Socket code to enable websockets
import socket from './socket';
```

Now, we'll hop over to the socket code and start adding code line-by-line to get the functionality working for our new Polls channel and Lobby topic! Open up `assets/js/socket.js` and delete everything in there to start, since we're building everything ourselves! Next, we'll start by setting up our import statement to bring the Phoenix Socket library for JavaScript into our code:

```
// Import Phoenix's Socket Library
import { Socket } from 'phoenix';
```

This imports the `Socket` as a class that we can reference in our current code file, which we'll be doing a lot of over the next couple of lines! Now let's actually use this import:

```
// Next, create a new Phoenix Socket to reuse
const socket = new Socket('/socket');
```

Here we're creating a reference to a variable called `socket` that will be responsible for storing the user socket that we're creating on the backend! Remember that the socket acts as the gateway between the client and the channels/topics, so this is essentially opening up that line of real-time communication that we can start listening to and sending messages on! Now that we have the socket, let's actually connect to it:

```
// Connect to the socket itself
socket.connect();
```

The socket is in place and (hopefully) we're seeing connections to it now! This means that we've established a line of communication between our client and our server, so we should be ready to move on to actually attempting to start subscribing to a particular channel and topic:

```
// Create a channel to handle joining/sending/receiving
const channel = socket.channel('polls:lobby', {});
```

Notice that here is where we're actually specifying which topic we want our client to be listening to! In our case, we care about the `polls:lobby` topic only, so we'll only create a channel on that topic (although it is entirely possible to create multiple channels for multiple topics). Okay, we have our socket, we have our channel, so everything should be all set up and ready to go for us to be able to actually join the topic we care about! This one actually relies on a few lines of code:

```
// Next, join the topic on the channel!
channel
  .join()
  .receive('ok', res => console.log('Joined channel:', res))
  .receive('error', res => console.log('Failed to join channel:', res));
```

Every new Socket created has a few functions attached to it. First, we have a `join/0` function, which tells the JavaScript code that it is time to join the channel topic and set the client up as a listener for any messages on that topic that are sent over the socket. Next, we check the data returned back with the `receive/2` function. Remember those tuples I said we'd use later as part of our response to the join function? `{:ok, socket}` and `{:error, socket}`? Well, since we can't exactly use pattern matching, we do the best approximation we can and look for those same messages. The first part of the tuple, the `:ok` or `:error`, tells us which of these receive functions we'll hit in the JavaScript code. The next part is our response, which in our case is the `socket` that we're returning back for each of these.

Finally, we need to export the socket that we've created and connected to our Phoenix backend so that the app.js file knows to include this code as part of its JavaScript code. We do this through something called an "export statement":

```
// Finally, export the socket to be imported in app.js
export default socket;
```

If we've done everything correctly, when we open up our web browser and visit the home page for the app we're building, we should expect to see a message in our JavaScript developer console about being able to successfully join a channel with the message `"Joined channel: {}"`!

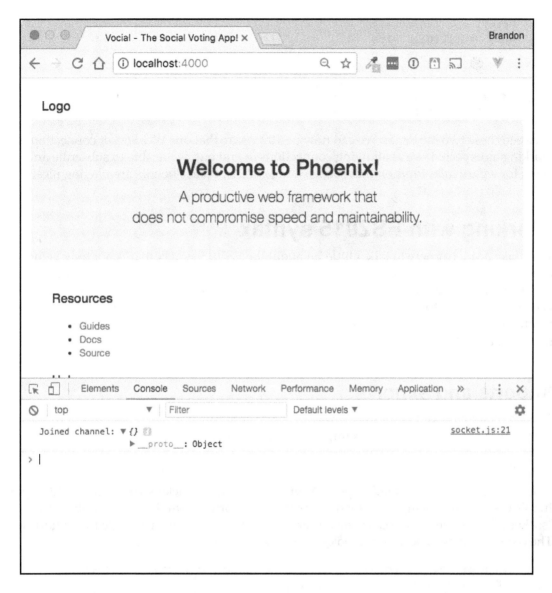

In addition to this, if we take a look in our terminal that's running our Phoenix server, we should see a message telling us that Phoenix is also doing everything right and responding out that the attempt to join the channel and topic was successful:

```
[info] GET /
[debug] Processing with VocialWeb.PageController.index/2
  Parameters: %{}
```

```
    Pipelines: [:browser]
[info] Sent 200 in 72ms
[info] JOIN "polls:lobby" to VocialWeb.PollsChannel
    Transport: Phoenix.Transports.WebSocket (2.0.0)
    Serializer: Phoenix.Transports.V2.WebSocketSerializer
    Parameters: %{}
[info] Replied polls:lobby :ok
```

Between these two messages, we can now be 100% sure that our WebSocket connection is working as expected; we're allowing connections in and out, we're able to subscribe and listen for a particular topic on that socket, and JavaScript and Phoenix are playing nicely!

Working with ES2015 syntax

We'll take a sidebar here to talk a little bit about the ES2015 syntax that is not only being used in the preceding examples but will be used in pretty much every code sample, snippet, or tutorial you'll read, especially in the context of modern Phoenix code. Just in case, we'll take a few minutes to talk about the syntax used in the preceding examples and what they mean. The first line we wrote in the `socket.js` was an `import` statement and our first introduction to ES2015 syntax!

Imports and exports

`import` statements can work in two ways; either through working with default imports or named imports. Looking at the example we wrote for the first line:

```
import { Socket } from 'phoenix';
```

This is an example of a **named** import. Anything we put in brackets will be a named import. In this case, we're looking for something that was exported from the Phoenix library as "socket". This is usually the case when there are multiple exports in a single file or library. The corresponding export might look something like this:

```
// This is not the actual code, just an example of how this could look
let Socket = {};
export { Socket };
```

This is the way that we're going to be able to work with other libraries and how we're going to be able to create our own libraries as well. If we take a look at the `socket` file, we had a line at the bottom that corresponded with our code:

```
export default socket;
```

Here, we were setting up our socket as a "default" export, which means that when we import it, we don't have to write the name of the export as part of the import statement. If we remember all the way back to when we looked at app.js, we had this line in it:

```
import socket from './socket';
```

Again, note the lack of curly braces on our import statement (much like how there were no curly braces on our export statement). The only other important thing you'll need to know to be able to work with the code effectively is how libraries are referenced in import statements. In the from '...' part of the import statement we specify our library as being either a local library or a global library. If you see './File', then it is a file path that is referencing a local file (in our case, "File.js" in the current directory). If you see 'File', then it is a global library (likely something installed via NPM) called File. In our case, we have import socket from './socket', so that means that app.js is looking for a file named socket.js in its current directory!

let and const

Next, we'll move on to variable declarations in JavaScript. In addition to the original var cat = "meow"; syntax, ES2015 introduces two new forms for declaring different variables: let and const. We won't go into extreme detail on these and why they were specifically implemented, but the important things to note are things that will cause errors later on. For example, with let statements, let variables can never be redeclared in the same scope. You can, however, reassign the value in the variable:

```
let greeting = "hello";
let greeting = "world"; // This will result in an error!
greeting = "world"; // This will not!
```

const, on the other hand, makes it so you cannot reassign a variable. It does not make it immutable, mind you; it just means you cannot take the variable name and reassign it later. Take a look at this example to get a better picture:

```
const greeting = "hello";
greeting = "world"; // This will result in an error!
```

For the most part, I just stick to using const for everything unless I specifically know I need it to be a variable I can reassign later (which is very rare).

Fat-arrow functions

ES2015 also introduces a new syntax for declaring functions called "fat arrow functions." Let's look at a simple variable function definition:

```
var greet = function(name) {
  console.log("Say hello to ", name);
};
```

We could instead write that function definition with fat arrow syntax as follows:

```
const greet = (name) => {
  console.log("Say hello to ", name);
};
```

Fat-arrow syntax also has a number of extra shortcuts you can use to make the amount of code even smaller! For example, if your function just has a single line or is just a return statement, you can rewrite your function as follows:

```
const greet = (name) => console.log("Say hello to ", name);
```

Alternatively, you can wrap your return statement in parentheses as well, like this (and you'll have to remember this if you want to return an object as your shorthand function's return):

```
const greet = (name) => (console.log("Say hello to ", name));
```

Now, this is very important. If you only have one line as your statement for a shorthand syntax like the preceding example, it will be what is returned no matter what! That means that you can do something like this:

```
const greet = (name) => name.toUpperCase();
```

If you passed in a name to that function, it would implicitly return that name uppercased! Yes, even without a return statement; again, remember that this becomes an implicit return. You can even make this shorter; you only need the parentheses around the arguments if there is more than one argument or no arguments. All of these are valid function declarations:

```
const greet = () => "Hello!";
const greet = name => "Hello " + name + "!";
const greet = (message, name) => message + " " + name + "!";
```

The last thing about arrow functions is that they retain the context of `this` from where the functions are declared, which leads to weird scenarios where this is suddenly some anonymous function and you have to write code to get around `this` not meaning what you expect it to mean. Again, there's a lot more detail surrounding this and what it means; there are plenty of resources out there to help you understand these at a much deeper level!

Variable and argument destructuring

This is the last piece that you'll need to understand, as it tends to appear in a lot of JavaScript code tied to Phoenix channels. This last concept is centered around destructuring variables and arguments and it actually works a lot like what you're used to in Elixir. It basically allows you to do things like this:

```
const person = {
  firstName: "Jane",
  lastName: "Smith",
  age: 30
};

const { firstName, lastName, age } = person;

console.log(firstName); // Will output "Jane"
console.log(lastName); // Will output "Smith"
console.log(age); // Will output "30"
```

This is a nice, cleaner way of doing something that previously required as much code as this:

```
const person = {
  firstName: "Jane",
  lastName: "Smith",
  age: 30
};

const firstName = person.firstName;
const lastName = person.lastName;
const age = person.age;

console.log(firstName); // Will output "Jane"
console.log(lastName); // Will output "Smith"
console.log(age); // Will output "30"
```

It can also be used in functions, as well:

```
const greeting = { firstName, lastName } => "Hello " + firstName + " " +
lastName + "!";
```

This does the same thing as the other destructuring code we wrote earlier! This should be enough ES2015 for you to be able to understand everything you might need as we work through the JavaScript code that we'll need to write to finish implementing the channels for our application!

Sending and receiving messages with channels

We have a channel that we can join and some basic JavaScript, but without it actually doing something more interesting I don't think we'll have enough people using the site to make it worthwhile. We need to get some code in place that will help us mediate the sending and receiving of messages between our client and our server! The good news is that the code to do that is just as simple as the code we've already written to handle our client joining and subscribing to a particular topic. The problem right now, however, is that our code dealing with the polls topic is always firing, no matter what page it's on.

Conditionally loading our socket

Let's quickly add a little check into our code to make that problem go away. In `assets/js/socket.js`, we're going to wrap our channel connection code inside of a conditional:

```
// Only connect to the socket if the polls channel actually exists!
if (document.getElementById('enable-polls-channel')) {
  // Create a channel to handle joining/sending/receiving
  const channel = socket.channel('polls:lobby', {});

  // Next, join the topic on the channel!
  channel
    .join()
    .receive('ok', res => console.log('Joined channel:', res))
    .receive('error', res => console.log('Failed to join channel:', res));
}
```

If we refresh our browser on the homepage of our app we'll no longer see that `'Joined channel'` message, which is good! If we browse over to `/votes`, however, we still don't get anything showing up, so we'll want to clear that up too. At the top of `lib/vocial_web/templates/poll/index.html.eex`, add the following line:

```
<i id="enable-polls-channel" />
```

Now when you refresh that page, you should see the same `"Joined channel: {}"` message in your developer console. We'll also need to add in something that will send a message, so we'll add a quick mostly useless button that will allow us to send a single message across our socket so that we can verify that functionality is working as expected.

Sending messages on the socket

For us to be able to start sending messages and continue testing the overall functionality of our channels, we'll need some sort of input from the user to initiate the message across. To do that, we'll just add a dummy button to the page that allows us to ping the server from the client across the WebSocket. Add the following button code to that same template:

```
<button id="polls-ping" class="btn btn-primary">Ping Websocket</button>
```

We'll next need to hop back over to `socket.js` and add a new few lines of code that will be responsible for hooking this button up to be able to broadcast something out to the server. Open up `assets/js/socket.js` and add this to the bottom of the conditional (the enable-polls-channel conditional):

```
document.getElementById("polls-ping").addEventListener("click", () => {
  channel
    .push("ping")
    .receive("ok", res => console.log("Received PING response:",
res.message))
    .receive("error", res => console.log("Error sending PING:", res));
});
```

There's a little bit going on here, so let's take a few minutes to explain. First off, we grab the document out of the page and look for an element on the page with an ID of `"polls-ping"`. Next, we add an event listener to it that will register every time a user clicks on the button. `addEventListener` takes a function as the second argument, so we'll use the fat arrow syntax to create a new function in-line.

Next, we use the `push` function on the channel object that we created. Push takes in arguments for the message we want to send out, and optionally, any additional payload information we want included as part of that message. In our case, we don't care about any payload; we just care that we're sending the `"ping"` message across. If we receive a successful message, we send it back out to the developer console! If we get an error message back from the server, we'll deal with that accordingly as well!

Now we'll need to actually implement the server side of this. Heading back to `lib/vocial_web/channels/polls_channel.ex`, you'll want to add the following function:

```
def handle_in("ping", _payload, socket) do
  {:reply, {:ok, %{message: "pong"}}, socket}
end
```

Again, we're keeping our code VERY simple to start. We use the `handle_in/3` function to deal with incoming messages from the server. If we want to send something back, we can do that too. The help documentation from running `h Phoenix.Channel` in IEx says this about `handle_in/3`:

> *After a client has successfully joined a channel, incoming events from the client are routed through the channel's* `handle_in/3` *callbacks. Within these callbacks, you can perform any action. Typically you'll either forward a message to all listeners with* `broadcast!/3`, *or push a message directly down the socket with push/3. Incoming callbacks must return the socket to maintain ephemeral state.*

Since this is a ping message, the server should reply back to the client that it received and processed the message, so we need to include a reply from the server. The same help page has this to say about replies:

> *In addition to pushing messages out when you receive a* `handle_in` *event, you can also reply directly to a client event for request/response style messaging. This is useful when a client must know the result of an operation or to simply track messages.*

We include a reply, include the state and payload of the reply back to the client, and include the socket as the final piece of the tuple. This should now be enough code for us to actually test this out. Go back to your page, refresh, and if you followed all of the instructions, you should be able to click on the button on your page at the top, send out a ping message to the server, and get a reply back from the server, all through our `socket.js` code:

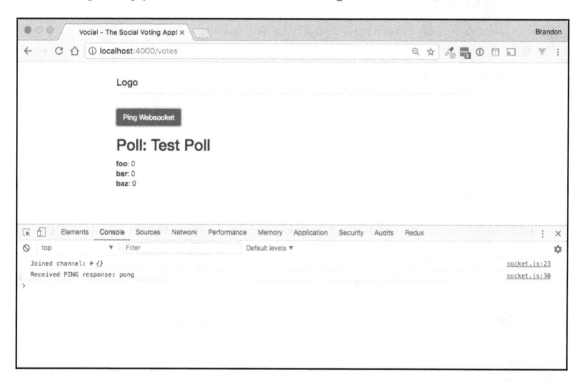

In addition to this, if we start looking at the messages showing up in our Phoenix logs, we should see the successful results we need to be confident that this whole thing is functioning from both sides:

```
[debug] INCOMING "ping" on "polls:lobby" to VocialWeb.PollsChannel
  Transport: Phoenix.Transports.WebSocket
  Parameters: %{}
```

We still need a way to test out receiving messages from the server, since WebSockets are a bidirectional communication method! Let's head back to `lib/vocial_web/channels/polls_channel.ex` and add some code to broadcast a message out to all of the clients that someone has pinged the server:

```
def handle_in("ping", _payload, socket) do
  broadcast socket, "pong", %{message: "pong"}
  {:reply, {:ok, %{message: "pong"}}, socket}
end
```

And we'll need to open up `assets/js/socket.js` as well to add code that will handle these broadcasts from the server (again, add this code inside of the same `enable-polls-channel` conditional):

```
channel.on('pong', payload => {
  console.log("The server has been PONG'd and all is well:", payload);
});
```

This is where the Phoenix WebSocket stuff goes from being, *Hey, this is neat*, to *Wow, this is amazing*! Open up another web browser, also at `/polls` for your local server. When you click the **Ping** button on one browser, you should see the resulting broadcast on *all* of the browser windows that have this `page/socket/channel` open:

You can clearly see that the left browser window is the one that actually initiated the ping (and this is the only one getting the "Received PING response: pong" message in its developer console), yet both broadcast messages are being received nearly simultaneously! You can try this with one extra window or a hundred; the results will ultimately be the same. Congratulations! You are now successfully broadcasting messages bidirectionally on Phoenix channels!

Allowing users to vote on polls

We currently don't have any code in place that will actually allow anonymous users to vote, even outside of our socket code, so that's something we'll want to add in first. The reason that we're going to write in some non-socket code for voting is that everything WebSocket-based should generally have some way of manually performing whatever operations it is performing. That way the testing of your application is a little bit simpler and it also makes it easier for you to support older browsers and not just lock someone out of your application entirely.

First, we'll need to add the new route to be able to support voting on individual options. We'll make our own lives easier here by avoiding a complicated nested routing scheme that would give us a URL like `/polls/:vote_id/options/:id/vote`, as we can work directly with the Options and their primary key IDs.

Open up `lib/vocial_web/router.ex` and add the following to our listing of resources, fetching an option by its ID:

```
get "/options/:id/vote", PollController, :vote
```

This is referencing something that doesn't actually exist yet, so we'll need to get on that next. This is not by-the-books RESTful design, but this is by design; we want to make it dead simple for people to vote on things, and by avoiding the route of needing the vote ID, the option ID, and sending the whole thing over PUT, we can make it very simple to test our application. The nice thing about prototyping an application is that you can always improve on things later; keeping things as simple as possible as you're building up is often more important than nailing your implementation on your first pass. Now let's move on to our Poll controller over at `lib/vocial_web/controllers/poll_controller.ex`:

```
def vote(conn, %{"id" => id}) do
  with {:ok, option} <- Votes.vote_on_option(id) do
    conn
    |> put_flash(:info, "Placed a vote for #{option.title}!")
```

```
        |> redirect(to: poll_path(conn, :index))
    end
end
```

This is pretty standard code that we've written a hundred times, but we don't actually have a `Votes.vote_on_option/1` function yet in our context. This is another important part of building up a web application; learning how to prototype effectively. Sometimes you want to build your code in a way that's more intuitive than working backward; this helps you get better at naming your functions and modules in a way that's more conducive to what real developers would actually do and expect if they're ever working with your code!

The other nice thing about this is it helps us figure out where we need to go next with our code. Every time we build a piece we create a dependency on the next piece of our implementation, which can help you avoid turning your code into a scatter-brained spaghetti code mess! Our next dependency is implementing the `vote_on_option` function in our context, so navigate over to `lib/vocial/votes/votes.ex` and we'll add our new function:

```
def vote_on_option(option_id) do
end
```

Working from the code in the controller, remember that we had implied its implementation was a single argument. Given that we suffixed our function with `_on_option`, it's pretty easy to infer that our code is operating on options and should take an option ID as the single argument. We'll use a `with` statement for this code since that tends to result in very readable code, so the next line in our function is going to look something like this:

```
with option <- Repo.get!(Option, option_id),
```

Here we're expecting to receive an option back from our call to `Repo.get!/2`. When you see a bang as part of the function name, that means that if it fails to find the appropriate resource, it will error out instead of returning a nil. In our case, we don't want the user to be able to vote on a non-existing option, so that's the right choice for us. `Repo.get` takes in the query or schema as its first argument and the primary key (in our case, the ID) as the second argument. From the docs (for `Repo.get`, which shares an almost identical usage except that it does not throw the `Ecto.NoResultsError` if it fails):

Fetches a single struct from the data store where the primary key matches the given ID.

We've fetched our option (assuming everything has gone well up to this point), so now we'll need to figure out the current vote count and add one to it:

```
votes <- option.votes + 1
```

Finally, we can close out our function with the actual update operation. This will very closely match the code that we already have in place to do updates for the polls themselves:

```
do
   update_option(option, %{votes: votes})
end
```

Following our dependency chain down, here's yet another function that we haven't actually implemented yet! The only value that we're changing the option is the number of votes, so we just include that as the updated attributes passed into our option update function. This one is also almost identical to the other updated code, so let's implement our update_option/2 function:

```
def update_option(option, attrs) do
   option
   |> Option.changeset(attrs)
   |> Repo.update()
end
```

That's all that we need to implement in our manual update code to serve as the actual infrastructure and backbone and make it all work! If you followed everything along you should have some new code like this in your votes context:

```
def vote_on_option(option_id) do
   with option <- Repo.get!(Option, option_id),
        votes <- option.votes + 1
   do
      update_option(option, %{votes: votes})
   end
end

def update_option(option, attrs) do
   option
   |> Option.changeset(attrs)
   |> Repo.update()
end
```

The last piece is for us to jump into our interface and add some sort of buttons to allow users to vote on options in polls as they appear. Again, we're going to opt for the simplest implementation for this, even if it is not the most aesthetically-pleasing option!

Remember to keep starting simple and building up, instead of jumping immediately into the most complicated solutions! In all of my experience doing development, the best experiences I've ever had building projects have been the ones where I started off small and gave myself the room and agility to iterate and adjust my initial assumptions as I went along!

Let's spend some time editing `lib/vocial_web/templates/poll/index.html.eex` and change the option display a little bit to add our new buttons. We'll just modify the loop responsible for displaying the options instead of the entire template:

```
<%= for option <- poll.options do %>
  <strong><%= option.title %></strong>:
  <span id="vote-count-<%= option.id %>" class="vote-count"><%=
option.votes %></span>
  <a href="/options/<%= option.id %>/vote" class="btn btn-primary vote-
button-manual" data-option-id="<%= option.id %>">Vote</a>
  <br />
<% end %>
```

We had to change quite a bit to really make this all work the way we'll need it to later on. If we're thinking about how our voting system might be implemented, we will need a simple way to update the number of votes in the element, as well as a way to figure out/reassign what those buttons will do. To address this, we start by wrapping the count of votes inside of a span with a very specific ID (mapped to the option's primary key). This will allow us to very quickly find and change the number of votes displayed in the user's browser.

Also, the vote button has been given an extra CSS class (outside of the Bootstrap styling) called `vote-button-manual`. We've also assigned a data attribute to it to store the current option ID; we will need to do this to be able to modify the behavior of the button and have it interact with the server (specifically, to cast the vote for that one specific option)! For now, though, go back to your UI, and you should see something like this:

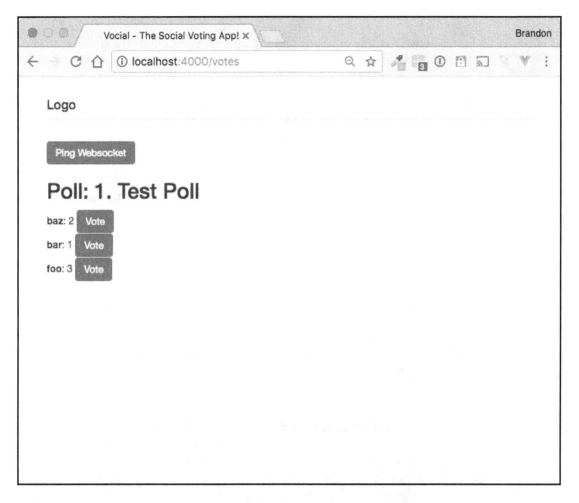

It's not perfect, but if you go through and test each of the buttons, you'll see that they DO work! You may run into one issue with the UI, though, that's a little strange: every time you vote and the page refreshes, the order of the options changes! That's because the default ordering is never guaranteed for us! We can go back to the line responsible for handling the iteration of our options and modify the `for` statement slightly to fix this little bug:

```
<%= for option <- Enum.sort(poll.options, &(&1.id >= &2.id)) do %>
```

This will give us a list of sorted options by their primary key instead of whatever random ordering we're happening to get at the time, which is a more consistent experience and definitely less jarring for the user!

> If you do not specify any ordering in your database queries, you should always be very cautious about making assumptions about the order that things will appear in!

In the process of doing this, we'll actually break a test back in `test/vocial_web/controllers/poll_controller_test.exs`, since we're changing the formatting. We'll correct the `GET /polls` test:

```
test "GET /polls", %{conn: conn, user: user} do
  {:ok, poll} =
    Vocial.Votes.create_poll_with_options(%{title: "Poll 1", user_id:
user.id}, [
      "Choice 1",
      "Choice 2",
      "Choice 3"
    ])

  conn = get(conn, "/polls")
  assert html_response(conn, 200) =~ poll.title

  Enum.each(poll.options, fn option ->
    assert html_response(conn, 200) =~ "#{option.title}"
    assert html_response(conn, 200) =~ "#{option.votes}"
  end)
end
```

We'll want to write up a few tests to cover this new behavior (especially our `Votes.vote_on_option/1` function as we'll be reusing that for our socket code as well)! First, we'll write up our new Votes context test by adding a new test to the `describe "options"` block in `test/vocial/votes/votes_test.exs`:

```
test "vote_on_option/1 adds a vote to a particular option", %{user: user}
do
  # Code goes in here...
end
```

We'll need the user to create an appropriate poll to use; otherwise, this is a pretty standard test. We'll use the `create_poll_with_options` function we made earlier to make our lives simpler and create an appropriate poll with an option for us:

```
with {:ok, poll} = Votes.create_poll(%{ title: "Sample Poll", user_id:
user.id }),
     {:ok, option} = Votes.create_option(%{ title: "Sample Choice", votes:
0, poll_id: poll.id }),
     option <- Repo.preload(option, :poll)
```

```
do
   # Next bits of code go here...
end
```

The next bit is the actual asserts of the test itself. We've created a poll, we've created an option, and now we want to verify that when we vote on the option its vote count goes up by one:

```
votes_before = option.votes
```

First, we store the current value of the option's votes before we do any further actions. This will give us our baseline assertion to see how the data changes over the course of this test. Next, we'll actually update the option with one additional vote:

```
{:ok, updated_option} = Votes.vote_on_option(option.id)
```

This will give us the output we can use to verify the overall functionality of our test. Since the function we wrote has the express and sole purpose of just adding one to the overall vote count of the options, we write that as our specific assertion:

```
assert (votes_before + 1) == updated_option.votes
```

Now we'll run our test to verify the results! Our test should be passing here, so we've verified the functionality of our context separate from that of our controller. Let's finish this functionality up by also adding a test for our controller since we're already doing a pretty good job of keeping the total test coverage decently high! Open up `test/vocial_web/controllers/poll_controller_test.exs` and we'll start implementing our test. First, we'll need to modify our setup block so that there is a good pre-existing poll with options we can use. Add this line (and change the return at the end of the function to include this new variable):

```
{:ok, poll} = Vocial.Votes.create_poll_with_options(
   %{ "title" => "My New Test Poll", "user_id" => user.id },
   ["One", "Two", "Three"]
)
{:ok, conn: conn, user: user, poll: poll}
```

Now we can reference the pre-created poll by pattern matching inside of our test declarations for `poll`. To that point, let's now start adding our test further down in this file:

```
test "GET /options/:id/vote", %{conn: conn, poll: poll} do
end
```

We start off by declaring our test in the same way that we've gone through previously and described our tests and set them up. Next, similar to the other test that we wrote that covers this same functionality, we'll need to make it so that we can start with a baseline count of votes for a particular option:

```
option = Enum.at(poll.options, 0)
before_votes = option.votes
```

Then, we can make a request to the actual endpoint that is responsible for incrementing the vote count for that particular option, and record the newly modified option vote count:

```
conn = get(conn, "/options/#{option.id}/vote")
after_option = Vocial.Repo.get!(Vocial.Votes.Option, option.id)
```

We have everything we need as the framework for this test to be able to finally write our final assertions! We do a redirect as part of that controller, so we'll want to double-check that our returned HTTP status code is 302 and that we're getting redirected to a particular endpoint. We'll also want to verify that the number of votes increased by one:

```
assert html_response(conn, 302)
assert redirected_to(conn) == "/polls"
assert after_option.votes == (before_votes + 1)
```

If we run our controller tests we should also likewise see green tests! Our code is now ready, our test suite is green, and we can start working on the much cooler functionality by implementing some real-time application code!

Making voting real-time

We have our manual methods for voting, so we have a nice fallback should we be working with a browser that doesn't support anything fancy, but let's also build the good stuff into our application! If we return back to the JavaScript code that lives in assets/js/socket.js, we can go into our conditional and start by adding a new bit of code by modifying our current join code. Again, when we're building functionality we always want to be building our functionality up from the simplest implementation, so we'll start with some dummy code!

Building our dummy functionality

We'll want to start off by modifying our `join` function to turn off the event handlers for the buttons with the `vote-button-manual` CSS class attached to them (remember I said we'd be dealing with those again later). We'll also have it output something to the developer logs so that we can verify things are working before we start implementing the next pieces:

```
// Next, join the topic on the channel!
channel
  .join()
  .receive('ok', res => {
    document.querySelectorAll('.vote-button-manual').forEach(el => {
      el.addEventListener('click', event => {
        event.preventDefault();
        console.log('Do something special!');
      });
    });
    console.log('Joined channel:', res);
  })
  .receive('error', res => console.log('Failed to join channel:', res));
```

We take what used to be a very simple `receive('ok'...)` function and build it up a lot more. First of all, we no longer want to click on those buttons to vote and refresh the page; instead, we'll want this functionality to work through our channels when we've successfully joined a channel! This code is pretty messy right now, though, so let's start creating a new function to handle this work, otherwise, we'll quickly get ourselves into a scenario where this code is incredibly difficult to maintain or add on to. We'll start by implementing an `onJoin` function up near the top of our file (right under our `import` statement):

```
// Utility functions
const onJoin = res => {
  document.querySelectorAll('.vote-button-manual').forEach(el => {
    el.addEventListener('click', event => {
      event.preventDefault();
      console.log('Do something special!');
    });
  });
  console.log('Joined channel:', res);
};
```

Return next back to the `join` code and we'll tell it to use our new helper function instead:

```
// Next, join the topic on the channel!
channel
  .join()
  .receive('ok', res => onJoin(res))
  .receive('error', res => console.log('Failed to join channel:', res));
```

Much cleaner! Now if you go back to the UI and click on one of the **Vote** buttons, you should see **Do something special** appear in the developer logs:

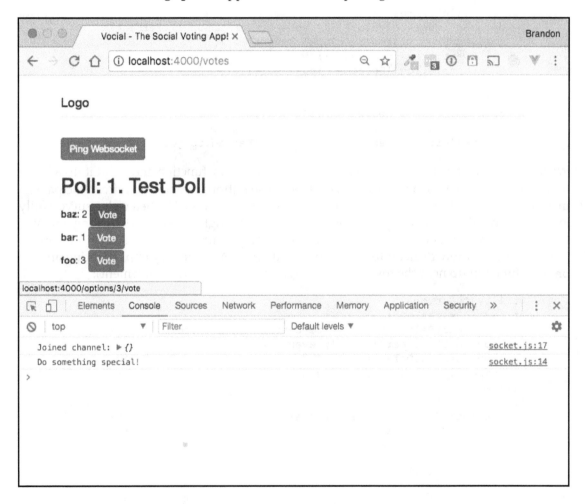

Changing our dummy code to push to the server

The dummy code is there, but it's not doing anything other than validating that we've done something good to start. Let's expand on that more by pushing a socket message up to the server. We'll start off by writing a function that is responsible for actually pushing the vote back up to the server. Place this function preceding to your `onJoin` function for now:

```
// Push the vote up to the server
const pushVote = (el, channel) => {
  channel
    .push('vote', { option_id: el.getAttribute('data-option-id') })
    .receive('ok', res => console.log('You Voted!'))
    .receive('error', res => console.log('Failed to vote:', res));
};
```

We want to grab the current option ID for the button clicked and use that as part of the payload for the vote command that we'll push up via the socket. If all is successful, we'll display something out to the user to let them know their vote was recorded; otherwise, we'll also record whatever failure message we may get displayed back out!

We'll also need to modify the `onJoin` function we wrote previously. It will need to have access to the channel so it can pass that along to the `pushVote` function, so we'll need to modify the function's signature to include the ability to pass in the channel. In addition, we'll need to modify the body of the click event handler to call out to our new `pushVote` function:

```
// When we join the channel, do this
const onJoin = (res, channel) => {
  document.querySelectorAll('.vote-button-manual').forEach(el => {
    el.addEventListener('click', event => {
      event.preventDefault();
      pushVote(el, channel);
    });
  });
  console.log('Joined channel:', res);
};
```

We'll need to modify where we call our `onJoin` function as well since we can now no longer just pass in the response; we'll need the channel as well:

```
// Next, join the topic on the channel!
channel
  .join()
  .receive('ok', res => onJoin(res, channel))
  .receive('error', res => console.log('Failed to join channel:', res));
```

Finally, we'll need a function to handle what happens when the server broadcasts out to us that we've received a new vote on one of the options from another client. We'll arbitrarily call that message a `'new_vote'` message and assume that it will need to send to us an option ID and the new vote count for that option:

```
channel.on('new_vote', ({ option_id, votes }) => {
  document.getElementById('vote-count-' + option_id).innerHTML = votes;
});
```

Writing our server channel code for live voting

The last piece to the puzzle for all of this work is that we need to tell Phoenix how to deal with the "vote" message that is getting pushed from the client. Remember that our preceding implementation used the "push" message with an `option_id` parameter; we'll use those rules to implement the appropriate `handle_in` function. Back in `lib/vocial_web/channels/poll_channel.ex`, add the following:

```
def handle_in("vote", %{"option_id" => option_id}, socket) do
  with {:ok, option} <- Vocial.Votes.vote_on_option(option_id) do
    broadcast socket, "new_vote", %{"option_id" => option.id, "votes" =>
option.votes}
    {:reply, {:ok, %{"option_id" => option.id, "votes" => option.votes}},
socket}
  else
    {:error, _} ->
      {:reply, {:error, %{message: "Failed to vote for option!"}},
socket}
  end
end
```

In the preceding block of code, we start with just our `handle_in` function pattern matching on "vote" messages coming from the client. We're expecting them to provide an `option_id` parameter (because how else would we know what it is that they're trying to vote on?), and with that option ID we'll try to cast that vote. If we succeed, we'll broadcast out to all listening clients, *Hey, we just received a new vote for this particular option ID. The new vote count should be X!*

If all went well, we'll broadcast out a message repeating the same information we received, and we'll include a reply to the sender that the server received the message successfully! Otherwise, we'll fail out with an error reply that lets the user know that they failed to vote for the option they clicked the button for!

Refactoring our channels away from the index

We have our WebSockets running on the index page for our Polls, but that'll actually be very difficult for us to support in the future, especially if we want to add anything like per-poll chat options or another similar feature that relies very specifically on the display of a single poll. Because of that, let's take a few minutes to implement a show action and template for our poll, and move our socket code there instead! We'll also have to change some of the topics that we were previously relying on since right now we're using the lobby as the identifier for the polls channels. We'll instead want to switch that over to be more along the lines of: "polls:(poll id)". First, hop on over to `lib/vocial_web/router.ex` and modify the "polls" resource line to also include `:show` as one of the options:

```
resources "/polls", PollController, only: [:index, :new, :create, :show]
```

We'll also need a controller addition and a context addition, since there is no `get_poll/1` function to retrieve a specific poll, and there is no show action either. We'll start with our controller, and we'll stub out what we think the `get_poll` function should look like. In `lib/vocial_web/controllers/poll_controller.ex`, add the following:

```
def show(conn, %{"id" => id}) do
  with poll <- Votes.get_poll(id), do: render(conn, "show.html", %{ poll:
poll })
end
```

We've created a line that references a Votes context function called `get_pol`", but we haven't actually written that yet, so now let's hop over to `lib/vocial/votes/votes.ex` and write that function:

```
def get_poll(id), do: Repo.get!(Poll, id) |> Repo.preload(:options)
```

We're not doing anything too exciting here; we need to fetch a poll out of the database with a specific ID (and we want it to return with a failure if it couldn't find it - this is why we are using the `Repo.get!/2` function instead of `Repo.get/2`).

We wouldn't want to add new functionality without also updating our tests, so we'll wander over to `test/vocial/votes/votes_test.exs` and add a single test inside of our `describe "polls"` block:

```
test "show_poll/1 returns a specific poll", %{user: user} do
  poll = poll_fixture(%{user_id: user.id})
  assert Votes.get_poll(poll.id) == poll
end
```

A quick run of mix test should give us a fully-green test suite, so now we'll hop on over to write our controller test at `test/vocial_web/controllers/poll_controller_test.exs` and write a simple test:

```
test "GET /polls/:id", %{conn: conn, poll: poll} do
  conn = get conn, "/polls/#{poll.id}"
  assert html_response(conn, 200) =~ poll.title
end
```

This test, however, will fail right now! We've not written any templates for this show action, so if we run our test suite we'll get a nice big error in our test suite. Let's fix that now. We'll end up reusing the Poll display template, so let's create a partial template first. Create `lib/vocial_web/templates/poll/_poll.html.eex` as follows:

```
<div class="poll-display">
  <h2>Poll: <%= @poll.id %>. <%= @poll.title %></h2>

  <%= for option <- Enum.sort(@poll.options, &(&1.id >= &2.id)) do %>
    <strong><%= option.title %></strong>:
    <span id="vote-count-<%= option.id %>" class="vote-count"><%=
option.votes %></span>
    <a href="/options/<%= option.id %>/vote" class="btn btn-primary vote-
button-manual" data-option-id="<%= option.id %>">Vote</a>
    <br />
  <% end %>
</div>
```

We'll also create `lib/vocial_web/templates/poll/show.html.eex`:

```
<%= render("_poll.html", %{ poll: @poll }) %>
```

All we did was copy and paste our Poll display code out of the index and place it here. This also means we can refactor our `index.html.eex` file to just use this template instead of duplicating logic! Open up `lib/vocial_web/templates/poll/index.html.eex`, remove the "enable-polls-channel" line at the top, and change the Poll loop to use the partial instead. Our new index template should look like this:

```
<%= for poll <- @polls do %>
  <%= render("_poll.html", %{ poll: poll }) %>
<% end %>
```

Moving the channel functionality to show

The next step in polishing up our application is moving our channel logic to instead be poll-specific instead of all sitting in the lobby. Open up `show.html.eex` and change the template to include the WebSocket-specific code that used to live in `index.html.eex`. We'll need to modify it slightly as well since we'll need to have a way to tell JavaScript what poll ID it needs to use to find the right topic:

```
<i id="enable-polls-channel" data-poll-id="<%= @poll.id %>"></i>
<button id="polls-ping" class="btn btn-primary">Ping Websocket</button>
```

We'll also need to open up `socket.js` and change the code to start using this new code. Modify the old `if` statement that checked if polls were enabled for that page to instead grab the enable socket tag:

```
// ...

// Only connect to the socket if the polls channel actually exists!
const enableSocket = document.getElementById('enable-polls-channel');
if (enableSocket) {
  // Pull the Poll Id to find the right topic from the data attribute
  const pollId = enableSocket.getAttribute('data-poll-id');
  // Create a channel to handle joining/sending/receiving
  const channel = socket.channel('polls:' + pollId, {});

  // ...
```

If we take a look over at our server we're probably going to start seeing a lot of warnings in our terminal:

```
[warn] Ignoring unmatched topic "polls:1" in VocialWeb.UserSocket
```

This is good! This tells us that our JavaScript code is actually working and doing everything we expect it to! Now we need to change our socket and channel code to use these new topics, which means we're going to be working with topic wildcards now! Open up `lib/vocial_web/channels/user_socket.ex` and change the polls channel line to use a wildcard instead of "lobby" as the subtopic:

```
channel "polls:*", VocialWeb.PollsChannel
```

Finally, hop over to `lib/vocial_web/channels/polls_channel.ex` and change our join function to be able to listen for this new wildcard:

```
def join("polls:" <> _poll_id, _payload, socket) do
  {:ok, socket}
end
```

That will be it! Our functionality now should be otherwise unchanged from what we had before, except it will be much more specific to that specific poll. This will enable us to be able to do fun things with charts and graphs later on, as well as implementing features and functionality like live chat on each of the polls!

Starting our channel tests

We'll also want to finish up by writing some appropriate tests for our channels. We'll create `test/vocial_web/channels/polls_channel_test.exs` and start off by declaring our test module, including the appropriate set of testing macros and alias statements:

```
defmodule VocialWeb.PollChannelTest do
  use VocialWeb.ChannelCase

  alias VocialWeb.PollsChannel
end
```

Similar to our controller tests, we'll also need to create a nice big setup block that will create a user account that we can use:

```
setup do
  {:ok, user} = Vocial.Accounts.create_user(%{
    username: "test",
    email: "test@test.com",
    password: "test",
    password_confirmation: "test"
  })
```

We'll also need to make a pre-created poll:

```
  {:ok, poll} = Vocial.Votes.create_poll_with_options(
    %{ "title" => "My New Test Poll", "user_id" => user.id },
    ["One", "Two", "Three"]
  )
```

Now, we'll need to create a socket that we can simulate our tests against. Phoenix provides a built-in helper via ChannelCase that allows us to create a fake socket and subscribe to a particular topic (remember that our topic was mapped to a specific poll):

```
{:ok, _, socket} =
  socket("user_id", %{user_id: user.id})
  |> subscribe_and_join(PollsChannel, "polls:#{poll.id}")
```

Finally, we'll need to return all of that out to let our tests pick and choose which they need:

```
  {:ok, socket: socket, user: user, poll: poll}
end
```

The first WebSocket event that we created was our `ping` event because it was by far the simplest to implement, so let's do that for the first channel test we've ever written:

```
test "ping replies with status ok", %{socket: socket} do
  ref = push socket, "ping", %{}
  assert_reply ref, :ok, %{message: "pong"}
end
```

We apply pattern matching against the arguments to our test to get the socket out, and then we push a `ping` message onto that with an empty payload. This returns back to us a reference to the mock socket (you can think of this as our modified conn object from our controller tests, although it's not precisely identical).

We then pattern match our reply, asserting that the ping should respond back with an `:ok` status and a message of `pong`! The next test that we're going to have to write, though, is going to be much more complicated, unfortunately. This is the test of our vote, and there's a lot we're going to have to do here to make it work, so let's step through it bit-by-bit to make sure we truly understand it:

```
test "vote replies with status ok", %{socket: socket, poll: poll} do
```

We start off by pattern matching our arguments to pull the socket and poll out of the setup block. This will give us a good starting point. Similar to what we did in our controller tests, we'll also want to grab the first option from the poll, and then, similar to our ping WebSocket test, we'll want to simulate a ping message on to the server:

```
option = Enum.at(poll.options, 0)
ref = push socket, "vote", %{"option_id" => option.id}
```

Now we'll want to actually verify the reply and the broadcast that we send out as part of the `handle_in` function for the `vote` message. This has one *very* tricky part to it that is very easy to get caught on, so I'll write the code out first and then explain it:

```
assert_reply ref, :ok, %{"option_id" => option_id, "votes" => votes}
assert option_id == option.id
assert votes == option.votes + 1
```

`assert_reply` works by looking for a success or failure message, and then the next statement is not asserting a value; instead, it is assigning new variables (`option_id` and `votes`) and those values returned are getting pattern matched into those variables. This is why we have the two extra assertions as follows; we need to verify that the returned `option_id` and `votes` values match what we're expecting. We then do the same thing with `assert_broadcast`, except for this we do not need to use the ref variable we used with `assert_reply`:

```
assert_broadcast "new_vote", %{"option_id" => option_id, "votes" => votes}
assert option_id == option.id
assert votes == option.votes + 1
```

The same rules apply regarding the value/variables as with `assert_reply`. If you assume that it works like a simple assertion, you will likely end up getting error messages about not being able to invoke remote functions or unused variables!

Run our tests again now that we've written our channel tests! If you've followed everything closely and carefully, you should have a fully-green test suite here!

Summary

This was a huge chapter, filled with tons of Phoenix real-time application building! We've covered adding actual voting functionality and ES2015 syntax, written a great deal of non-Elixir code, and dove into arguably one of the coolest portions of built-in functionality on the Phoenix side!

We've done a lot of the hardest pieces of work, as well; we've covered all of our new work with tests as part of our development lifecycle and written JavaScript code to swap out functionality depending on what level of features our browsers support!

7
Improving Our Application and Adding Features

We are now in a place with our application where we have some very basic functionality and even a few cool little-advanced touches. This is a great first step for us to be in right now, but an application with just one core feature set is not going to be a very popular application for very long. We've been pretty happy just chugging along and writing the code that we needed to support our MVP product, but now that we have that first bit of work in place, it is time for us to start building on top of it in a real, meaningful way.

In this chapter, we will add a few new features onto our platform to demonstrate how to iterate on a Phoenix application and to showcase some of the other common features and libraries that people will find themselves building over time. By the conclusion of this chapter, we should have the following features implemented:

- Image uploads for polls
- Voting restrictions so people can't vote in the same poll multiple times

Honestly, there are a lot of other features we could implement here as well, but we'll try not to get too carried away and stick to things that are probably the most commonly requested recipes and tutorials out there!

Designing and implementing our new features

One thing we'll want to get into the habit of doing it, before adding new features, sitting down and taking a nice, thoughtful look at how we'll be designing our features. We want to figure out what the use cases are: why do we want to add these features? What do they add to the experience that makes our application more compelling for the user to use and continue using? What benefits do they add, and just as importantly, what will it cost us to add them?

This isn't just a question of straight-up money or initial time sink, but it is a long-term question as well. How hard will it be to support? How much extra work will we need to do to be able to support this feature? Not only that but is it the kind of feature that is required for the application to succeed? When you sit down and start answering these questions, you can learn a lot more about your own application and intentions!

We laid out three new features that we'll be adding to our application, so we'll come up with some quick guidelines and designs for each feature so that we'll know what we'll need to do to be able to implement each feature to some sort of baseline standard. The first feature we laid out is the ability to implement image uploads for our polls.

For image uploads, we will need the following:

- Somewhere that we can store our images
- A way to link an image to a user or a poll
- A way to display the image as part of the poll

So what will we need to fulfill this criteria?

- Either a local file/directory or somewhere online to store images:
    - To keep things simple, we'll stick to using an uploads directory in our application instead of S3
- A new schema and database table to store images:
    - The images must be linked to polls
    - Images should also be linked to users
    - We'll need a table on which to store the URL or path, the poll ID, the user ID, the alt text, and a caption
    - We should have a maximum of one image per poll

- The image should be displayed on the actual page:
    - Where should the image be displayed?
    - The image should include the caption and the alt text
    - There must be a way to remove an image from a poll
    - Images should be deleted when a poll is deleted

If we were to describe the new UI for our **New Poll** page, we'd probably want it to look something like this:

```
┌──────────────────────────────────────────┐
│  ┌──────────────────────────────────────┐ │
│  │                                      │ │
│  │   New Poll                           │ │
│  │                                      │ │
│  │   Title:                             │ │
│  │                                      │ │
│  │   ┌───────────────────────────┐      │ │
│  │   └───────────────────────────┘      │ │
│  │                                      │ │
│  │   Options (separated by commas):     │ │
│  │                                      │ │
│  │   ┌───────────────────────────┐      │ │
│  │   └───────────────────────────┘      │ │
│  │                                      │ │
│  │   Poll Image:                        │ │
│  │                                      │ │
│  │   Choose File to Upload...  ┌───────┐│ │
│  │                             │Browse ││ │
│  │                             └───────┘│ │
│  │   ┌──────────┐                       │ │
│  │   │  Create  │                       │ │
│  │   └──────────┘                       │ │
│  │                                      │ │
│  └──────────────────────────────────────┘ │
└──────────────────────────────────────────┘
```

That's probably all of the information that we'll need to be able to implement our first additional feature, so let's start off by getting our image uploads feature up and running correctly!

Implementing file uploads in Phoenix

File uploads are probably one of the most common features you'll end up having to implement over the course of a web application, so it's a good feature to use to cut our teeth on some of the other form handlers built into Elixir. This will also provide us a nice opportunity to start messing around with some of the custom options for configuring our Phoenix application (since we'll need to tell Phoenix that it's okay to serve certain types of files out of certain folders that aren't in our current application layout), as well as an opportunity to really dive into Elixir's file-handling functionality.

Working with uploads in Phoenix

Phoenix doesn't have anything built into its directory structure to store uploaded files, so that's something we'll have to write ourselves. We'll start off by creating a new directory in the root of our application called `uploads` in the root directory of our Phoenix application. We'll also want to make sure that the directory is included if we're using something like Git for source control:

```
$ mkdir uploads
$ touch uploads/.gitkeep
```

We'll also have to modify our endpoint to allow serving files from this new directory. To do this, you tell Phoenix that, as part of the plugs responsible for keeping the server alive and moving, you'll also include a line for `Plug.Static` telling it that there is a new directory for it to watch and serve out to the client appropriately. Open up `lib/vocial_web/endpoint.ex` and look for the existing `Plug.Static` line (it should be around *line 10*), and then add the following line:

```
plug Plug.Static, at: "/uploads", from: "./uploads"
```

This tells Phoenix that we're going to be serving static content at a URL relative to our application's domain on the `/uploads` path. It also tells Phoenix that we're going to be serving these static files from the `uploads` directory in the root of the application (note the `./` prefixing the uploads path).

We can quickly verify that our application is serving files from the `uploads` directory by putting a sample text file in our `uploads` directory and then attempting to visit that path on our local development server. You can run the following command:

```
$ echo 'Hello World' && uploads/test.txt
```

Then, open up your browser to `http://localhost:4000/uploads/test.txt` and verify that when you load that URL, you get the text **Hello World** back in your browser! If you do that and everything works, then we're ready to move on to the next step of our implementation process: writing the file upload UI.

Adding file uploads to our new poll UI

We have a nice `uploads` directory now, and we have a way for Phoenix to serve files out of that new directory, but we don't have a way for any of that to actually get into our application! We'll need to fix this by adding a file-handling functionality into our application. Let's start by updating our template. Open up `lib/vocial_web/templates/poll/new.html.eex` and add the following code just following to the options input:

```
<label>
  Poll Image:
  <%= file_input f, :image %>
</label>
<br />
```

You'll also need to return back to the `form_for` call at the top of that template and pass in the multipart option, set to `true`:

```
<%= form_for @poll, poll_path(@conn, :create), [multipart: true], fn f ->
%>
```

This will give us a browser-native file input handler, passed as part of the poll's passed-in parameters. Next, we'll need to take that image and turn it into something usable on the Elixir side of things. The way it's currently set up, the image will come in as a `%Plug.Upload` struct in the poll's parameters under the key of `image`, so that's where we'll look for our image. We don't have to do anything in our controller to make this all work; instead, we will be looking to implement this in our votes context. Open up `lib/vocial/votes/votes.ex` and let's add some new code to make this all work!

We'll need to start off by adding a new step in our `create_poll_with_options` with statement pipeline. The new `with` statement should look something like this:

```
# ...
with {:ok, poll} <- create_poll(poll_attrs),
     {:ok, _options} <- create_options(options, poll),
     {:ok, _filename} <- upload_file(poll_attrs, poll)
do
# ...
```

Don't worry—`upload_file/2` has not been implemented yet! Right now, we're just starting a little small and trying to prototype out what our code should look like and how it should perform in general. We're going to build up to something a lot more exciting! One thing that we're guessing we're going to need (other than the image itself, for obvious reasons) is the poll. We'll want a good way to link an image to a poll (especially later when we start diving into hooking the upload code up to the database to make the image storage more permanent!).

The next step is going to be writing the `upload_file/2` function itself. We'll need to do some work to get the image moved from a temporary directory to a more permanent directory, a way to set what the filename should be, and a way to get the current image extension (at a minimum). Let's try to come up with a general method signature (we can always modify this later based on our needs):

```
defp upload_file(%{"image" => image, "user_id" => user_id}, poll) do
    # ...
end
```

Again, we'll need the image (which, remember, is a `%Plug.Upload{}` struct). We'll also need the user ID since we'll need a good way to link the uploaded image to the user that performed the upload in the first place. We'll also likely want the information about the poll that the image is going to be associated with. Remember the original design of our feature, where we said that we were likely to want to be able to associate an image both with the poll and probably also the user that did the upload?

The next thing we can do is get the extension of the file from `Path.extname`. From our IEx terminal, we can run `h Path.extname` to get more information on how to use this library, enabling it to function a little bit better:

```
iex> h Path.extname

def extname(path)

Returns the extension of the last component of path.

## Examples

    iex> Path.extname("foo.erl")
    ".erl"

    iex&> Path.extname("~/foo/bar")
    ""
```

That gives us the extension of the file! Based on that, let's write a new line into our function that captures the file's current extension in a variable that we can use for later.

```
extension = Path.extname(image.filename)
```

We'll also want to construct some sort of unique filename for this image that we're uploading. The default filenames that Phoenix creates for temporary files are hardly the prettiest things in the world and might make things very difficult to debug later on without some sort of reference. Arbitrarily, I'm choosing the following template for the filename: (user id)-(poll id)-image.ext. Here's the next line of the code based on that template:

```
filename = "#{user_id}-#{poll.id}-image#{extension}"
```

Finally, we'll copy the file out to the filesystem with our new filename and return a tuple to indicate that everything was a success!

```
File.cp(image.path, "./uploads/#{filename}")
{:ok, filename}
```

We'll also probably want a version of our function that doesn't do anything if we don't include an image as one of the arguments, so we'll write that version of our upload_file function very quickly. The end result should be the following block of code:

```
defp upload_file(%{"image" => image, "user_id" => user_id}, poll) do
  extension = Path.extname(image.filename)
  filename = "#{user_id}-#{poll.id}-image#{extension}"
  File.cp(image.path, "./uploads/#{filename}")
  {:ok, filename}
end
defp upload_file(_, _), do: {:ok, nil}
```

Note that we'll need to send back a structure of {:ok, nil} even if we don't end up uploading a file; without that line, our with statement will actually fail when we're expecting it to work!

We'll need just the filename instead of the full path name because later on we're going to want to easily store that URL in the database and have it be appropriately linked up to the poll. Let's shift our focus now onto the database side of this problem and start getting everything stored in our database! You can also test out this UI with the image uploads and verify that the images are getting uploaded appropriately into your `uploads` directory in your root directory. The new UI should resemble the following screenshot when you load up the new vote form in your browser:

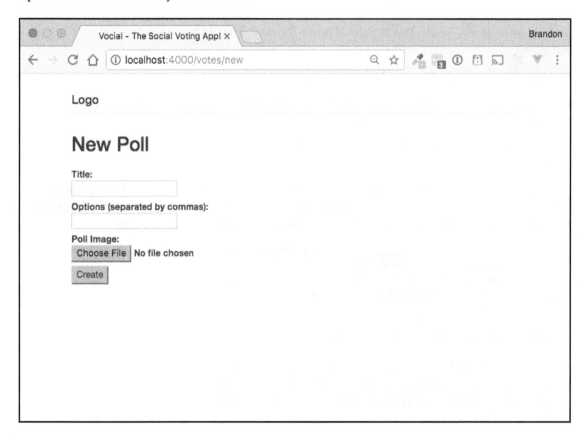

Hooking up the uploads to our database

Now that we have images and they're getting uploaded into our file structure, we need to make sure we're actually storing information about those files in a way that allows us to easily retrieve them later on. To do this, we'll need to create a new database table to store information about those uploads and link those both to users and polls.

Writing the migration file

If we look back to our planned design for the uploads table, we came up with the following criteria for what we figured we'd need: *We'll need a table to store the URL or path, the poll ID, the user ID, the alt text, and a caption.* Let's create our migration and do all of the work the hard way so that we can reinforce all of these concepts and continue to learn how to build an Elixir and Phoenix app at a deep level! We'll start by generating the migration and then editing that generated file:

```
$ mix ecto.gen.migration create_images_table
* creating priv/repo/migrations
* creating priv/repo/migrations/20171117232649_create_images_table.exs
```

Then, we open up the migration file:

```
defmodule Vocial.Repo.Migrations.CreateImagesTable do
  use Ecto.Migration

  def change do
    create table(:images) do
      add :url, :string
      add :alt, :string
      add :caption, :string
      add :poll_id, references(:polls)
      add :user_id, references(:users)

      timestamps()
    end
  end
end
```

What we're adding here is a URL that will keep track of what the display URL should be for the user, some alt text to display should the image not load (and for accessibility reasons (such as to enable screen readers)), a caption to display with the image, and then, finally, references back to the poll that state what this image is associated with and the user that uploaded the image in the first place.

This is a good minimum amount of information that will enable us to allow the user to upload images associated with their polls, give them clever captions, and store all of that information in the database and display it later. There are a lot of other ways to handle user uploads—for example, you could use something like Amazon S3 and store the images that you upload into an S3 bucket, and then store that as the URL for the image.

The nice thing about this particular schema is that it easily allows for that sort of behavior since, at the end of the day, it is just storing a URL, some extra display information about the image, and some of the image's general metadata regarding its relation to the rest of the database structure. It'd be pretty easy to swap out a filesystem-based upload system with something like S3!

Our migration is complete, so let's give it a quick run and make sure everything is good before we start moving on to implementing the schema!

```
$ mix ecto.migrate
[info] == Running Vocial.Repo.Migrations.CreateImagesTable.change/0 forward
[info] create table images
[info] == Migrated in 0.0s
```

If we take a look at the table structure, we should also see all of the columns in place, as expected!

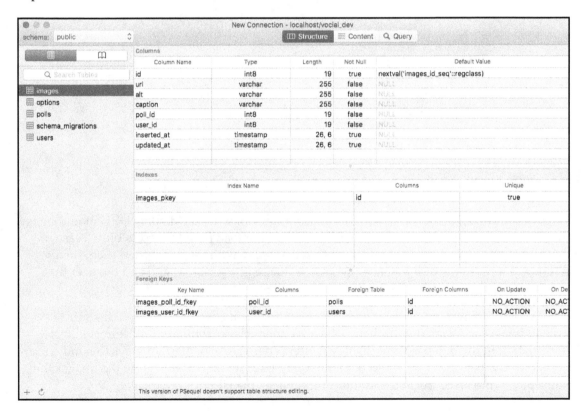

Modifying the schema and the context code

Now that the migration is in place, we've run it successfully, and we've verified the new table structure, we're ready to start tackling the actual code necessary to make this all work. We built out our UI to allow us to upload things and now we have the database table in place to store the information in a more permanent way, but we also need to keep track of where the files are getting uploaded to and build a way to serve them back out when people want to view those polls in the future!

One thing that we neglected to put into our original UI is the image caption and alt text since our primary concern at the time was just adding in the upload image support. We'll need to quickly add this as well, otherwise, our images will be captionless and alt textless until we do! Go back to `lib/vocial_web/templates/poll/new.html.eex` and add the following block of text:

```
<label>
  Image Caption:<br />
  <input type="text" name="image_data[caption]" />
</label>
<br />
<label>
  Image Alt Text:<br />
  <input type="text" name="image_data[alt_text]" />
</label>
<br />
```

This should leave us with a UI that includes fields for the image caption and alt text:

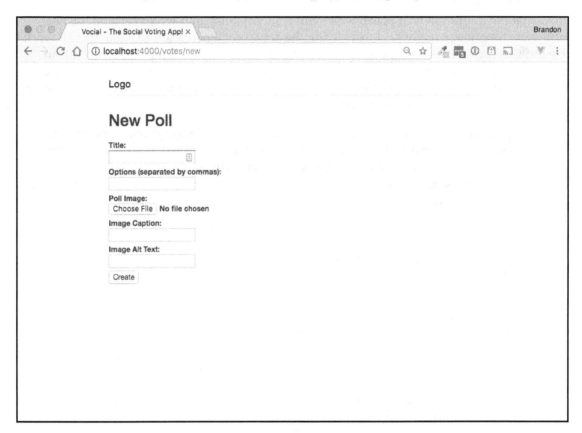

The other thing this will do is leave us with an extra set of data getting sent into our controller that we'll need to handle appropriately. Return to `lib/vocial_web/controllers/polls_controller.ex`. We'll modify the top of the `create` function to deal with the new `image_data` map that will get passed in:

```
def create(conn, %{"poll" => poll_params, "options" => options,
"image_data" => image_data}) do
  split_options = String.split(options, ",")
  with user <- get_session(conn, :user),
       poll_params <- Map.put(poll_params, "user_id", user.id),
       {:ok, _poll} <- Votes.create_poll_with_options(poll_params,
split_options, image_data)
  # ...
```

We'll pass this down to our votes context, which will end up ultimately responsible for creating the database representation of the supplied image and image data. The nice thing, again, about this pattern is how lean this is leaving our controllers! We are doing a lot to keep our code simple, readable, and independent of anything outside of a single abstraction whose sole responsibility is gluing the controllers to our schemas!

That raises a good point: What about our schema? We've written the database migration and tweaked the UI, but we never stopped to actually add the code for our schema! We'll need to create a new file for this to work, so let's create `lib/vocial/votes/image.ex` and start building it piece by piece:

```
defmodule Vocial.Votes.Image do
  use Ecto.Schema
  import Ecto.Changeset

  alias Vocial.Accounts.User
  alias Vocial.Votes.Poll
  alias Vocial.Votes.Image
  # ...
end
```

We start off by declaring our image schema in our `Vocial.Votes` context. We tell Elixir that this is using the `Ecto.Schema` macros and we import the `Ecto.Changeset` functions we'll need to construct our `changeset` function.

Next, we'll need access to the user schema in the `Vocial.Accounts` context and the poll schema in the `Vocial.Votes` context, since images exist relative to both of those. We'll also need to reference the current module to be able to use its struct without having to also declare its namespace and context, so we include `Vocial.Votes.Image`. Now we have defined the base structure for our schema, we need to define the schema itself:

```
schema "images" do
  field :url, :string
  field :alt, :string
  field :caption, :string

  belongs_to :user, User
  belongs_to :poll, Poll

  timestamps()
end
```

Most of this should just be going over old ground at this point! We store the URL, the alt text (as the `alt` column), and the caption. We set up the relationships of this schema to the users and polls tables, and end with the Ecto standard timestamp columns for auditing (`inserted_at` and `updated_at`)!

The final part of implementing our schema file is creating our `changeset/2` function! This is going to require a little more thoughtful planning before we implement it, since we'll need to consider what fields should be required and which ones should not. We will likely want to restrict ourselves to creating images that have no URL associated with them, since it would be rather difficult to display an image without knowing where to point the user's browser in order for them to view the image! We should also likewise require a `user_id` and `poll_id` to be present, since images are supposed to be uploaded in reference to both a poll and a user. That should give us a `changeset` function that looks something like this:

```
def changeset(%Image{}=image, attrs) do
  image
  |> cast(attrs, [:url, :alt, :caption, :user_id, :poll_id])
  |> validate_required([:url, :user_id, :poll_id])
end
```

We want to allow someone to set the rest of the fields in the changeset, but we don't want to *need* them to! We'll also want to modify the poll schema and the user schema to include a reference to these images. We'll say that a poll can only have one image associated with it, but since users can have multiple polls, that means the relationship on `User` will be `has_many` and the relationship on `Poll` will be `has_one`:

In the schema for `lib/vocial/accounts/user.ex`, add the following line:

```
has_many :images, Vocial.Votes.Image
```

In the schema for `lib/vocial/votes/poll.ex`, add the following line:

```
has_one :image, Vocial.Votes.Image
```

Returning back to our votes context, we can finish the work that we started and get the image uploads to work!

Completing the votes context for the image uploads

We have almost everything in place, except for the final code necessary to get our image uploads into the context. We've started the work in the `create_poll_with_options/3` function of `lib/vocial/votes/votes.ex`, but now we need to expand that work significantly and add to the function's signature. We'll want to pass in the `image_data` hash that we constructed as part of the modified template that included the caption and the `alt_text` for our image, and we'll also want to add a new line to our `with` statement that saves the uploaded file into the database! At the top of `lib/vocial/votes/votes.ex`, you'll want to add an `alias` statement for the image module:

```
alias Vocial.Votes.Image
```

Then we'll continue by modifying the function to take in a new argument that is the image-specific data, leaving us with a three-argument `create_poll_with_options` function:

```
def create_poll_with_options(poll_attrs, options, image_data) do
```

Next, we'll want to go into the `with` statement, modify the `upload_file` call, and add a new line to it as well, since now we actually care about the returned filename, and will need to persist that to the database!

```
{:ok, filename} <- upload_file(poll_attrs, poll),
{:ok, _upload} <- save_upload(poll, image_data, filename)
```

We don't have a `save_upload/3` function defined yet but don't worry, we're getting there! The `save_upload` function will need data from the poll (this will give us the `poll_id` and `user_id` data), the `image_data` map that contains the caption and alt text, and finally the actual filename that we decided on for the user! Since this is a pretty custom data structure we're building out that will essentially be our attributes, we'll start constructing the `attrs` map that we'll use to create the image struct. We'll also need to catch the scenario where we get a `nil` filename since that will happen if the user does not upload any images:

```
defp save_upload(_poll, _image_data, nil), do: {:ok, nil}
defp save_upload(poll, %{"caption" => caption, "alt_text" => alt_text},
filename) do
  attrs = %{
    url: "/uploads/#{filename}",
    alt: alt_text,
    caption: caption,
    poll_id: poll.id,
    user_id: poll.user_id
  }
  # ...
end
```

Again, remember the structure we wrote in our `with` statement? That's why, if we have no upload, we just carry on as if all is well since it is perfectly valid for us to not want to upload an image to our poll! The rest of the code to make this work is pretty standard stuff that you've seen a million times before at this point, so we won't go into excruciating detail on it:

```
%Image{}
|> Image.changeset(attrs)
|> Repo.insert()
```

This will successfully insert the poll into the database! We also need to adjust the `get_poll` and `list_polls` functions to include `:image` as part of their preloads:

```
  def get_poll(id), do: Repo.get!(Poll, id) |> Repo.preload([:options,
:image])

  def list_polls do
    Repo.all(Poll) |> Repo.preload([:options, :image])
  end
```

And there we are! The code to create, upload, and display our images is *nearly* complete! We just need to modify the code template for showing the poll in `lib/vocial_web/templates/vote/_poll.html.eex` to include a conditional `div` to display the associated image!

```
  <%= if @poll.image do %>
    <div class="image-display">
      <img src="<%= @poll.image.url %>" alt="<%= @poll.image.alt %>"
style="width: 350px;" />
      <br />
      <small><%= @poll.image.caption %></small>
    </div>
  <% end %>
```

Voila! We are done! We should be able to navigate back to the **New Poll** page, fill in the new fields, and see the resulting poll with the image! Let's fill out the poll information, as shown in the following screenshot:

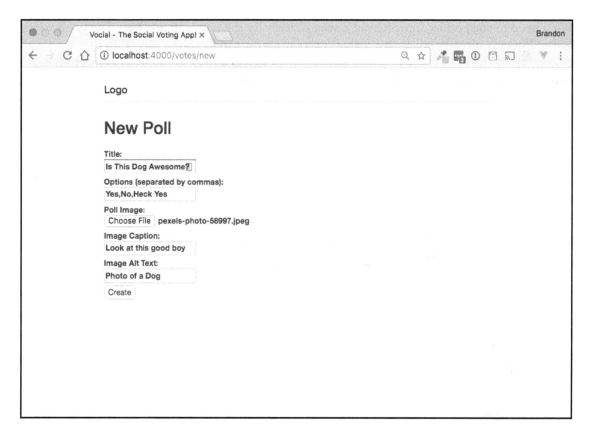

We should expect to see our completed poll with an image in its display.

We're done! We can now move on to the next missing feature in our application: Restricting people from voting more than once!

Implementing voting restrictions

Right now, anybody on the internet can essentially stuff the ballot with as many votes as our poor system will allow them to! This doesn't make for very fair polls, so we'll take a naive approach and implement an IP-based list of people who have already voted on each particular poll!

We'll need to start off by figuring out a way to identify the user's IP address. The good news is that Phoenix already has that information ready for us in the `conn` object! In the `conn` object, one of the keys in the map is `remote_ip`, which is a tuple of the four octets in the IP address of the connecting user! We can verify this either by placing an `IEx.pry` statement in one of our controller actions and taking a look at the output for `conn.remote_ip`:

```
require IEx

def index(conn, _params) do
  IEx.pry
  polls = Votes.list_polls()
  render conn, "index.html", polls: polls
end
```

Which, when we load up the `/votes` path (since the preceding code is in our votes controller), we'll get a request in our IEx shell to open up `pry`:

```
Request to pry #PID<0.784.0> at VocialWeb.PollController.index/2
(lib/vocial_web/controllers/poll_controller.ex:10)

    8:
    9: def index(conn, _params) do
   10: IEx.pry
   11: polls = Votes.list_polls()
   12: render conn, "index.html", polls: polls

Allow? [Yn] y

Interactive Elixir (1.5.2) - press Ctrl+C to exit (type h() ENTER for help)
pry(1)> conn.remote_ip
{127, 0, 0, 1}
```

If we say yes here, we'll get access to the controller's function call for the index, which means we'll have access to any local variables that are set at this time. In our case, we're specifically checking the value of `remote_ip` as reported by the `conn` object (that has indeed been passed in). In our case, we get a four-digit tuple that represents our IP address!

If we wanted to store this as a string instead of the tuple (which would be very hard to store in the database), we could convert the tuple to a list with `Tuple.to_list/1` and then call `Enum.join/2` on that result, which would look something like the following:

```
ip = conn.remote_ip
|> Tuple.to_list()
|> Enum.join(".")
```

This would result in (using the same preceding example) 127.0.0.1. This will give us all of the information that we need to be able to handle blocking extra votes per IP address! Well, I should say that this just gives us the basic information; we still don't have anything more to block vote attempts!

Creating the vote record migration

To do this, we'll need to add another table to our database. This new table will have the explicit purpose of recording votes for each poll, which right now can just be something as simple as a list of IP addresses that have voted on a particular poll. It's a pretty simple feature and design, so we'll keep the table structure equally simple. Let's first create the migration for our `vote_records` table, which will record the `poll_id` and the `ip_address`:

```
$ mix ecto.gen.migration add_vote_records_table
* creating priv/repo/migrations
* creating priv/repo/migrations/20171125044437_add_vote_records_table.exs
```

We'll give it a very simple migration since our table design is also very simple:

```
defmodule Vocial.Repo.Migrations.AddVoteRecordsTable do
  use Ecto.Migration

  def change do
    create table(:vote_records) do
      add :ip_address, :string
      add :poll_id, references(:polls)

      timestamps()
    end
  end
end
```

Let's run it quickly as a sanity check:

```
$ mix ecto.migrate
[info] == Running Vocial.Repo.Migrations.AddVoteRecordsTable.change/0
forward
[info] create table vote_records
[info] == Migrated in 0.0s
```

Great! The table is in place without any issues, so we can start implementing the schema next!

Creating the vote record schema

With our database structure ready to go, we can create our schema file to accompany it! Create `lib/vocial/votes/vote_record.ex` and we'll start it off the same way we start off most of our new schemas: with macros, imports, and aliases first!

```
defmodule Vocial.Votes.VoteRecord do
  use Ecto.Schema
  import Ecto.Changeset

  alias Vocial.Votes.VoteRecord
  alias Vocial.Votes.Poll
  # ...
end
```

The next step in building out our schema is always specifying that the schema will house our data and the shape of that schema, so we'll implement that next:

```
schema "vote_records" do
  field :ip_address, :string

  belongs_to :poll, Poll

  timestamps()
end
```

Finally, we'll need to implement the `changeset/2` function. This follows the same template you're used to, but we'll want both to cast and make mandatory both the `ip_address` and `poll_id` fields, since this doesn't make sense without both values there!

```
def changeset(%VoteRecord{}=vote_record, attrs) do
  vote_record
  |> cast(attrs, [:ip_address, :poll_id])
  |> validate_required([:ip_address, :poll_id])
end
```

We'll also want to return to our poll schema and add a reference to having many vote records! Add the following to the poll schema defined in `lib/vocial/votes/poll.ex`:

```
has_many :vote_records, Vocial.Votes.VoteRecord
```

Next, we'll want to hit up our poll controller for the code where the voting takes place and modify that to record the voter's IP address. Open up `lib/vocial_web/controllers/poll_controller.ex`, where we'll add the `remote_ip` logic from the `conn` object that we discussed earlier. The new `vote` action should look like this:

```
def vote(conn, %{"id" => id}) do
  voter_ip = conn.remote_ip
  |> Tuple.to_list()
  |> Enum.join(".")
  with {:ok, option} <- Votes.vote_on_option(id, voter_ip) do
    conn
    |> put_flash(:info, "Placed a vote for #{option.title}!")
    |> redirect(to: vote_path(conn, :index))
  end
end
```

Note the new additions—we have all of the code that converts a tupled IP address of `{127, 0, 0, 1}` into a string that the database (and most people) can understand: `"127.0.0.1"`. This value is then passed into the votes context's `vote_on_option` function as the last argument! We can now tackle the votes context and start adding in the code that will allow us to record who is voting on each poll! At the top of `lib/vocial/votes/votes.ex`, add the following `alias` statement:

```
alias Vocial.Votes.VoteRecord
```

We'll also want to adjust the preloads that are used in the index and the show page, so we'll change `get_poll` and `list_polls` to the following:

```
def get_poll(id), do: Repo.get!(Poll, id) |> Repo.preload([:options,
:image, :vote_records])

def list_polls do
  Repo.all(Poll) |> Repo.preload([:options, :image, :vote_records])
end
```

Next, we can tackle the `vote_on_option` function, but we'll need to alter it pretty significantly. Previously, we'd just blindly return the result of `update_option/2`, but now we actually need that data to be correct for us to proceed. Here is the new `vote_on_option/2` function:

```
def vote_on_option(option_id, voter_ip) do
  with option <- Repo.get!(Option, option_id),
       votes <- option.votes + 1,
       {:ok, option} <- update_option(option, %{votes: votes}),
       {:ok, _vote_record} <- record_vote(%{ poll_id: option.poll_id,
ip_address: voter_ip })
  do
    {:ok, option}
  end
end
```

So now we depend on the `update_option` function returning us the standard "everything was good" response of `{:ok, struct}`, and then we take that `option` information and pass it in to the `record_vote/1` function (that we haven't written yet!). Remember that we need the `poll_id` and the `ip_address` as the only two really important bits of data. It's time to move on to write our `record_vote/1` function!

```
def record_vote(%{poll_id: _poll_id, ip_address: _ip_address}=attrs) do
  %VoteRecord{}
  |> VoteRecord.changeset(attrs)
  |> Repo.insert()
end
```

Easy! There's not really anything special that this code does; it's just a standard database insert! We make sure that we actually get the `poll_id` and the `ip_address`, but otherwise, we proceed! We will also need to update the JavaScript code around the channel to record the user's IP address on each vote, but this is a much more complicated endeavor because of how the Phoenix WebSocket implementation needs to remain transport agnostic! There is a way around this, but it's a little convoluted.

First, we'll need to add a new meta tag in `lib/vocial_web/templates/layout/app.html.eex`:

```
<meta name="remote_ip" content="<%= @conn.remote_ip |> Tuple.to_list() |>
Enum.join(".") %>">
```

Next, we'll need to modify our JavaScript code in `assets/js/socket.js` to seek out this meta tag and pull the remote IP address value out. In the `enableSocket` conditional statement, after we set the `pollId`, add the following line:

```
// Get the stored remote IP for a user
const remoteIp =
document.getElementsByName('remote_ip')[0].getAttribute('content');
```

Then, modify the `socket.channel` call in the next line to pass in the `remoteIp` value as part of the join payload:

```
// Create a channel to handle joining/sending/receiving
const channel = socket.channel('polls:' + pollId, {remote_ip: remoteIp });
```

Now, we'll need to modify our join handler for the poll channel to set an assign value on the socket. Open up `lib/vocial_web/channels/poll_channel.ex` and change the `join` function:

```
def join("polls:" <> _poll_id, %{"remote_ip" => remote_ip}, socket) do
  {:ok, assign(socket, :remote_ip, remote_ip)}
end
```

And that's all of the foundation code we'll need to get the remote IP address in our vote handler code in the same poll channel module! Scroll down to the `handle_in("vote", ...)` function. We'll want to pattern-match out the socket's `remote_ip` value in the assigns and pass that down to the `vote_on_option` function call:

```
def handle_in("vote", %{"option_id" => option_id}, %{assigns: %{remote_ip:
remote_ip}}=socket) do
  with {:ok, option} <- Vocial.Votes.vote_on_option(option_id, remote_ip)
do
```

That's it! Now we can actually start recording all of the votes that happen as part of our voting application! Make a couple of votes, some through the index (not using the WebSocket code) and some on the show page (using the WebSocket code). The end result should be that our IP address is getting recorded for each vote that we cast!

Hooking up restrictions

We're nearing the end of this exercise! We can finally start denying people based on their IP addresses if they've already voted, since we now know that they are indeed being recorded properly! The first thing we'll want to do is implement some sort of check for whether or not a user has already voted for a particular poll. For this, we'll return to our votes context (`lib/vocial/votes/votes.ex`) and implement an `already_voted?` function:

```
def already_voted?(poll_id, ip_address) do
  votes = (from vr in VoteRecord, where: vr.poll_id == ^poll_id and
vr.ip_address == ^ip_address)
  |> Repo.aggregate(:count, :id)
  votes > 0
end
```

Here we take in the `poll_id` and the `ip_address` and just grab a count out of the database with the `Repo.aggregate/3` function! We then take that count and, if there are more than 0 votes for that particular poll's ID/IP address combination, then we'll return true!

Now, we'll modify our `vote_on_option` function to check the return of our `already_voted?` function. We're using a `with` statement here, so we just verify that `already_voted?` returns false. We'll also want to be safe and implement an `else` clause:

```
def vote_on_option(option_id, voter_ip) do
  with option <- Repo.get!(Option, option_id),
       false <- already_voted?(option.poll_id, voter_ip),
       votes <- option.votes + 1,
       {:ok, option} <- update_option(option, %{votes: votes}),
       {:ok, _vote_record} <- record_vote(%{ poll_id: option.poll_id,
ip_address: voter_ip })
  do
    {:ok, option}
  else
    _ -> {:error, "Could not place vote"}
  end
end
```

Finally, we'll need to return back to our poll controller's `vote` action and implement similar logic:

```
def vote(conn, %{"id" => id}) do
  voter_ip = conn.remote_ip
  |> Tuple.to_list()
  |> Enum.join(".")
  with {:ok, option} <- Votes.vote_on_option(id, voter_ip) do
    conn
```

```
    |> put_flash(:info, "Placed a vote for #{option.title}!")
    |> redirect(to: poll_path(conn, :index))
  else
    _ ->        conn
      |> put_flash(:error, "Could not vote!")
      |> redirect(to: poll_path(conn, :index))
  end
end
end
```

The good news is that the code in our polls channel is already handling this case, so we're done implementing the code to make this all work! Let's take a look at the result in our UI if we try to vote more than once on a poll:

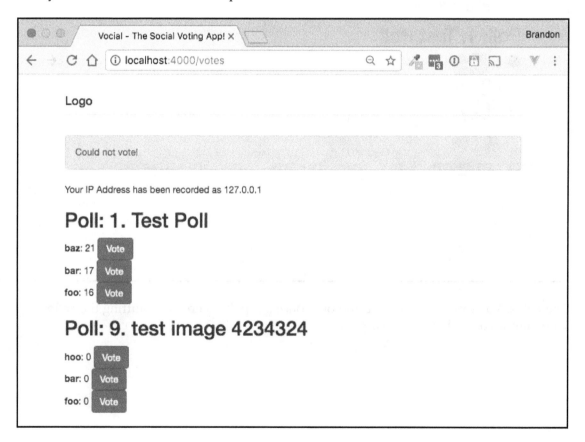

In our web socket, we should see the following (we'll have to look in the JavaScript developer console to see this one):

There it is! You can now vote once and only once per poll, so no more stuffing the ballot with your favorite choice in these polls!

Fixing the broken tests

If we run our tests right now, we're not going to see very promising results. In the process of us changing our function signatures around, we also ended up breaking a good portion of our test suite, and that's going to make development and debugging other issues significantly more difficult over time!

```
$ mix test
...
Finished in 11.7 seconds
41 tests, 15 failures

Randomized with seed 60247
```

We're going to want to go in and start cleaning up a lot of these broken tests as we go along, since if we leave them broken, it is going to be increasingly difficult for us to understand when we're introducing code-breaking changes or not! Generally speaking, when I have a large broken test suite, I try to make my life easier by just focusing on a single test at a time. This keeps me from feeling overwhelmed as I look at the list of broken tests, and you never know when fixing one test might fix other related tests! Let's look at one example of a failed test out of our 15 total failures:

```
  1) test polls create_poll_with_options/2 returns a new poll with options
(Vocial.VotesTest)
     test/vocial/votes/votes_test.exs:44
     ** (UndefinedFunctionError) function
Vocial.Votes.create_poll_with_options/2 is undefined or private. Did you
mean one of:

          * create_poll_with_options/3

     code: {:ok, poll} = Votes.create_poll_with_options(%{title: title,
user_id: user.id}, options)
     stacktrace:
       (vocial) Vocial.Votes.create_poll_with_options(%{title: "Poll With
Options", user_id: 8}, ["Choice 1", "Choice 2", "Choice 3"])
       test/vocial/votes/votes_test.exs:47: (test)
```

Okay, so here is an example where us changing one part of the function (in this case, the number of arguments) introduced some failing tests. Let's pop over to that particular test and take a look at it:

```
    test "create_poll_with_options/2 returns a new poll with options",
%{user: user} do
        title = "Poll With Options"
        options = ["Choice 1", "Choice 2", "Choice 3"]
        {:ok, poll} = Votes.create_poll_with_options(%{title: title, user_id:
user.id}, options)
        assert poll.title == title
        assert Enum.count(poll.options) == 3
    end
```

So, we have no handler to deal with certain scenarios, such as when there are is no image data associated with our poll. We can fix this by modifying the `image_data` parameter to have a default value of `nil`, which will fix the issue with the function having no matching signature! The good news is that our `upload_file/2` and `save_upload/3` functions are already set up to be able to handle scenarios where there is no actual image data passed in!

We'll make that change in `lib/vocial/votes/votes.ex`:

```
    def create_poll_with_options(poll_attrs, options, image_data \\ nil) do
      Repo.transaction(fn ->
        with {:ok, poll} <- create_poll(poll_attrs),
             {:ok, _options} <- create_options(options, poll),
             {:ok, filename} <- upload_file(poll_attrs, poll),
             {:ok, _upload} <- save_upload(poll, image_data, filename) do
          poll |> Repo.preload(:options)
        else
          _ -> Repo.rollback("Failed to create poll")
        end
      end)
    end
```

If we rerun `mix test` now, we should expect to see fewer failures than previously:

```
$ mix test
...
Finished in 12.6 seconds
41 tests, 7 failures

Randomized with seed 462215
```

Let's take a look at our next failure:

```
 1) test options vote_on_option/1 adds a vote to a particular option
(Vocial.VotesTest)
    test/vocial/votes/votes_test.exs:78
    ** (UndefinedFunctionError) function Vocial.Votes.vote_on_option/1 is
undefined or private. Did you mean one of:

        * vote_on_option/2

    code: {:ok, updated_option} = Votes.vote_on_option(option.id)
    stacktrace:
      (vocial) Vocial.Votes.vote_on_option(46)
      test/vocial/votes/votes_test.exs:84: (test)
```

This particular test is failing because when we updated the logic in our voting function to record the user's IP address, we made recording the IP address a requirement. We can fix up our test by changing the following line in the "`vote_on_option/1 adds a vote to a particular option`" test:

```
{:ok, updated_option} = Votes.vote_on_option(option.id)
```

Let's change it to the following:

```
{:ok, updated_option} = Votes.vote_on_option(option.id, "127.0.0.1")
```

Now we're down to six errors! The next test's failure is due to the way that the polls controller handles the `Create` action. Again, this is due to us pattern matching aggressively and not accounting for the modified usage and parameters. Let's look at the failure:

```
 1) test POST /polls (with valid data) (VocialWeb.PollControllerTest)
    test/vocial_web/controllers/poll_controller_test.exs:50
    ** (Phoenix.ActionClauseError) could not find a matching
VocialWeb.PollController.create clause
    to process request. This typically happens when there is a
    parameter mismatch but may also happen when any of the other
    action arguments do not match. The request parameters are:

      %{"options" => "One,Two,Three", "poll" => %{"title" => "Test Poll"}}
```

We can add a new implementation in
`lib/vocial_web/controllers/poll_controller.ex` for `create` that does not check
for image data underneath the first implementation. This implementation looks as follows:

```
def create(conn, %{"poll" => _poll_params, "options" => _options}=params)
do
  create(conn, Map.put(params, "image_data", nil))
end
```

Now we're down to four failures! The next failure we need to deal with is the following:

```
  1) test polls show_poll/1 returns a specific poll (Vocial.VotesTest)
     test/vocial/votes/votes_test.exs:62
     Assertion with == failed
     code: assert Votes.get_poll(poll.id()) == poll
     left: %Vocial.Votes.Poll{__meta__: #Ecto.Schema.Metadata<:loaded,
"polls">, id: 168, inserted_at: ~N[2018-02-05 21:38:16.179993], options:
[], title: "Hello", updated_at: ~N[2018-02-05 21:38:16.180002], user:
#Ecto.Association.NotLoaded<association :user is not loaded>, user_id: 297,
image: nil, vote_records: []}
     right: %Vocial.Votes.Poll{__meta__: #Ecto.Schema.Metadata<:loaded,
"polls">, id: 168, inserted_at: ~N[2018-02-05 21:38:16.179993], options:
[], title: "Hello", updated_at: ~N[2018-02-05 21:38:16.180002], user:
#Ecto.Association.NotLoaded<association :user is not loaded>, user_id: 297,
image: #Ecto.Association.NotLoaded<association :image is not loaded>,
vote_records: #Ecto.Association.NotLoaded<association :vote_records is not
loaded>}
     stacktrace:
       test/vocial/votes/votes_test.exs:64: (test)
```

If you're running your tests in a terminal that supports colors, you'll see these two fields
highlighted:

```
..., image: #Ecto.Association.NotLoaded<association :image is not loaded>,
vote_records: #Ecto.Association.NotLoaded<association :vote_records is not
loaded>, ...
```

This is telling us that we're missing preloads in our `poll_fixture/1` function at the top of
the `votes_test` file. Modify the `Repo.preload` statement in `poll_fixture` to the
following:

```
poll <- Repo.preload(poll, [:options, :image, :vote_records]) do
```

Now we're down to two failing tests!

```
1) test vote replies with status ok (VocialWeb.PollChannelTest)
   test/vocial_web/channels/polls_channel_test.exs:33
   ** (EXIT from #PID<0.439.0>) an exception was raised:
       ** (FunctionClauseError) no function clause matching in
VocialWeb.PollsChannel.join/3
           (vocial) lib/vocial_web/channels/polls_channel.ex:4:
VocialWeb.PollsChannel.join("polls:190", %{}, %Phoenix.Socket{assigns:
%{user_id: 330}, channel: VocialWeb.PollsChannel, channel_pid:
#PID<0.441.0>, endpoint: VocialWeb.Endpoint, handler: nil, id: "user_id",
join_ref: 2211, joined: false, private: %{log_handle_in: :debug, log_join:
:info}, pubsub_server: Vocial.PubSub, ref: nil, serializer:
Phoenix.ChannelTest.NoopSerializer, topic: "polls:190", transport:
Phoenix.ChannelTest, transport_name: :channel_test, transport_pid:
#PID<0.439.0>, vsn: nil})
           (phoenix) lib/phoenix/channel/server.ex:188:
Phoenix.Channel.Server.init/1
           (stdlib) gen_server.erl:365: :gen_server.init_it/2
           (stdlib) gen_server.erl:333: :gen_server.init_it/6
           (stdlib) proc_lib.erl:247: :proc_lib.init_p_do_apply/3
```

This is just another example of a modified function signature breaking our test suite. Pop over to `test/vocial_web/channels/polls_channel_test.exs` and modify the block of code that creates your socket to the following:

```
{:ok, _, socket} =
  socket("user_id", %{user_id: user.id})
  |> subscribe_and_join(PollsChannel, "polls:#{poll.id}", %{"remote_ip"
=> "127.0.0.1"})
```

If we rerun our test suite now, we should be back to a fully green test suite! This will give us the confidence we need to know that when we start implementing the next couple of parts of our application, we can do so safely!

Summary

We've now implemented some more quality-of-life features for our application that are things most people would come to expect from a modern application! Images are a major driver of internet applications nowadays (one only needs to look at the popularity of Facebook, Instagram, and Tumblr for examples of this), so it makes sense that we'd try to implement our own image handling code, and the issue of how to implement this functionality that shows up all the time in places such as Stack Overflow and other troubleshooting forums. It made sense to include it here to provide a more thorough reference on how to do it yourself!

We also implemented an IP address-based vote restriction system into our application to make sure that a couple of malicious users couldn't just make sure that all of their favorite choices in each poll always won! It took a bit of running around, and we had to write some code all over the place to make it come together in the end, but in the process, we got to learn a little more about some of the restrictions that exist when working with our controllers and our channels, and we even got to mess around a little bit with socket assigns as part of this process!

In our next chapter, we'll start diving head-first into implementing another common feature in Phoenix applications: chat! We'll create a way for users to interact with each other while watching the results of the voting happen live!

8
Adding Chat to Your Phoenix Application

When we last left off, we had organized our application and touched on a few of the missing areas of functionality that we really needed to make our application feel a little more finished. Our application is largely functional, and if we were so inclined, we could easily polish and ship this initial pass as a decent MVP (minimally viable product)! Take a moment to pat yourself on the back; getting anything completed can be a very difficult thing to do, and you're already well on your way to launching the next unicorn product! Of course, launching any kind of social app nowadays without something to enable some sort of real-time communication would never fly with investors, so the next thing we'll tackle is integrating chat into the polls. We also have a little bit of minor code cleanup to do as part of our development process. It can sometimes be nice to sprinkle in small, easy wins to keep you motivated in longer feature development sessions, which this will absolutely be one of, so we'll try to work that same rule in to this chapter as well to keep your momentum up!

In this chapter, we'll learn a few new things and dive into a few other missing elements:

- Understanding a data model for a chat application
- Building the data model for a chat application
- Integrating chat with the data model into Phoenix
- Cleaning up the navigation layout of our application

Adding chat to a Phoenix application

Adding chat is one of the more fun projects to work on in any web application. Often with development projects, there is a lot of "build this, see if anyone uses it after a month" and relying on metrics to really determine whether the feature that you developed added value or not. The nice thing about all of these real-time channel features is that they provide a level of immediate feedback and a clear picture of usage.

If you want to know who is using your application and how, you will now have a very clear way to check in on the health of your site. Visit some of the most popular polls and see how many people are on and using the chat portions of your application! It also is really fun to open up two browsers and see that instant flow of data simultaneously between multiple windows. Without any further ado, let's start designing this feature out a little bit more (since we probably should not just jump into the development of this feature blind).

It'll probably help us to start off with some sort of mockup of what we think that this application may look like when it is completed. We'll need a few diagrams:

1. What does the chat section look like when the user is not signed in but viewing a poll?
2. What does the chat section look like when the user is signed in and viewing their poll?
3. What does the chat section look like when the user is signed in and viewing someone else's poll?
4. What does the chat section look like when the user is not viewing a poll?

We'll start by looking at what the mockup for our application looks like right now:

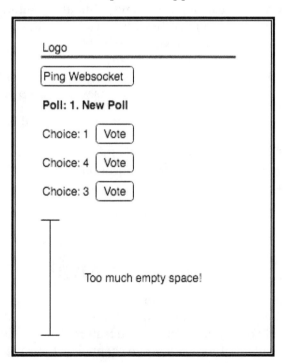

Right now, if you just pull up any poll, you'll notice that there is a ton of unused space, especially if there aren't that many options available on your poll. We'll fill up that extra space with the chat window that we'll be using to power the chat portion of our application. We'll design the chat application to function in the way that most chat applications work. You'll have your text box that you'll enter your messages into to speak with other users, and we'll also have a chat log that we can view that will display some amount of history about the chat application. Let's take a look at a mockup of our same application, but this time with a chat window:

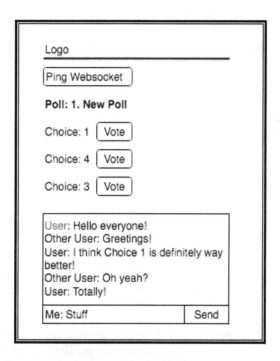

It's not too radically different, and the feature shouldn't look too complicated overall, so we should be able to use this as the framework to determine the design of the schema that we'll need to implement. If we look closely at our chat window, we can see a few different pieces of information that we'll need to track for history reasons:

- The message
- The author of the message
- Timestamps of the message (to provide ordering)
- The poll the message is associated with (if any)

We may also want to implement a system of logical deletes for messages to allow people to hide/remove chat messages on their polls, but we'll tackle that a little bit later. It's always good to go for the simplest implementation first and then iterate on it later, so we'll do precisely that.

Working with the chat schema

From the previous mockups, we can pretty comfortably design out what the schema for our chat information should look like. We'll want to store enough information to be able to rebuild the display when a user goes to the page, as well as information related to who said what and when. We'll stick with that to start since it is the simplest implementation:

```
table: messages
------------------------
   id : integer, primary key
   message : string, not null
   author : string, not null
   poll_id : integer, references polls, nullable
   inserted_at : timestamp
   created_at : timestamp
```

We have the standard columns that are created as a part of every Ecto table (`id`, `inserted_at`, and `created_at`), so we'll skip those. The key fields in this implementation are `message`, `author`, and `poll_id`. Message is pretty straight-forward, so I don't think we really need to spend too much time dissecting that and what it's used for. It'll store some arbitrary length of string and it shouldn't be null (so that people can't just spam empty messages).

Next, we have author, another string. This one also disallows null values, since we should know who wrote what and when. Again, nothing too particularly tricky or anything. We're starting off with a very simple implementation here, so we're not tying a specific message to a specific user. We may end up wanting to do that for auditing purposes, but for right now, we'll stick with just storing the author as a string representation.

Finally, we have the `poll_id`, which is a reference to the polls table. This will help us link the message back to a specific poll so that we know which poll to display the message under. We need this column, in particular, to be nullable and not-required because we're also going to implement a chatroom lobby into our application.

Building the chat schema

Let's get to writing some code to put this all together! We'll start off by building our `add_messages_table` migration:

```
$ mix ecto.gen.migration add_messages_table
* creating priv/repo/migrations
* creating priv/repo/migrations/20171206203035_add_messages_table.exs
```

We'll want to explicitly have it create the standard Ecto timestamps, as well as our `message`, `author`, and `poll_id` columns. `id` will be created by default every time, so there's not much we need to do there. Also, since we're relying on a foreign key that will likely be used pretty frequently in our queries, we want to make sure that we're creating an index for that particular column in reference to the correct table. In the `priv/repo/migrations/*_add_messages_table.exs` file (the timestamp prefix of the migration file will be different for you), add the following:

```
defmodule Vocial.Repo.Migrations.AddMessagesTable do
  use Ecto.Migration

  def change do
    create table(:messages) do
      add :message, :string
      add :author, :string
      add :poll_id, references(:polls)

      timestamps()
    end

    create index(:messages, [:poll_id])
  end
end
```

Now, we'll want to run the migration to verify that everything is working the way we expect it to:

```
$ mix ecto.migrate
[info] == Running Vocial.Repo.Migrations.AddMessagesTable.change/0 forward
[info] create table messages
[info] create index messages_poll_id_index
[info] == Migrated in 0.0s
```

There we go! We should now have our new messages table ready to go in our database, so the next step will be writing up the code for everything so that we can start actually using this to store our chat messages! We'll need to create a new schema file under a context. Since we're tying messages so closely to voting and polls, it makes sense for us to place the messages schema and code files under the votes context. Let's create `lib/vocial/votes/message.ex` and begin! We'll start off by creating the base file structure for our schema, which we've done plenty of times and don't need to explain anymore:

```
defmodule Vocial.Votes.Message do
  use Ecto.Schema
  import Ecto.Changeset

  alias Vocial.Votes.Message
end
```

Next, we'll need to build out the messages schema so that Ecto knows how to map the database table to our internal `%Message{}` struct:

```
schema "messages" do
  field :message, :string
  field :author, :string

  belongs_to :poll, Vocial.Votes.Poll

  timestamps()
end
```

Again, remember that each message is (optionally) attached to a poll. Finally, we'll need to implement the changeset function so that we can actually make modifications to chat messages, whether it is through updates or inserts (deletes don't go through changesets):

```
def changeset(%Message{}=message, attrs) do
  message
  |> cast(attrs, [:message, :author, :poll_id])
  |> validate_required([:message, :author])
end
```

Note that in our call to `cast/3`, we're saying that `message`, `author`, and `poll_id` are all valid values to set as part of a changeset. However, in our `validate_required` function, we're saying that only the message and author fields need to be set as part of a valid function.

Another thing we'll need to do is modify the existing Poll schema to have a `has_many` reference to the `Message` schema that we just created. In our schema for `lib/vocial/votes/poll.ex`, we'll add just one line:

```
has_many :messages, Vocial.Votes.Message
```

Designing our message functionality

Next, we need to determine what functionality should be tied to messages in our application so that we can figure out what code we should be writing in our context. While you can always just default to implementing full **CRUD** (create, read, update, delete) for each of your schemas, you may specifically want to avoid doing this. One good thing about not just implementing these by default is you standardize the API for your database models that other developers can see and interpret. Doing so allows you to specify safe boundaries for how to interact with various models (for example, there may be a database table of constants that you do not want the user to be able to modify). In the case of our application, with messages for our chat application, maybe we don't intend for a user to ever be able to edit their own messages. This is a sound reason for us to completely avoid implementing an edit or update function in our context and controllers! Now we have less code to write, less code to maintain, and fewer entry points for bad data into our table. The surface area is reduced while the intended functionality remains the same, and of course, we can always go back and add more code later to cover any gaps.

Let's design the functionality for our chat messages just to make sure we cover these same rules and assumptions:

- Users should be able to make new messages
- Users should be able to see chat messages for polls
- Users should be able to see chat messages for the lobby

That's a good first pass and tells us that we will need to implement a list function for messages (and one with the poll ID specified), as well as a create function. That's an easy first pass of functionality to implement in our context!

Implementing message functions in our context

We'll start with the easiest functionality to implement and then we'll spend a little bit of time writing some tests for our new functions as well. One thing we'll also need to do is clean up some of the broken tests that are the result of the work from the last chapter; we'll tackle that as well. First, in our Votes context (`lib/vocial/votes/votes.ex`), we'll need to add an alias statement for our new message schema:

```
alias Vocial.Votes.Message
```

Next, we'll continue by implementing the simplest bit of functionality: the `list_messages/0` function. This will give us a list of messages not associated with a Poll. We'll add this to our votes context:

```
def list_lobby_messages do
  Repo.all(
    from m in Message,
    where: is_nil(m.poll_id),
    order_by: [desc: :inserted_at],
    limit: 100
  )
end
```

Instead of just using `list_messages/0` as our function name, we should make it clear that we're not attempting to get every message that exists, just the ones that do not have a poll associated with them! By naming this `list_lobby_messages/0`, we're making it very clear that this function's purpose is 100% to get the messages not associated with a poll! In keeping consistent with the name of the function and what the name implies, we also need to specifically tell Ecto that we're looking for messages with a null (nil in the case of Elixir) poll ID value! We don't need any additional preloads or anything as part of this function, but we do need to make sure that we're ordering our messages by when they were inserted into the database and we also want to limit how many messages we're pulling at a time. Right now, we've arbitrarily set that limit to 100, but it could be any amount depending on what you want or how you can scale your application!

Now, we'll write up the function that will handle giving us a list of messages that are associated with a poll! We'll call this function `list_poll_messages/1`, again keeping the intent of the function very clear for anyone else that might be working on this application with us. Let's take a look at what this function looks like:

```
def list_poll_messages(poll_id) do
  Repo.all(
    from m in Message,
    where: m.poll_id == ^poll_id,
```

```
      order_by: [desc: :inserted_at],
      limit: 100,
      preload: [:poll]
    )
  end
```

This isn't too dramatically different from the lobby messages function, but one thing we are including here is a preload statement to make sure the poll is preloaded into our list of poll messages.

Finally, we'll need to implement a function to create new messages, but this is just the same sort of code we've implemented everywhere else, nothing too fancy:

```
def create_message(attrs) do
  %Message{}
  |> Message.changeset(attrs)
  |> Repo.insert()
end
```

Now that we have the code in place, the next step is for us to write some tests to make sure our code is actually doing what we expect it to!

Writing our unit tests

We're going to go in and start modifying `test/vocial/votes/votes_test.exs`. We'll create a new "messages" describe block in our test, and we're going to mess around with chaining `setup` blocks in tests to do a better job of doing test creation. Remember that the process for `setup` functions is to return information in the form of a tuple where the first element in the tuple is the atom `:ok` and the second part is a keyword list of any of the other information you want to pass down to other tests. We can test this out very quickly by writing our new describe block and then putting a new test in it:

```
describe "messages" do
  test "message is hello", %{message: message} do
    assert message == "Hello"
  end

  test "user is not blank", %{user: user} do
    assert !is_nil(user)
  end
end
```

This will give us a little room to experiment with our `setup` block. We set up a couple of baseline tests; one to verify that when passed a new variable from the `setup` block that it matches, and the second to verify we did not break anything in the original `setup` block. Now, in that same messages block, we're going to write up a new `setup` block to get a good feel for how those work and how to effectively use them in our tests:

```
setup do
  {:ok, message: "Hello"}
end
```

When we rerun our tests we will see both tests pass now! There is a weird gotcha here, however; where did the `user` variable get set from in our *user is not blank* test? We can dive into this a little more with another modification to our `setup` block; this time, modify the tuple returned to set `user` explicitly to `nil`:

```
setup do
  {:ok, message: "Hello", user: nil}
end
```

If you rerun the tests for this file now (and only this file), you'll get a failure about a non-truthy value:

```
$ mix test test/vocial/votes/votes_test.exs
  ...
  3) test messages user is not blank (Vocial.VotesTest)
     test/vocial/votes/votes_test.exs:110
     Expected truthy, got false
     code: assert !is_nil(user)
     stacktrace:
       test/vocial/votes/votes_test.exs:111: (test)
  ...
```

What's happening here is that any `setup` blocks for tests are executed in order and then the results are all merged together. In our case, we're setting a new value for user (the value being nil), so the order goes something like this:

```
{:ok, user: %User{...}} -- merges with --> {:ok, user: nil, message:
"Hello" }
```

And that gives us the final value where message is set to "Hello" but user is set to nil! So, what if we want to use something passed in previously as part of our setup block (for example, to create some sample posts off of a user)? Simple, the setup block can also accept arguments to it, just like any of your tests! Take a look at this to get a good feel for how to write those changes in:

```
setup(%{user: user}) do
  {:ok, message: "Hello", user: user}
end
```

If you run your tests again from here, you'll be back to passing tests for those tests in the describe block! Let's start writing the real tests for our Votes context instead of these fake tests. Keep your setup block, but dump the "message" value you're passing out of the setup block and delete the two dummy tests we created as well. We'll start off by writing a test for create_message/1, since that's a pretty simple function to work with. This test isn't too complicated:

```
test "create_message/1 creates a message on a poll" do
  with {:ok, message} <- Votes.create_message(%{ message: "Hello World",
author: "Someone" }) do
    assert Votes.list_lobby_messages() == [message]
  end
end
```

This one also doesn't need a setup block yet, since we're not really relying on any outside information or setup information. Now let's tackle our two list functions, list_lobby_messages/0 and list_poll_messages/1! We know that these two functions rely on there being some messages either attached to a poll or attached to a lobby, so we'll jump in and start working on our setup block.

First, we'll need to create a poll, otherwise attaching messages to a Poll will fail. We'll also need the user information from previous setup blocks – that's why we needed to sidebar to talk about how to do that in chained setup blocks! We'll add this as the first line of our setup block:

```
{:ok, poll} = Votes.create_poll(%{ title: "Sample Poll", user_id: user.id
})
```

Next, we'll set up a few lists of messages to make our code a little cleaner:

```
poll_messages = [ "Hello", "there", "World" ]
lobby_messages = [ "Polls", "are", "neat" ]
```

Now we're going to write two `Enum.each` statements to iterate over these lists and create the right kind of message per each iteration:

```
Enum.each(poll_messages, fn m ->
  Votes.create_message(%{ message: m, author: "Someone", poll_id: poll.id
})
end)
Enum.each(lobby_messages, fn m ->
  Votes.create_message(%{ message: m, author: "Someone" })
end)
```

Finally, all we need to pass back out to the next tests in our run is the poll, so we'll end with a simple return for our `setup` block:

```
{:ok, poll: poll}
```

At the risk of being redundant, I'm going to include the full `setup` block here, since if you don't get this part right it will make your tests fail, and they may fail in ways that are very difficult to diagnose and correct:

```
setup(%{user: user}) do
  {:ok, poll} = Votes.create_poll(%{ title: "Sample Poll", user_id: user.id
})
  poll_messages = [ "Hello", "there", "World" ]
  lobby_messages = [ "Polls", "are", "neat" ]
  Enum.each(poll_messages, fn m ->
    Votes.create_message(%{ message: m, author: "Someone", poll_id: poll.id
})
  end)
  Enum.each(lobby_messages, fn m ->
    Votes.create_message(%{ message: m, author: "Someone" })
  end)
  {:ok, poll: poll}
end
```

Rerun our tests and...we'll get a failure! That's because our initial test for `create_message/1` was actually a little overly naive. Instead, we should be verifying that the list contains our created message instead of that the entire list of lobby messages contains just it. We'll do this lookup by checking the primary key for each message to make for an easier comparison:

```
test "create_message/1 creates a message on a poll" do
  with {:ok, message} <- Votes.create_message(%{ message: "Hello
World", author: "Someone" }) do
    assert Enum.any?(Votes.list_lobby_messages(), fn msg -> msg.id ==
message.id end)
```

```
      end
   end
```

This will make our tests significantly less brittle and better at telling us when real issues happen rather than when our tests change in the course of development. Having tackled that, we can move on to writing the first of the tests for the list functionality. We'll start off by testing `list_lobby_message/0`:

```
test "list_lobby_messages/1 only includes lobby message" do
  assert Enum.count(Votes.list_lobby_messages()) > 0
  assert Enum.all?(Votes.list_lobby_messages(), &(is_nil(&1.poll_id)))
end
```

We first make sure that we have ANY lobby messages, since if that count is 0, then the next test will unfortunately pass. Next, we verify that all of the messages have a nil `poll_id` value. We do this through a little bit of anonymous function shorthand. Consider this statement in particular:

```
&(is_nil(&1.poll_id))
```

The preceding code is actually just shorthand for writing this:

```
fn p ->
  is_nil(p.poll_id)
end
```

Finally, we'll write a test for `list_poll_messages/1`, which is almost identical, except we want to verify that every message returned has a poll ID that matches the supplied poll. We will need to catch the poll value out of the `setup` block to write this test effectively:

```
test "list_poll_messages/1 only includes poll message", %{poll: poll} do
  assert Enum.count(Votes.list_poll_messages(poll.id)) > 0
  assert Enum.all?(Votes.list_poll_messages(poll.id), &(&1.poll_id ==
poll.id))
end
```

We again make sure that messages exist for that poll (which we set up in our `setup` block), and then we also make sure that every message returned is a message for that one particular poll!

That's it! Our new context code is appropriately covered under tests, we have the functionality we need to start building our chat application further, and we're ready to go! To give ourselves a quick break, though, we need to fix one part of our application, so we'll weave that in to give us a breather and get a quick win in. Verify that we're at a fully-green test suite and we'll move on!

Fixing navigation in our application

Right now, if you just visit the root of your application, you're almost immediately stuck. There's no concept of navigation or anything to make anyone's lives easier, and it even makes it difficult for us to be able to navigate around and fix up our application quickly. This is the root view of our application right now:

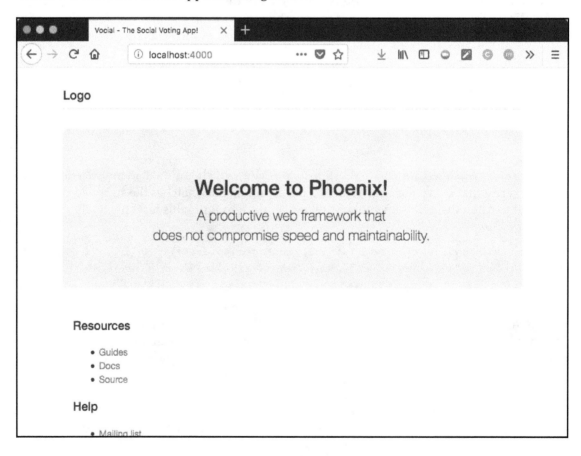

This is not a great user experience, so we should highlight it as one area for us to fix up. We'll start off by moving that top "logo" bit into a partial template for Phoenix that we'll create as `lib/vocial_web/templates/layout/_nav.html.eex`. In this case, we use the underscore prefix on the filename to indicate that it is a partial template and not a template that is specifically tied to a controller action. Create that file, open it up, and then we'll give it the following contents:

```
<header class="header">
  <h4>Vocial</h4>
</header>
```

The underscore in front of the file is not necessarily a community standard, but something I personally use to make it clear which templates are going to be reused.

Now, we'll hop over to `lib/vocial_web/templates/layout/app.html.eex` and replace the three preceding lines with the following line:

```
<%= render "_nav.html" %>
```

Refresh your page and everything will be (basically) identical! Now we can start modifying our navigation a little bit better and keep our `app.html.eex` file cleaner as part of that. Refresh the page, verify that everything is still the same, and then we'll start improving the nav component to our site.

Back in `lib/vocial_web/templates/layout/_nav.html.eex`, we're going to (heavily) modify the content. Phoenix includes, by default, a minified version of Bootstrap, so we're going to use some Bootstrap conventions to create a nice navigation header:

```
<nav class="navbar navbar-default">
  <div class="container-fluid">
    <div class="navbar-header">
      <a class="navbar-brand" href="/">Vocial</a>
    </div>
    <ul class="nav navbar-nav navbar-right">
      <li><a href="/polls">Polls/a></li>
      <li><a href="/login">Login</a></li>
    </ul>
  </div>
</nav>
```

This should give us a usable navigation header that looks something like this:

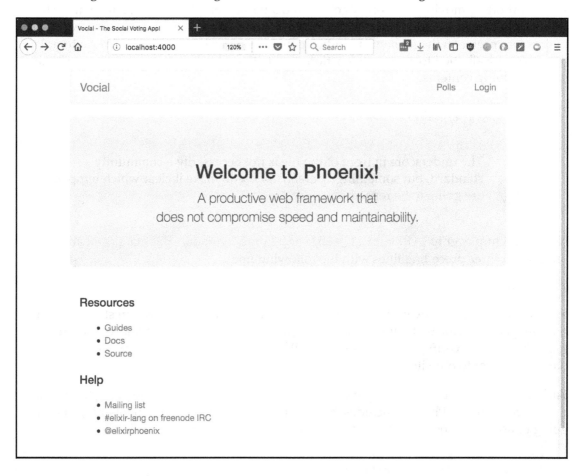

We'll also quickly want to tune up the list of Polls so that we can navigate to a specific one easier. To do this, we'll need to change what we pass in for the "_poll.html" partial, since we'll need to pass in the @conn variable to be able to use the Phoenix HTML link helper. Open up lib/vocial_web/templates/poll/index.html.eex and change the render line for _poll.html to this:

```
<%= render("_poll.html", %{ poll: poll, conn: @conn }) %>
```

And then open up lib/vocial_web/templates/poll/show.html.eex to do the same:

```
<%= render("_poll.html", %{ poll: @poll, conn: @conn }) %>
```

Finally, we'll hop into `lib/vocial_web/templates/poll/_poll.html.eex` and change the portion that displays the title of the poll to also be a link (using Phoenix's link helper) to allow you to quickly navigate to the poll:

```
<h2><%= link "Poll: #{@poll.id}. #{@poll.title}", to: poll_path(@conn,
:show, @poll) %></h2>
```

The link header above is why we needed to change our partials to pass `@conn` into the partial render! Now, when we pull up the list of polls, we can navigate quickly to the poll we want to test! If you navigate back to the polls index now, you should see the titles of the polls have turned into links that we can click on to navigate to the right poll, like in the following screenshot:

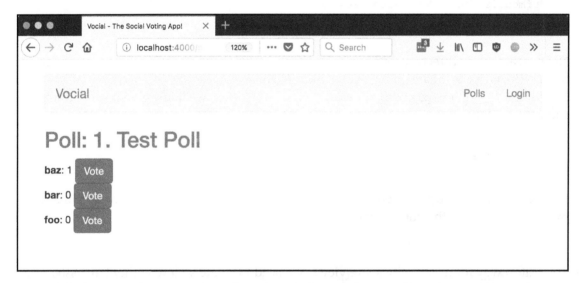

We have what we need and we have a nice quick win under our belts, so let's move back into development on the chat portion of our application!

Creating the chat UI

Now that we have an easier way to get to our actual polls and we have the backend code framework in place, we can start to move forward a little bit more with the actual development of the chat component itself. We'll need to start off by building out the UI in the simplest way possible first, since without that it will be very difficult to actually accomplish anything else.

Another consideration that we're going to have to make is that we likely will want it to be easy to place chat into our application anywhere, which means we're going to have to build out a shared component.

Building the UI Itself

Phoenix, unfortunately, does not have a built-in concept of shared templates or views, so we're going to have to make one ourself! We'll start off by creating a new view called `VocialWeb.SharedView`. Create `lib/vocial_web/views/shared_view.ex` and give it the base view code:

```
defmodule VocialWeb.SharedView do
  use VocialWeb, :view
end
```

Next, create a new directory under `lib/vocial_web/templates` called `shared`, and in there we're going to create `_chat.html.eex`. Then, in `lib/vocial_web/templates/shared/_chat.html.eex`, we'll just give it some dummy code:

```
<div>
  <h1>CHAT</h1>
</div>
```

Finally, we can open up `lib/vocial_web/templates/poll/show.html.eex` and add the following line to the bottom of our template:

```
<%= render(VocialWeb.SharedView, "_chat.html") %>
```

To create a way for us to easily share views, we need to create a view without an associated controller and a template directory to match that view. The nice thing about this is that it makes it clear what the intent of those templates are and let us reuse them for other templates along the way. We don't need the controller because nothing is going through the full stack of a Phoenix request. The first controller that routes the browser's request handles all of the `setup` and output, so all we need is a view and a template itself.

 If you don't specify a view module for a template in a render call, it is assumed that the view module is whatever the current view module is.

Refresh your browser while viewing a poll and you should see `"CHAT"` in big letters underneath the voting options for your application. Now we can start building up the UI for our chat window a little more! I'm going to provide the code for this; a lot of this work is just in making the chat window slightly presentable, so there's not too much to explain:

```
<br/><br/>
<div class="chat-window container well" id="enable-chat-channel" >
  <div class="row col-md-12">
    Your name:
    <input type="text" class="form-control author-input" placeholder="Name"
/>
  </div>
  <div class="row col-md-12">
    <h3>Chat</h3>
    <ul class="list-unstyled chat-messages">
      <li>&lt;Person&gt; Hello World!</li>
      <li>&lt;Other Person&gt; Greetings to you all!</li>
    </ul>
  </div>
  <div class="row">
    <div class="col-md-10">
      <input type="text" class="form-control chat-input"/>
    </div>
    <div class="col-md-2">
      <button class="btn btn-primary chat-send">Send</button>
    </div>
  </div>
</div>
```

One thing that I included is two sample messages so that we can flesh out the UI a little bit more and see what it looks like populated with real data. We also create our initial text box and send button, which right now won't do anything because they're not actually hooked up to any real code!

The end result is we should now have a Poll View and chat window that looks like this:

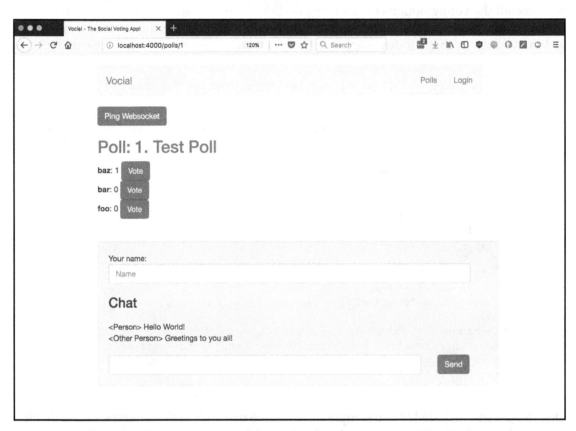

We can now start building up the WebSockets, channels, and topics to really give this the kind of functionality that will make our app stand out! We also built in the concept of a chat lobby, so we'll head over to `lib/vocial_web/templates/page/index.html.eex` and replace its contents (previously the Phoenix marketing materials) with this:

```
<div class="jumbotron">
  <h2><%= gettext "Welcome to %{name}!", name: "Vocial" %></h2>
  <p class="lead">A social voting app!</p>
</div>

<%= render(VocialWeb.SharedView, "_chat.html") %>
```

Again, notice that we're just reusing that chat template, so our shared views and templates have already served us well! This will be the chat that powers our lobby chat, so we'll start off building up this chat and then we'll start implementing the chat system for each individual poll as well.

Creating our chat channel

To start implementing chat in our application, we'll need to start building out the chat channel and setting up all of the framework code necessary for us to support the new channel. We'll need to start by adding the new channel to `lib/vocial_web/channels/user_socket.ex`:

```
channel "chat:*", VocialWeb.ChatChannel
```

We don't actually have a Chat Channel module yet, so that will be the next file that we will have to start building up. In the same directory, we'll create a `chat_channel.ex` file and start it off with a simple channel skeleton:

```
defmodule VocialWeb.ChatChannel do
  use VocialWeb, :channel

  def join("chat:lobby", _payload, socket) do
    {:ok, socket}
  end
end
```

We'll also have to refactor our JavaScript in the `socket.js` file since we had originally written that to be very specific to the live polls work. We'll create a new file in `assets/js` called `poll.js`, and move all of the poll-specific code there:

```
// Push the vote up to the server
const pushVote = (el, channel) => {
  channel
    .push("vote", { option_id: el.getAttribute("data-option-id") })
    .receive("ok", res => console.log("You Voted!"))
    .receive("error", res => console.log("Failed to vote:", res));
};

// When we join the channel, do this
const onJoin = (res, channel) => {
  document.querySelectorAll(".vote-button-manual").forEach(el => {
    el.addEventListener("click", event => {
      event.preventDefault();
      pushVote(el, channel);
```

```
      });
    });
    console.log("Joined channel:", res);
  };

  const connect = socket => {
    // Only connect to the socket if the polls channel actually exists!
    const enableLivePolls = document.getElementById("enable-polls-channel");
    if (!enableLivePolls) {
      return;
    }

    // Pull the Poll Id to find the right topic from the data attribute
    const pollId = enableLivePolls.getAttribute("data-poll-id");
    // Get the stored remote IP for a user
    const remoteIp = document
      .getElementsByName("remote_ip")[0]
      .getAttribute("content");
    // Create a channel to handle joining/sending/receiving
    const channel = socket.channel("polls:" + pollId, { remote_ip: remoteIp
});

    // Next, join the topic on the channel!
    channel
      .join()
      .receive("ok", res => onJoin(res, channel))
      .receive("error", res => console.log("Failed to join channel:", res));

    document.getElementById("polls-ping").addEventListener("click", () => {
      channel
        .push("ping")
        .receive("ok", res => console.log("Received PING response:",
res.message))
        .receive("error", res => console.log("Error sending PING:", res));
    });

    channel.on("pong", payload => {
      console.log("The server has been PONG'd and all is well:", payload);
    });

    channel.on("new_vote", ({ option_id, votes }) => {
      document.getElementById("vote-count-" + option_id).innerHTML = votes;
    });
  };

  export default { connect };
```

We'll also refactor our `socket.js` file to be more minimal:

```
// Import Phoenix's Socket Library
import { Socket } from "phoenix";

// Next, create a new Phoenix Socket to reuse
const socket = new Socket("/socket");

// Connect to the socket itself
socket.connect();

// Finally, export the socket to be imported in app.js
export default socket;
```

Finally, we'll need to modify our `app.js` file to use this new code:

```
// Import the default Phoenix HTML libraries
import "phoenix_html";

// Import the User Socket code to enable websockets
import socket from "./socket";

// Import the polls channel code to enable live polling
import LivePolls from "./poll";
LivePolls.connect(socket);
```

We need to do this all because our poll code needs to be properly separated out from our chat code, and the socket itself needs to be more reusable than it is currently. We are also now ready to start building up our chat code, so let's create another new file in that same directory called `chat.js`, which we'll give a similar structure to our live polls code. We'll start off explicitly targeting the chat lobby but we'll eventually move into being able to support either version of chat:

```
// Import Phoenix's Socket Library
import { Socket } from "phoenix";

// Utility functions

// When we join the channel, do this
const onJoin = (res, channel) => {
  console.log("Joined channel:", res);
};

// Next, create a new Phoenix Socket to reuse
const socket = new Socket("/socket");

// Connect to the socket itself
```

```
socket.connect();

const connect = (socket) => {
  // Only connect to the socket if the chat channel actually exists!
  const enableLiveChat = document.getElementById("enable-chat-channel");
  if (!enableLiveChat) {
    return;
  }
  // Create a channel to handle joining/sending/receiving
  const channel = socket.channel("chat:lobby");

  // Next, join the topic on the channel!
  channel
    .join()
    .receive("ok", res => onJoin(res, channel))
    .receive("error", res => console.log("Failed to join channel:", res));
};

// Finally, export the socket to be imported in app.js
export default { connect };
```

Finally, we'll hop back over to `app.js` and import/enable this code as well:

```
// // Import the Chat Socket code to enable chat
import LiveChat from "./chat";
LiveChat.connect(socket);
```

Sending chat messages

To actually send chat messages back and forth things are going to be a bit more complicated than our voting code. We'll need to modify a little more of the code to allow this to work. In our `assets/js/chat.js` file, we'll need to add a few new utility functions. We'll need utility functions for:

- Sending chat messages to the server
- What to set up when we join the chat channel
- A way to add messages to our ongoing list of chat messages

Sending chat messages to the server will be pretty simple overall, so we'll start with implementing that:

```
// Push a new message to the server
const pushMessage = (channel, author, message) => {
  channel
    .push("new_message", { author, message })
    .receive("ok", res => console.log("Message sent!"))
    .receive("error", res => console.log("Failed to send message:", res));
};
```

This will take in the channel (since we need to know how to push this message from the client to the server), the author (since we need to know who is sending the message), and finally the message itself (since it won't be very helpful for us to send a message with only the author filled in). The code is otherwise just a normal WebSocket push. We'll call the message for a new message being sent or received "new_message" and we'll include the author and the message as part of that payload! Next, we need to clean up and build more onto the onJoin function that we started:

```
const onJoin = (res, channel) => {
  document.querySelectorAll(".chat-send").forEach(el => {
    el.addEventListener("click", event => {
      event.preventDefault();
      const chatInput = document.querySelector(".chat-input");
      const message = chatInput.value;
      const author = document.querySelector(".author-input").value;
      pushMessage(channel, author, message);
      chatInput.value = "";
    });
  });
  console.log("Joined channel:", res);
};
```

We're adding an event listener to anything with a "chat-send" class attached to it. This event will prevent the default behavior for that element from firing, grab the values stored in the author and chat message input fields, and then call our previous pushMessage function to send that information to the server. Next, we'll need to implement a way to add new messages onto our list (our chat window), so we'll write an addMessage function that will take in an author and a message as the arguments:

```
// Add a message to the list of chat messages
const addMessage = (author, message) => {
  const chatLog = document.querySelector(".chat-messages");
  chatLog.innerHTML += `<li>
```

```
            <span class="author">&lt;${author}&gt;</span>
            <span class="message">${message}</span>`;
};
```

Finally, down in our `connect()` function, we'll add a handler for when we receive a `new_message` event from the server. At the bottom of the `connect` function, add the following block of code:

```
channel.on("new_message", ({ author, message }) => {
  addMessage(author, message);
});
```

Right now, this code will not do anything worthwhile, because we don't have any of the Phoenix code behind the scenes to back up this functionality. Let's tackle that next!

Hooking up the new JavaScript code to Phoenix

All of this code doing all of this cool stuff in JavaScript doesn't mean much if we can't actually hook it up for broadcasting and storing messages! The good news is that there really isn't that much code we need to write! First, we'll want to update our chat channel code to be able to handle this `new_message` event and store the message in the database.

Back in `lib/vocial_web/channels/chat_channel.ex`, we'll need to add an alias to the Votes context:

```
alias Vocial.Votes
```

And then we'll add a new `handle_in/3` function:

```
    def handle_in("new_message", %{"author" => author, "message" => message},
socket) do
      with {:ok, _message} <- Votes.create_message(%{author: author, message:
message}) do
        broadcast socket, "new_message", %{author: author, message: message}
        {:reply, {:ok, %{author: author, message: message}}, socket}
      else
        _ -> {:reply, {:error, %{message: "Failed to send chat message"}},
socket}
      end
    end
```

Here, we watch for a `new_message` sent from the client through WebSockets with an author and message field in the body. If we successfully write the message to the database, we broadcast back out that we have a new message for everyone. We also reply to the sender so that they know that their message was received. Otherwise, we record an error message!

Next, we'll want to make it so that if you load up the chat in a new browser session, it will give you the last messages, so we'll want to modify some code in `lib/vocial_web/controllers/page_controller.ex` to fetch those:

```
alias Vocial.Votes

def index(conn, _params) do
  messages = Votes.list_lobby_messages() |> Enum.reverse()
  render conn, "index.html", messages: messages
end
```

We need to alias the Votes context since that provides the `list_lobby_messages/0` functionality. Also, as a quirk, we need to fetch the list of messages but then reverse them! We need to do this because we need the most recent `N` messages, but then we want to display those messages in a chronological order (oldest at the top and newest at the bottom), so we just reverse the list in Elixir before sending it back out to the template.

 Remember that in our `list_lobby_messages/0` function we order the messages by time in reverse chronological order to allow us to limit the number of messages returned and give us the correct results.

Now, we'll need to modify our `lib/vocial_web/templates/page/index.html.eex` template to pass these messages to the partial template:

```
<%= render(VocialWeb.SharedView, "_chat.html", messages: @messages) %>
```

And at last, the final piece of this is that we need to implement is in our `_chat.html.eex` partial (located in `lib/vocial_web/templates/shared/_chat.html.eex`). We need to change the list of messages to build the chat log from what the database gives us:

```
<ul class="list-unstyled chat-messages">
  <%= for message <- @messages do %>
    <li><span class="author">&lt;<%= message.author %>&gt; <span
class="message"><%= message.message %></span>
  <% end %>
</ul>
```

That's it! If you open up multiple chat windows in the lobby (just the root window, for us), you should be able to have a nice conversation with yourself:

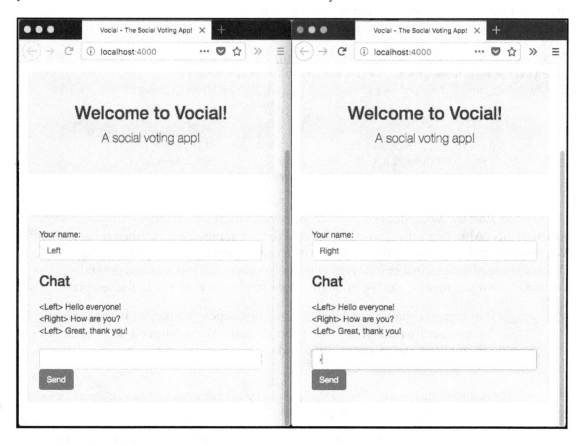

Now that the lobby chat is working, we also need to start working on the chat for individual polls and fix up our tests as well!

Refactoring for poll chats

We need a way to be able to specify which chatroom to connect to for our polls-specific chat. To do that we'll need to start specifying the chatroom (we'll use that as part of the topic to connect to). We'll start by placing a data attribute on our chat-window in `lib/vocial_web/templates/shared/_chat.html.eex` that we will reference later in our `chat.js` file:

```
<div class="chat-window container well" id="enable-chat-channel" data-
chatroom="<%= @chatroom %>">
```

We'll need to actually pass a value to that that will enable us to reference `@chatroom` since right now we're not setting that anywhere. We'll also need to hop out to our `lib/vocial_web/templates/poll/show.html.eex` and set that as part of the call to render:

```
<%= render(VocialWeb.SharedView, "_chat.html", messages: @poll.messages,
chatroom: @poll.id) %>
```

This will currently break, as we're not including messages as a part of our preloads for our query, so we'll also need to hop over to `lib/vocial_web/votes/votes.ex` and change our `get_poll/1` and `list_polls/0` functions:

```
def get_poll(id) do
  Repo.get!(Poll, id)
  |> Repo.preload([:options, :image, :vote_records, :messages])
end

def list_polls do
  Repo.all(Poll) |> Repo.preload([:options, :image, :vote_records,
:messages])
end
```

We'll want to do the same in `lib/vocial_web/templates/page/index.html.eex` as well (this one being set to `"lobby"` instead of the poll's ID):

```
<%= render(VocialWeb.SharedView, "_chat.html", messages: @messages,
chatroom: "lobby") %>
```

Next, we'll need to change the JavaScript code in `assets/js/chat.js` to use this new data attribute. We'll start off by getting that information out and putting that in our connect function, and we'll also change what channel we join by default:

```
// Get the chatroom that we're supposed to connect to
const chatroom = document
  .getElementById("enable-chat-channel")
  .getAttribute("data-chatroom");
// Create a channel to handle joining/sending/receiving
const channel = socket.channel("chat:" + chatroom);
```

Finally, we'll modify our `join` function for the Chat Channel module (in `lib/vocial_web/channels/chat_channel.ex`). We'll also need to modify our `handle_in` function to also be able to pull the `poll_id` (or lobby) out of the socket:

```
def join("chat:" <> _poll_id, _payload, socket) do
  {:ok, socket}
end
```

Nothing special here! The last piece we need to do is flesh our `handle_in` function. It's mostly the same, but we'll start by pulling the `poll_id` out of the socket's topic (since it goes in the format of `"chat:(poll ID or lobby)"`.

```
poll_id = case socket.topic do
  "chat:lobby" -> nil
  "chat:" <> id -> id
  _ -> nil
end
```

Finally, we need to modify our `create_message` function in our `with` statement to pass in the poll ID:

```
with {:ok, _message} <- Votes.create_message(%{author: author, message:
message, poll_id: poll_id}) do
```

The end result is that we should now have chats that are separate between the lobby and specific polls; we finally have that social edge to our application that we wanted to build! This is a pretty great portion of functionality and the kind of thing that allows us to really elevate our application!

Let's take a look at what the chat window looks like embedded in a Poll view, which should pretty closely match our original mockup:

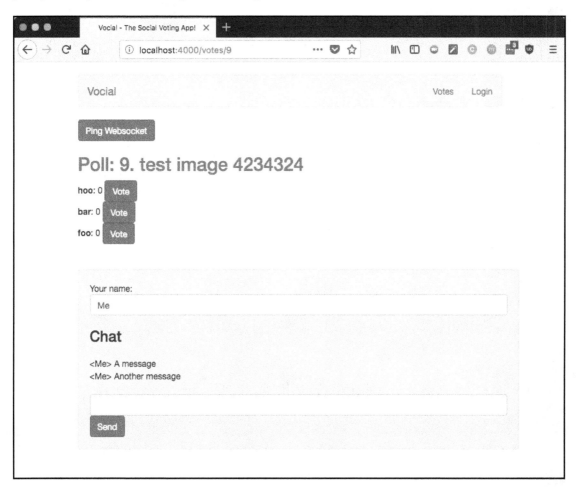

Fixing up our tests

We'll need to fix up our tests very quickly as well. For the most part, we can just reuse the code from the poll channel tests. We'll start off with a standard channel test skeleton. Create `test/vocial_web/channels/chat_channel_test.exs` and we'll start it off simply enough:

```
defmodule VocialWeb.ChatChannelTest do
  use VocialWeb.ChannelCase

  alias VocialWeb.ChatChannel
end
```

Next, we'll add a `setup` block. We'll start off by creating a user and a poll to give us our baseline:

```
setup do
  {:ok, user} = Vocial.Accounts.create_user(%{
    username: "test",
    email: "test@test.com",
    password: "test",
    password_confirmation: "test"
  })
  {:ok, poll} = Vocial.Votes.create_poll_with_options(
    %{ "title" => "My New Test Poll", "user_id" => user.id },
    ["One", "Two", "Three"]
  )
```

Then we'll create a mock socket that will join the chat lobby and the chat for the created poll:

```
  socket = socket("user_id", %{user_id: user.id})
  {:ok, _, poll_socket} = subscribe_and_join(socket, ChatChannel,
"chat:#{poll.id}", %{})
  {:ok, _, lobby_socket} = subscribe_and_join(socket, ChatChannel,
"chat:lobby", %{})
```

Finally, we return out the information that we've created as a part of this `setup` block:

```
  {:ok, poll_socket: poll_socket, lobby_socket: lobby_socket, user: user,
poll: poll}
end
```

Next, we'll write a test that makes sure we get a reply from the socket and a broadcast from the socket that matches the author/message format we specified in the channel itself:

```
test "new_message replies with status ok for chat:poll_id",
%{poll_socket: socket} do
    ref = push socket, "new_message", %{"author" => "test", "message" =>
"Hello World"}
    assert_reply ref, :ok, %{author: author, message: message}
    assert author == "test"
    assert message == "Hello World"

    assert_broadcast "new_message", %{author: author, message: message}
    assert author == "test"
    assert message == "Hello World"
end
```

Finally, we duplicate the test for the chat lobbies as well:

```
test "new_message replies with status ok for chat:lobby", %{lobby_socket:
socket} do
    ref = push socket, "new_message", %{"author" => "test", "message" =>
"Hello World"}
    assert_reply ref, :ok, %{author: author, message: message}
    assert author == "test"
    assert message == "Hello World"

    assert_broadcast "new_message", %{author: author, message: message}
    assert author == "test"
    assert message == "Hello World"
end
```

And that's it! If we run our tests for the chat channel now, we should see nice green tests:

```
mix test test/vocial_web/channels/chat_channel_test.exs
..

Finished in 1.2 seconds
2 tests, 0 failures

Randomized with seed 933948
```

Returning to a passing test suite

We also have a few random test failures that we'll want to correct very quickly before we close out this chapter. The first is a result of us adding new preloads:

```
  1) test polls show_poll/1 returns a specific poll (Vocial.VotesTest)
     test/vocial/votes/votes_test.exs:62
     Assertion with == failed
     code: assert Votes.get_poll(poll.id()) == poll
     left: %Vocial.Votes.Poll{__meta__: #Ecto.Schema.Metadata<:loaded,
  "polls">, id: 84, image: nil, inserted_at: ~N[2018-02-06 16:33:20.390976],
  options: [], title: "Hello", updated_at: ~N[2018-02-06 16:33:20.390987],
  user: #Ecto.Association.NotLoaded<association :user is not loaded>,
  user_id: 131, vote_records: [], messages: []}
        right: %Vocial.Votes.Poll{__meta__: #Ecto.Schema.Metadata<:loaded,
  "polls">, id: 84, image: nil, inserted_at: ~N[2018-02-06 16:33:20.390976],
  options: [], title: "Hello", updated_at: ~N[2018-02-06 16:33:20.390987],
  user: #Ecto.Association.NotLoaded<association :user is not loaded>,
  user_id: 131, vote_records: [], messages:
  #Ecto.Association.NotLoaded<association :messages is not loaded>}
     stacktrace:
       test/vocial/votes/votes_test.exs:64: (test)
```

The good news is that this one is very easy for us to fix. In our `poll_fixture/1` function in `test/vocial/votes/votes_text.exs`, just change the line in the `with` statement that adds the preloads to:

```
poll <- Repo.preload(poll, [:options, :image, :vote_records, :messages]) do
```

This leaves us with one failing test on page controller, which is happening since we ripped out the boilerplate code but left the test in place. The failing test is:

```
  1) test GET / (VocialWeb.PageControllerTest)
     test/vocial_web/controllers/page_controller_test.exs:4
     Assertion with =~ failed
     code: assert html_response(conn, 200) =~ "Welcome to Phoenix!"
```

Open up `test/vocial_web/controllers/page_controller_test.exs` and change the failing test to this instead:

```
test "GET /", %{conn: conn} do
  conn = get(conn, "/")
  assert html_response(conn, 200)
end
```

Now everything is back to green and fully-passing tests!

Summary

That was a lot! We spent a lot of time in JavaScript in this chapter (just like last chapter), but it's important to understand on a deep level how to properly break up JavaScript code and hook into separate channels! There's a lot of work that goes into building a really good live application, and we tackled a good portion of this!

This work also underscored a very significant part of the software development workflow: mocking up your frontend before you start working on it can go a long way towards making sure your application functions the way you expect. It also becomes easier to build and maintain!

On the database side of things, in this chapter we spent a long time working on hooking up our chat, working through our created mockups, and building our data models just to start. This was a good way to build up our foundation to make sure when we started heavily modifying the JavaScript code, our backend was there to support it.

We then transitioned on to refactoring our Javascript to allow for multiple channels, and we also broke up the logic of our code a little bit further to set up multiple topics, which we then broke apart into separate chat rooms!

We have a lot to show for our efforts! In the next few chapters, we'll start to dive headfirst into some of the more advanced Elixir and Phoenix features, such as Phoenix Presence, and other major performance tweaks. We'll also dive a bit more into OTP to get a better foundation in some of the more advanced features and functionality that is working for us behind the scenes!

Using Presence and ETS in Phoenix

9

In the last chapter, we explored the best ways to increase the social abilities of your application. We walked through the process of implementing a chat system in your application, which allowed your users to talk to each other as they visited and voted on various polls, which is a great way to really get your users talking and excited about your platform! These are the kinds of features that are currently in high-demand, so being well-versed in understanding how to write them will go a long way!

We're now preparing to move into some of the more advanced topics behind Elixir and Phoenix. A robust, performant application will also utilize a lot of the more advanced language and framework features that are generally behind the scenes of such applications. Two of these features are Presence and **Erlang Term Storage** (**ETS**).

In this chapter, we'll be covering a few different topics:

- An introduction to Phoenix Presence
- How to utilize Phoenix Presence in your application
- How to implement the Elixir code for Presence
- How to implement the JavaScript code for Presence
- An introduction to ETS
- How to use ETS in an IEx window
- How to use ETS in Your Phoenix application
- Using ETS to store vote data
- Using ETS to store chat data
- Writing a fallback for ETS if there is no data

Utilizing Presence and ETS to make our app more robust

As we start scaling our application, we'll very quickly find that in Phoenix applications, the bottleneck moves away from what our connections are doing and how long they're sitting around for and moves toward the database. In addition, the concept of determining the state of connections (when they are established, how long they've been active, what their current state is, and so on) becomes a more important question to answer. The good news is that Elixir and Phoenix both have built-in tools that you get for free that allow you to solve these problems!

Elixir provides access to ETS through the `:ets` namespace. This allows you to create tables, insert/retrieve/delete data, and so on. ETS specifically stores any information you enter into it in memory, which means any access to it is incredibly fast!

In addition, Phoenix provides access to Presence, which allows you to track and update the existence of connections. You can think of this as a list of users in a chat application—you'll want to store who is online, who is not, and what the status is for each of those users. That's the kind of feature that is almost just assumed at this point, so we'll want to include it as part of our application's chat system.

What is Presence?

We have already briefly talked about Presence, but there's actually a lot more to it. Presence works through the concept of **conflict-free replicated data types** (**CRDTs**). The general premise behind Presence and how it was built is that, to actually be able to track users as they join/leave/go away, you need to be able to track the state change over time and resolve that change with other servers as well, since most applications today are clustered in some way.

The difficulty comes from when you have multiple servers that are all in charge of recording a user's state. If you have three servers and one goes down, and another server records a user signing off, and then another server records the user signing on, which one wins?

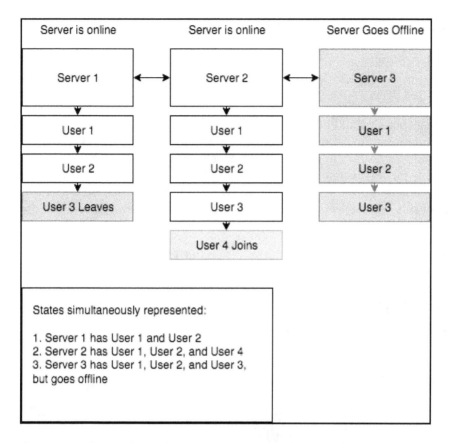

In the preceding example, we have three separate states that are all represented at the same time. What happens if the offline server comes back online? What is the current accurate state of the users that are connected? The right answer is **User 1**, **User 2**, and **User 4**, but how does the server know that? Without anything to help resolve the conflicts here, the server will just make its best guess with the data it has and hope for the best. Eventually, the server will catch back up and be at the appropriate state (think *eventual consistency* here), but for a while, the server might incorrectly think that **User 3** is still active, or it may ignore **User 4**.

This is just a recipe for confusion, and not just for the server. Ultimately, it will likely fall to you, intrepid application developer, to solve this problem somehow. You could come up with a wonderful solution, but then you'd have to maintain that wonderful solution, and over time that might get trickier as new servers are added, new user states are added, and so on.

The good news here is that Phoenix just gives this ability to you as a built-in feature, and it sits on top of a mountain of computer science research! One only needs to visit the Wikipedia page for CRDTs to get a good overview of just how much science and research sits behind this powerful concept. CRDTs power Phoenix's Presence modules, and even the JavaScript code to support Presence is there. This dramatically drops the overhead required to implement this system (both from an actual lines-of-code perspective, but also from the extreme cognitive load that comes with something like this).

If we want to tap into Presence in our application, we'll need to slightly adjust the overall design of our chat application and add a section displaying the users. We'll probably also want to add new messages into our chat application showing when people join, leave, or change their status. Let's take a look at what a new design for this might look like:

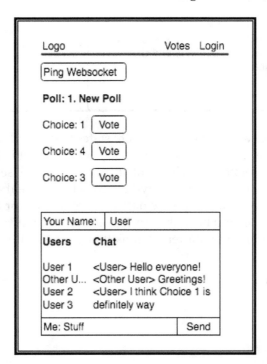

You can see here that we have a list of users (each with various statuses), and in the chat logs themselves, we can see a few messages related to people joining, leaving, or with another status. Another thing we'll want to implement is something that requires a user to enter their username before being allowed to participate in the chat, so we'll also tackle that as part of our implementation. We'll change the text entry at the bottom to first ask the user for their name before we allow them to actually begin chatting; this will then *join* them to the Presence system and start keeping track of them.

The final thing we'll want to implement is an idle/away tracker, which will just be a simple state on the user's JavaScript window that sets a timeout that gets canceled when the user types anything into the chat window (even if they don't hit **Send**). The following is a very simple state diagram of how that might look:

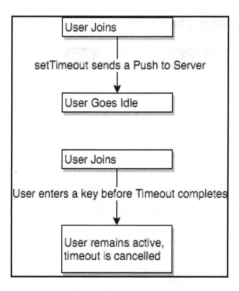

Updating our chat UI

We'll want to start off by modifying the UI to allow for the display of users and write in a couple of examples of what different join, leave, or status change messages might look like. We'll make a couple of assumptions in doing this, and this is the kind of thing where if you were building this as a fully-fledged startup or anything like that, you'd likely want to clean up the design and UI of all of this. That's okay, though—we're interested in quick results! Besides, after we launch and get our 10 million dollar valuation, then we can go back and hire a designer to make everything look beautiful!

The few assumptions that we're going to be making throughout this process are as follows:

- Users will have three statuses: active, idle, and leaving
- Users will be displayed on the user list if they're active or idle
- If users leave, we'll display a notification in the chat window that they left
- If users join, we'll display a notification in the chat window that they joined
- If users go idle, we'll display a notification in the chat window that they are now idle
- Status change messages will not be recorded by the server
- If a user is idle, their username will be grayed out
- Status change messages will be grayed out

The end result will look something like the following:

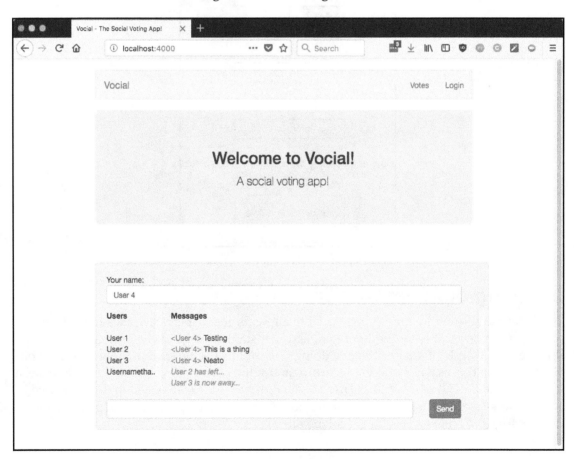

Nothing too complicated here. We'll need to refactor our chat window a little bit to use a few different CSS classes and fix up a few little implementation details with the chat window. Open up `lib/vocial_web/templates/shared/_chat.html.eex` and we'll start stepping through the changes line by line:

```
<div class="chat-window container well" id="enable-chat-channel" data-
chatroom="<%= @chatroom %>">
```

We don't need the original spacer at the top (since that is a problem that we can and should solve via CSS), and the first `div` on the page will remain otherwise unchanged. We will need to change our username input, however, since we need it to store its own class. We're also going to use Bootstrap's grid to space things out a little more. One of the things we're going to need here is a button that tells our application when it is safe to attempt to connect to the socket and display the chat window:

```
<div class="row">
  <div class="col-sm-2">
    <h4>Name:</h4>
  </div>
  <div class="col-sm-8 name-input">
    <input type="text" class="form-control author-input"
placeholder="Name" />
  </div>
  <div class="col-sm-2">
    <button class="btn btn-primary join-chat">Join</button>
  </div>
</div>
```

Next, we need to wrap the chat display in a row, since we're going to offset it a little bit to display our list of users. In addition, we're going to give it a class to denote that it's part of the main chat user interface. Finally, we're going to add a special utility class that we'll expand on a little bit later called `hidden`. Essentially, we want anything that is marked as hidden to—you guessed it—be hidden by default! Let's start off by entering the first part of our UI:

```
<div class="row chat-ui hidden">
```

Now it's time to write up the mockup for our user list. This is actually a pretty straightforward thing that we're building, so there's not a ton of UI work that we need to do for all of this. It is just going to be another unstyled list. We're going to include an example of an idle user as well, so that we can get a feel for what things might look like:

```
<div class="col-sm-2 user-list">
  <strong>Users</strong>
  <ul class="username-list list-unstyled">
    <li>User 1</li>
    <li>User 2</li>
    <li>User 3</li>
    <li class="idle">User 4</li>
    <li>Usernametha...</li>
  </ul>
</div>
```

Since we've created our list of users and given it a size of two columns, we'll need to adjust our chat display to only be 10 columns instead of the full 12. We'll also want to include a couple of examples of users either leaving or changing status, so we'll just include a few mock status messages at the end of our message list for now:

```
<div class="col-md-10 chat-display">
  <strong>Messages</strong>
  <ul class="list-unstyled chat-messages">
    <%= for message <- @messages do %>
      <li><span class="author">&lt;<%= message.author %>&gt;</span> <span
class="message"><%= message.message %></span>
    <% end %>
    <li class="status">User 2 has left...</li>
    <li class="status">User 3 is now away...</li>
  </ul>
</div>
```

Of course, we'll need to close out the row `div` that we opened up:

```
</div>
```

Finally, we have the code for our chat input and the closing of our wrapper chat-window `div`:

```
<div class="row chat-ui hidden">
  <div class="col-md-10">
    <input type="text" class="form-control chat-input"/>
  </div>
  <div class="col-md-2">
    <button class="btn btn-primary chat-send">Send</button>
  </div>
```

```
      </div>
    </div>
```

We'll also need to add some CSS to style our chat window appropriately. Open up
`assets/css/app.css`; the contents should currently be as follows:

```
/* This file is for your main application css. */
span.help-block {
  color: #f00;
}
.user-list {
  overflow-y: scroll;
  overflow-x: hidden;
  max-height: 500px;
}
.chat-window {
  min-height: 200px;
  margin-top: 20px;
}
.chat-display {
  overflow-y: scroll;
  max-height: 500px;
}
.user-list .idle {
  color: #888;
}
.chat-display .author {
  color: #f00;
}
.name-input {
  margin-bottom: 10px;
}
.chat-display .status {
  color: #888;
  font-style: italic;
}
.hidden {
  display: none !important;
}
```

This should give us all of the baseline stylings that we need to make this at least somewhat presentable. It's ultimately okay if it's not the most amazing thing in the world in terms of its aesthetics. That's the easiest thing to fix up later. When we open up our page, before doing anything else, we should see a screen that looks similar to the following screenshot. Note the lack of message and user list display; we'll work on what we need to do to display those later!

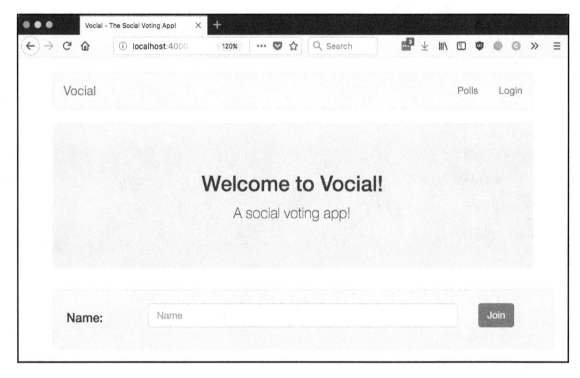

Let's move on to actually coding this thing!

Elixir implementation

We have our UI all setup and ready to go, so now we actually need to step through and start building this thing. We need to start off by telling Phoenix that we need to implement a Presence module that it can use to build things out. We'll need to create the Presence module ourselves, so we'll create a new file at `lib/vocial_web/channels/presence.ex`.

Any Presence module that we want to build will need to utilize the supplied Phoenix Presence module and describe how to actually interact with your application as a whole, including specifying what the OTP application is and which pubsub server the server and client should be using to communicate. We'll start off our Presence module by creating the file mentioned previously and giving it the following contents:

```
defmodule VocialWeb.Presence do
  use Phoenix.Presence,
    otp_app: :vocial,
    pubsub_server: Vocial.PubSub
end
```

From there, we'll go through the following steps:

1. We'll need to update the list of applications running for us in `lib/vocial/application.ex`. In the list of children in the `start/2` function, add the following line:

    ```
    supervisor(VocialWeb.Presence, [])
    ```

2. Similar to how we have to write views for our controller actions that are essentially dummy tasks, we're going to be doing roughly the same thing here. The bulk of our logic is going to go into our `chat_channel.ex` file in the same directory. In fact, let's open that up now and start making modifications to it to support the new Presence functionality we'll need to make this work. We'll start off by adding a line that adds our Phoenix module alias to this file:

    ```
    alias VocialWeb.Presence
    ```

3. We'll need to modify our two `join` functions. For Presence to work appropriately, we need to start recording the usernames (Presence won't work without a key to know how to map a state change back to a user), so we'll start by modifying the function signature:

    ```
    def join("chat:" <> _poll_id, payload, socket) do
    ```

4. We'll make sure that the socket is tracking the username that should be getting sent up as part of the payload.

    ```
    socket = assign(socket, :username, payload["username"])
    ```

5. We'll also need to send a special message to the chat channel that will be responsible for updating and dealing with the current state of active and connected users for every person that joins the channel. We'll accomplish this via a call of send, which will send a message to the current process (through the process mailbox, a topic we'll be exploring in much greater detail in Chapter 10, *Working with Elixir's Concurrency Model*). The code for this is pretty simple:

```
send(self(), :after_join)
```

6. Then we'll just close out the function in the same way that we have done previously:

```
  {:ok, socket}
end
```

We can ignore our handle_in function call dealing with new messages since nothing will be changing there. We're going to want to write a few new functions to handle broadcast messages for when a user goes idle or when a user is active again. We'll start with our user_idle message since that is the easiest logic to handle:

```
def handle_in("user_idle", %{"username" => username}, socket) do
  push socket, "presence_diff", Presence.list(socket)
  {:ok, _} = Presence.update(socket, username, %{
    status: "idle"
  })
  {:noreply, socket}
end
```

We'll want to be able to use the username as part of the payload to identify which user went idle; otherwise, this is a normal handle_in function. We'll want to push the fact that there is a change back out to the socket using the presence_diff message. The payload that we'll send will be the list of all the users and their current states. Then, we're going to go through and update the user's presence for the user that went idle. We'll use a status key that will denote if the user is active or idle. This will be the simplest implementation for us to track!

Dealing with when a user is active is quite a bit more complicated. We don't care if the user is being recorded as active if the user is active anyway! We should only really be tracking this when the user is active and was previously not active. Let's take a look at the full function for dealing with active users and we'll go through it step by step:

```
def handle_in("user_active", %{"username" => username}, socket) do
  presence = Presence.list(socket)
  [meta | _] = presence[username].metas
  if meta.status == "idle" do
    push socket, "presence_diff", Presence.list(socket)
    {:ok, _} = Presence.update(socket, username, %{
      online_at: inspect(System.system_time(:seconds)),
      status: "active"
    })
  end
  {:noreply, socket}
end
```

We start off with the same function signature that we were already working with, except this time we're watching for `user_active` messages with a username payload instead of `user_idle`. Next, we went to the current Presence state, which should be represented as a list of the users currently being tracked through Presence. This will return us a map in which each user's username is the key. Fetching that information will then return us an array of their state, referred to as their `metas`. The `metas` fetch a key value for the current state, a key value for the previous state, and then the actual information that we set as part of the `Presence.update` or `Presence.track` calls. In our case, we're working with a simple string of information that represents a user's status: currently either `"active"` or `"idle"`. We only care about the 0th element in the list (the head of the array) since that represents their current state.

We fetch the head off the list using pattern matching against the meta-list on that user. From there, we check to see if that user is currently idle. If they are, that means that they were idle and are now active again, so we'll want to update that user's status and push that back out to the socket. We also record the timestamp at which the user is online since this means they're back!

Finally, we have to write a `handle_info` function to deal with the message getting into our process's inbox. It takes two arguments, the first of which is just a pattern match against an atom and the second of which is the socket:

```
def handle_info(:after_join, socket) do
  push socket, "presence_state", Presence.list(socket)
  {:ok, _} = Presence.track(socket, socket.assigns.username, %{
    online_at: inspect(System.system_time(:seconds)),
    status: "active"
  })
  {:noreply, socket}
end
```

This is otherwise identical; we push out the current state of Presence back out to the socket, then we begin tracking the new user by their username (which we set in the socket assigns way back in our `join` call). This data includes an `online_at` timestamp and a marking that their current status is active. Finally, we pass a socket back out with no reply to the originator.

That's all of the code that we need to write to support our usage of Phoenix Presence for our application! Now we need to move on to the client side of our Presence code, which is arguably some of the most complicated JavaScript code that we'll need to write as part of our implementation.

JavaScript implementation

One of the first things that we'll want to do is install jQuery for us to use as part of the JavaScript code we'll need to write for Presence. We'll be doing a good amount of DOM manipulation, and that's the kind of thing that is complicated to do without something like jQuery behind it. To install a new library, we'll need to open up a terminal to our project root, and then move into the `assets/` directory. From there, run the following command:

```
$ npm install --save jquery
```

That will install jQuery for us and let us start using that as a part of our code. Next, we're going to hop over to `assets/js/chat.js` and start heavily modifying the code to start using and tracking Presence as part of our application.

First, we'll need to change our import statements at the top, since we'll need both Phoenix's Presence client code and the $ symbol to use for jQuery:

```
// Import Phoenix's Socket Library
import { Socket, Presence } from "phoenix";

import $ from "jquery";
```

Since we have jQuery available to us as part of our project, we should refactor some of our original functions to take advantage of this and clean up our code just a little bit. We don't have to do anything with the pushMessage function we've already written, but we can clean up onJoin:

```
// When we join the channel, do this
const onJoin = (res, channel) => {
  $(".chat-send").on("click", event => {
    event.preventDefault();
    const message = $(".chat-input").val();
    const author = $(".author-input").val();
    pushMessage(channel, author, message);
    $(".chat-input").val("");
  });
  console.log("Joined channel:", res);
};
```

Instead of making a bunch of querySelector and querySelectorAll elements, and then iterating through each to add event listeners manually, we can just use the on() helper supplied by jQuery. We can also directly select and get/set the values for each of the form inputs, so this helps clean up the code significantly!

Our addMessage function can also be cleaned up a little in the course of all of this!

```
// Add a message to the list of chat messages
const addMessage = (author, message) => {
  const chatLog = $(".chat-messages").append(
    `<li>
      <span class="author">&lt;${author}&gt;</span>
      <span class="message">${message}</span>
    </li>`
  );
};
```

We can use the `.append` call with backticks to give us a cleaner string-interpolated depiction of the new DOM elements we're adding as new chat messages are sent and received! We are now ready to start implementing the actual Presence JavaScript code itself!

We'll begin by storing a default state of Presence, which should just be an empty object. We'll also store the timer that we'll use to track when the user goes idle (or when it doesn't), and we'll store a constant representing what the idle timeout should be (arbitrarily, we'll set it to 30 seconds):

```
// Presence Functions

// Presence default state
let presences = {};

// The timer we'll use to check the user's idle status
let idleTimeout = null;

// How long we'll wait for the user to be marked as idle
const TIMEOUT = 30 * 1000; // 30 seconds
```

We'll also want an easy way to show/hide the chat UI, so we'll write a few quick utility functions for that:

```
// Provide a way to hide the current chat UI
const hideChatUI = () => {
  $("div.chat-ui").addClass("hidden");
};

// And a way to show the chat UI
const showChatUI = () => {
  $("div.chat-ui").removeClass("hidden");
};
```

Next, we'll need to change how we load and connect to the socket, since we're not just going to join and connect by default. We want to wait until the button is clicked to join the socket, but we also need to have a way of telling the JavaScript code how to join the channel and socket:

```
// Load the chat, display the UI, connect to the socket
const loadChat = socket => {
  // Set a handler that when the join-chat button is clicked, we verify
  that the username is not empty, and then show the UI and connect to the
  socket
  $(".join-chat").on("click", () => {
    const username = $(".author-input").val();
    if (username.length <= 0) {
```

```
      return;
    }
    showChatUI();
    connect(socket, username);
  });
};
```

We can now start diving into the code that is actually specific to Presence! We'll start with a handy little helper function that will give us the user's current status given an array of meta information:

```
// Given a metas array for a user, return their current status
const getStatus = metas => metas.length > 0 && metas[0]["status"];
```

So we can call `getStatus(metas)`, and if there is at least one meta in that array, we'll pull the `status` flag out of it! Our next function deals specifically with the data returned from our Phoenix server. This will be the function for syncing up the list of users to the current list of users returned from Presence:

```
// Sync up the list of users to the current Presence State
const syncUserList = presences => {
  $(".username-list").empty();
  Presence.list(presences, (username, { metas }) => {
    const status = getStatus(metas);
    $(".username-list").append(`<li class="${status}">${username}</li>`);
  });
};
```

So, given a list of presences, we'll clear out the entire user list (much easier than trying to diff against a bunch of DOM elements). Then, we'll view the list of all presence information and, for each, determine the status of the user and then add that list item to the overall list of users! Next, if a user starts typing again, we want to reset the current idle timer. We want to avoid marking the user as active and sending this information to the server when we don't need to, so we'll include the option to skip the initial active push to the server:

```
// Reset the timer when an interaction occurs
const resetTimer = (channel, username, skipPush = false) => {
  if (!skipPush) {
    channel.push("user_active", { username });
  }
  clearTimeout(idleTimeout);
  idleTimeout = setTimeout(() => {
    channel.push("user_idle", { username });
  }, TIMEOUT);
};
```

We'll also want a way to add messages to the chat window that say things such as *someone is away* or *someone is active again,* so we'll add a helper for adding status messages:

```
// Add a new status message to the chat display
const addStatusMessage = (username, status) => {
  $(".chat-messages").append(
    `<li class="status">${username} is ${status}...</li>`
  );
};
```

Next, we'll write a function to handle what happens when we get a `presence_diff` message from the server. We'll get a `diff` in the format of joins and leaves. Joins are any new status changes, whereas leaves are any old status changes, or people that have left and thus have an entry in the leaves, but not in the joins:

```
// When Phoenix reports a change in Presence status, determine the
differences
// and report the changes to the user
const handlePresenceDiff = diff => {
  // Separate out the response from the server into joins and leaves
  const { joins, leaves } = diff;
  if (!joins && !leaves) {
    // Throw out the diff if we're missing both joins and leaves!
    return;
  }
  // Next, based on the diff, get the new state of the presences variable
  presences = Presence.syncDiff(presences, diff);
  // Sync up the user list to the new state
  syncUserList(presences);
  // For all new statuses, add status messages to the chat log.
  Object.keys(joins).forEach(username => {
    const metas = joins[username]["metas"];
    const status = getStatus(metas);
    addStatusMessage(username, status);
  });
  // Finally, display messages for each person that leaves the chat too!
  Object.keys(leaves).forEach(username => {
    if (Object.keys(joins).indexOf(username) !== -1) {
      return;
    }
    addStatusMessage(username, "gone");
  });
};
```

We'll also need a (thankfully) much shorter function to handle the initial `presence_state` message from the server:

```
// When Phoenix reports the initial state of Presence status, sync up the
list of users
const handlePresenceState = state => {
  presences = Presence.syncState(presences, state);
  syncUserList(presences);
};
```

You'll also need to modify the `pushMessage` function to also call out to `resetTimer`; otherwise, the user will never be able to go active again:

```
// Push a new message to the server
const pushMessage = (channel, author, message) => {
  resetTimer(channel, author);
  channel
    .push('new_message', { author, message })
    .receive('ok', res => console.log('Message sent!'))
    .receive('error', res => console.log('Failed to send message:', res));
};
```

Finally, down in our `connect()` function, we'll want to add a couple of lines to handle the `presence_state` and `presence_diff` messages from the server, as well as start the idle timer. We'll start by changing the `connect()` function's signature to take in two arguments instead of just one:

```
const connect = (socket, username) => {
```

We'll need to change the `socket.channel` call to also pass in the username as part of the payload:

```
const channel = socket.channel('chat:' + chatroom, { username });
```

Then we'll add the new events and timer at the bottom:

```
    channel.on("presence_state", handlePresenceState);
    channel.on("presence_diff", handlePresenceDiff);

    resetTimer(channel, username, true);
```

We refactored the way we set up the initial connection, so we'll need to change our export at the bottom to expose the new `loadChat(...)` function:

```
// Finally, export the socket to be imported in app.js
export default { loadChat };
```

We'll also need to modify the bottom of app.js for all of the `LiveChat`-specific code:

```
// Import the Chat Socket code to enable chat
import LiveChat from './chat';
LiveChat.loadChat(socket);
```

That's it! We should now have a fully-working chat system that appropriately records the users' states without having to write a bunch of complicated CRDT logic to handle it ourselves! The end result should be a chat system that looks something like the following:

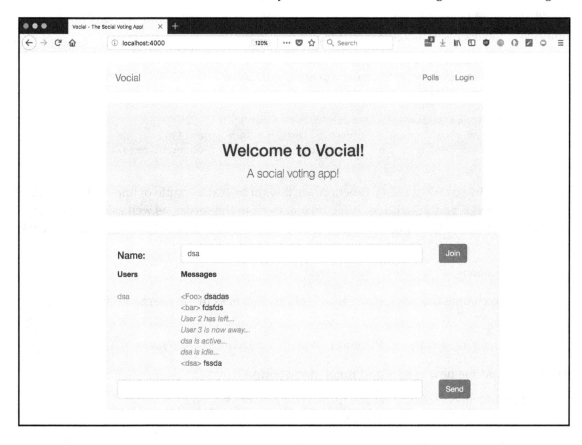

Given that we actually have a pretty decently full-featured chat application going on here, this is a pretty small amount of code and work overall! Presence is a really awesome feature. You get for free something that would be a pretty monumental and herculean effort to set up yourself! Since we are experts in Presence nowadays, it's time for us to move into another advanced Elixir feature that's rooted even deeper in the history of Elixir: ETS.

Using ETS

ETS is an in-memory storage system that stores pretty simple sets of information. ETS is insanely fast; imagine if every web application you ever wrote had something like Redis attached to it by default, for free, without any additional infrastructure! It's a very cool, but also often underutilized, feature that is rooted even deeper than Elixir itself. It can be used to store any data structure that Elixir and Erlang themselves can store. ETS works on the principle that each process itself can own up to 1,400 tables of information. However, this also means that all of the information in those tables goes away when that process goes away!

Why use ETS?

This, of course, begs the question of why we should use it if it can go away that quickly. The first reason is that it's fast! It's also very simple to implement and requires no additional infrastructure, which means if you need to cache temporary information, it's actually very simple to do so. Since this information is so incredibly temporary, however, we need to make sure that we don't store any information in it that is actually necessary to the function of our application, or at the very least information that is not also available somewhere in a more permanent form of storage.

That is honestly where ETS shines: using it for temporary caches of information that you have elsewhere, but maybe more expensive to fetch from. When you can do that, you can speed up your application pretty dramatically! That being said, this is also a cache, which means it carries with it a certain set of caveats:

- This data is transient—don't expect it to always be there
- Don't cache prematurely! This is provided as an example of how to cache via ETS, but that doesn't mean you should rush to do this!
- The data stored in ETS goes away when the process that created it goes away!

Experimenting with ETS in an IEx window

Let's begin by messing around a little bit with ETS inside of an IEx window. We can go to our application directory and run a new IEx session with `iex -S mix`:

```
$ iex -S mix
Erlang/OTP 20 [erts-9.1.5] [source] [64-bit] [smp:4:4] [ds:4:4:10] [async-
threads:10] [hipe] [kernel-poll:false] [dtrace]

Interactive Elixir (1.5.2) - press Ctrl+C to exit (type h() ENTER for help)
iex(1)>
```

We'll start this off simply enough. We'll create a table that can store a little bit of information in a set. Again, we can store any data structure that Elixir can understand, so this can actually be really handy! We can create a table with the `:ets.new(table_name, [:type])` command . This will return a table reference to us that we can use elsewhere to insert and fetch information. We can then use that same variable to insert data via `:ets.insert(table_reference, {:key, value})`. If we want to look up information, we can do it via the `:ets.lookup(table_reference, :key)` call! Let's see what this looks like in action:

```
iex(1)> table = :ets.new(:test_data, [:set])
#Reference<0.1390637660.3349544961.156677>
iex(2)> :ets.insert(table, {:key1, "value"})
true
iex(3)> :ets.lookup(table, :key1)
[key1: "value"]
iex(4)> :ets.insert(table, {:key2, %{username: "test"}})
true
iex(5)> :ets.lookup(table, :key2)
[key2: %{username: "test"}]
```

Let's explore some more of the options available to us to create tables. The first option that we saw is the type of the table, which can be any of the following:

- `:set`: This is the default type for tables; you are allowed to enter in one value per key, and all keys must be unique (much like a regular set)
- `:ordered_set`: Similar to `:set`, but the set itself is ordered by the keys
- `:bag`: You can have multiple items per key, but the items have to be unique (per key)
- `:duplicate_bag`: Similar to a regular bag, but the items do not have to be unique anymore

You can also control who else (that is, which another process) is allowed to access the information in these tables. The three options available to you are as follows:

- `public`: Any process can read or write information from these
- `protected`: The default choice; only writable by the owner process, but any process can read information
- `private`: Read and write are limited solely to the process that owns the tables

Finally, there's another option available to us called `:named_table`. This allows us to reference a table by using an atom instead of relying on storing a variable that we can use to grab the information. Let's take a look at using that to access ETS tables instead of holding on to a variable:

```
iex(6)> :ets.new(:test, [:bag, :named_table])
:test
iex(7)> :ets.insert(:test, {:user1, "Brandon"})
true
iex(8)> :ets.insert(:test, {:user1, "Richey"})
true
iex(9)> :ets.lookup(:test, :user1)
[user1: "Brandon", user1: "Richey"]
```

Here, you can see that we used the `:bag` table type, so we can store lots of different information in our bag, but no duplicates. If we try, nothing will happen:

```
iex(10)> :ets.insert(:test, {:user1, "Brandon"})
true
iex(11)> :ets.lookup(:test, :user1)
[user1: "Brandon", user1: "Richey"]
```

No error message, but nothing else either, so that's fine! Another thing we can do is delete entries in the tables using `:ets.delete(table, key)`:

```
iex(12)> :ets.delete(:test, :user1)
true
```

It's worth noting that a lot of the returns for functionality coming out of ETS tend to be a little stranger and more difficult to deal with than the standard returns that you see in a lot of standard Elixir libraries. There's less reliance on the `{:ok, result}` pattern, so it can admittedly sometimes be a little frustrating when trying to grab data.

Creating our Presence ETS table and GenServer

Let's start off with an ETS table that can store information about the various changes in Presence over the course of its lifetime. We'll need to wrap this inside of a GenServer, since we need a process that will live with our server rather than with each request (remember that ETS tables only live as long as their owner). Don't worry too much about the GenServer conventions at play here; we're going to dive into all of this in much, much more detail over the next chapter!

The important logic here will be all of the ETS-specific code! Let's start by creating a new file under `lib/vocial` called `chat_cache.ex`.

Setting up the GenServer

We'll begin by using the GenServer macro and setting up some configuration variables on the module:

```
defmodule Vocial.ChatCache do
  use GenServer

  @table :presence
  @key :statuses
```

Next, we'll need to implement two GenServer-specific functions, `start_link/0` and `init/1`. `start_link/0` is responsible for starting up the GenServer that we're building (and we'll also be giving it a name to make it easier to reference later):

```
def start_link do
  GenServer.start_link(__MODULE__, [], name: __MODULE__)
end
```

Then we'll need to implement `init/1`, which will just create our ETS table that we'll use for storing all of our Presence data over time:

```
def init(_) do
  table = :ets.new(@table, [:bag])
  {:ok, %{table: table}}
end
```

We're creating an ETS table of the `:bag` type so we can store a list of data instead of just single entries. Then, we just return a tuple of `{:ok, %{table: table}}`, which tells Elixir that we want the initial state of our GenServer to be a map that stores the ETS table that we've created! We could also use a named table here instead of an unnamed regular table (where we cannot look up the function and need to store the reference to the table's PID instead), but it's a good practice to get used to storing the concept of the state and learning how to pass it along over the course of the functions called in your GenServer.

Creating the public interface for the GenServer

Next, we'll need two utility functions to abstract away some of the GenServer logic. We'll start by creating the function responsible for writing new data to our ETS Presence cache:

```
def write(topic, username, status) do
  row = %{
    topic: topic,
    username: username,
    status: status,
    timestamp: DateTime.utc_now()
  }
  GenServer.cast(__MODULE__, {:write, row})
end
```

This function isn't doing nearly as much as it looks like it's doing: It takes in the topic, the user's username, and the status we want to record, builds a map from these, which includes the current timestamp, and then uses a `GenServer message` cast (an asynchronous call) to itself to write that row. We'll deal with this message later!

`lookup` is an even easier function! This time, we'll just want synchronous `GenServer` message call to get the data back out:

```
def lookup do
  GenServer.call(__MODULE__, {:lookup})
end
```

Implementing the cast and call logic

Now we'll need to write our handlers for the `cast` (async) and `call` (sync) functions. We'll start with our cast, which inserts the data into the ETS table. `handle_cast/2` is a function you need to implement for your `GenServer` to be able to deal with message casts, which takes in two arguments: the message you're sending (whatever data you're sending), and the current state of the `GenServer`, which in our case is going to store the table:

```
def handle_cast({:write, row}, %{table: table}=state) do
  :ets.insert(table, {@key, row})
  {:noreply, state}
end
```

In our `write` function, we sent the cast with a tuple of the message and the data we wanted to write. The message was `:write`, and the data was `row`. We also pattern matched against the `GenServer`'s state to get the table out. `GenServer`'s `handle_cast` calls usually end with a `{:noreply, state}` (remember that a GenServer maintains its state via function calls passing arguments, so this is our method for maintaining state for a GenServer).

Next, we need our lookup `handle_call` function. `handle_call` takes three arguments by default: the data being passed in, the originator process that sent the function, and the state. We don't care about the originator in our case, so we'll just mark that with an underscore for now:

```
def handle_call({:lookup}, _, %{table: table}=state) do
  case :ets.lookup(table, @key) do
    [] -> {:reply, [], state}
    data ->
      results = Enum.map(data, fn {_k, v} -> v end)
      {:reply, results, state}
  end
end
```

We perform our ETS lookup against the table stored in the state. If there's no data or no matching key, we'll get back a blank list, so we pattern against that first in our case statement. Otherwise, that means we have received data back from the server.

The key that we're using to store the data is `:statuses`, which means we'll get a data structure back from the server that looks like the following:

```
[ statuses: %{...}, statuses: %{...}, statuses: %{...}, ... ]
```

To make this data easier for our `lookup` function to deal with, we just enumerate over that data as if it were a list of tuples and match out the value from each of those entries. Finally, we respond back to where our call was sent from using the `{:reply, data, state}` response.

Hooking up the GenServer to our application

This gives us all of the supporting code that we need to be able to work with this, so let's add an entry into our application's list of workers and applications to make sure that our table is created when the application is started and is ready to go! Open up `lib/vocial/application.ex`, and in the `start/2` function, we'll add a new entry to the list of children:

```
# Define workers and child supervisors to be supervised
children = [
  # Start the Ecto repository
  supervisor(Vocial.Repo, []),
  # Start the endpoint when the application starts
  supervisor(VocialWeb.Endpoint, []),
  # Start your own worker by calling: Vocial.Worker.start_link(arg1,
arg2, arg3)
  # worker(Vocial.Worker, [arg1, arg2, arg3]),
  supervisor(VocialWeb.Presence, []),
  # Add support for our new ChatCache GenServer
  worker(Vocial.ChatCache, [])
]
```

If we restart our server now, we'll have a working GenServer up and running and ready to store and retrieve data out of ETS for us!

Storing Presence data in ETS

We should now start writing some data to ETS since we have all of the code and support in place to handle that! We'll also want to add a `ChatCache.write(...)` call in any place that we had any code that dealt with modifying Phoenix Presence data! Open up `lib/vocial_web/channels/chat_channel.ex`, and we'll start by adding a new alias to the top of our module to make accessing our `ChatCache` module a little easier:

```
alias Vocial.ChatCache
```

Next, our first function in our file that deals with Presence is our `handle_in` function for dealing with the `user_idle` status message, so we'll add a single line at the top of the function to handle that:

```
def handle_in("user_idle", %{"username" => username}, socket) do
  ChatCache.write(socket.topic, username, "idle")
  push socket, "presence_diff", Presence.list(socket)
  {:ok, _} = Presence.update(socket, username, %{
    status: "idle"
  })
  {:noreply, socket}
end
```

The format for our calls to write data to ETS consists of three arguments: the chatroom (or channel topic), the username, and their status. Since this is idle, we use `idle` for the status. We are already getting the username, so that's easy for us to handle, and the socket itself stores the topic that we're watching. Easy!

We then have our handler for dealing with `user_active` messages. This one is a little bit trickier since we don't want every trigger to denote that the user is active, just when the user is idle and becomes active again, so we'll throw the line into the `if` statement:

```
def handle_in("user_active", %{"username" => username}, socket) do
  presence = Presence.list(socket)
  [meta | _] = presence[username].metas
  if meta.status == "idle" do
    ChatCache.write(socket.topic, username, "active")
    push socket, "presence_diff", Presence.list(socket)
    {:ok, _} = Presence.update(socket, username, %{
      online_at: inspect(System.system_time(:seconds)),
      status: "active"
    })
  end
  {:noreply, socket}
end
```

Same call as before, except we're using `active` as the state to record. Finally, we need to modify our `handle_info` call for `:after_join` messages:

```
def handle_info(:after_join, socket) do
  ChatCache.write(socket.topic, socket.assigns.username, "active")
  push socket, "presence_state", Presence.list(socket)
  {:ok, _} = Presence.track(socket, socket.assigns.username, %{
    online_at: inspect(System.system_time(:seconds)),
    status: "active"
  })
  {:noreply, socket}
end
```

That's it! We're now properly recording user activity as a part of our Phoenix chat application! To verify that this is all working, we'll implement the final piece of this puzzle: retrieving data out of ETS!

Retrieving Presence data in ETS

The final piece of our puzzle is simple. We're going to do this purely as an exercise in understanding how the data is recorded in ETS. In reality, we'd want to lock this information down a little bit more to something like admins-only access. That's okay, though—the point of this is to learn and get a great handle on how to use this information. To make our lives easier, we'll implement a history action on our page controller and just build a simple list of all of the actions in the history logs:

1. We'll start by adding a new entry into our routes file at `lib/vocial_web/router.ex`. In our main scope, add the following line:

   ```
   get "/history", PageController, :history
   ```

2. In `PageController` (`lib/vocial_web/controllers/page_controller.ex`), we'll alias our `ChatCache` module and add the `history` function:

   ```
   alias Vocial.ChatCache

   def history(conn, _params) do
     render conn, "history.html", logs: ChatCache.lookup()
   end
   ```

3. For the final piece of this implementation puzzle, we'll create a new template under `lib/vocial_web/templates/page/history.html.eex`:

```
<div class="container">
  <h2>Chat History</h2>
  <ul class="list-unstyled">
    <%= for log <- @logs do %>
      <li>
        <em>#<%= log.topic %></em>
        &lt;<%= log.username %>&gt;
        <strong><%= log.status %></strong>
        at <%= log.timestamp %>
      </li>
    <% end %>
  </ul>
</div>
```

And that's it! If we head on over to our chat application, we can do a bunch of joins and idles and then open up our **Chat History** page, located at `/history`. We should see something like the following representing the user's status changing from **active** to **idle** periodically:

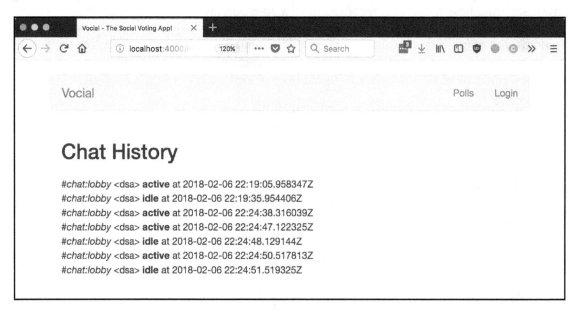

Summary

We've dealt with some very advanced pieces of functionality in the Phoenix development world, but also the kinds of functionality that really help us advance our application to the next level! Presence is an incredibly complicated concept powering an incredibly simple implementation and interface, and having that kind of weight behind our application means nothing but good things!

In addition, we spent a good chunk of time messing around with ETS and storing different types of data into different types of tables. We had to write our first GenServer to power everything behind the scenes, so that's something that we'll want to dive headfirst into over the next few chapters as well! ETS really requires a good GenServer to power it, since the lifetime of ETS tables is restricted almost solely to the lifetime of the process that created it, and when you have short-lived, temporary processes all over the place, it's important to abstract away that lifecycle into something that can afford to be a little more long-lived.

Also, it's worth reiterating that ETS is a cache, and that means that its use carries with it all of the advantages and caveats that come with any other forms of cache. Caching prematurely can cause complexity issues in your application later on down the line, so any time you're considering using ETS, you should think about it, and make sure you're not caching things to solve problems you don't have yet!

10
Working with Elixir's Concurrency Model

When you start working with your Phoenix application, you'll inevitably start marveling about how fast your application runs, how stable it is, and how well it handles an absolute ton of incoming connections. The great thing about working with Phoenix is that all of this is just something you get for free! No drama, no confusion, your application just scales for free to an amazing level. This is a wonderful thing to think about when you're architecting a site. Typically, there is a dance that happens somewhere along the implementation of your site where you need to start thinking and planning for how you're going to scale your app for 10x/100x/1000x growth in concurrent users.

If you're hosting your application in the cloud, you might just scale by throwing a ton of money at the problem until you can start making tweaks to your application. This is a high-up-front-cost method of scaling and tends to be a cost that is difficult to reduce in the lifetime of your application. In my personal experience, what usually happens is your patterns for scale, growth, and optimization tend to run very close to parallel with each other, so as you optimize your application you may end up just keeping the same number of cloud resources enlisted; you're just able to support more concurrent users as you make those optimizations. That makes these early decisions around scaling critical, and they affect your budget very early instead of allowing your application to scale organically with more users, more business, and more money!

If you're using a dedicated data center, you may have a much tougher life in this regard. You may have limited resources available to you for scaling and you may not be able to adjust them quickly, meaning your decisions need to be based around significant amounts of capacity planning and significant engineering, design, scale, and architecture plans and designs. You might be slower to react and acquiring new hardware might be locked behind multiple levels of approvals, purchase orders, installation, configuration, and so on. That being said, you might also be able to scale up long-term at a cheaper cost.

Elixir and Phoenix thrive on concurrency and parallelism! This means your capacity planning sessions and architecture designs can be significantly simpler and cheaper, both in the long-term and the short-term! If you're running on cloud services for running your application, you'll find Phoenix runs great on nearly all of the choices out there! You can reduce your needs for scaling and avoid running up a giant monthly cloud services bill! If you're running on a dedicated data center, you'll find your purchase orders for new hardware are greatly decreased (well, at least for your application's side of things)!

Generally speaking, you won't find yourself having to obsess about the BEAM/OTP concurrency model and how to optimize your application at insane levels. Of course, we would be remiss in our duties if we didn't spend a bit of time discussing what is going on behind the scenes and how to make the model work for your application! Maybe you find yourself wanting to write a library that makes your application easier to use and more reliable or maybe you just want to understand what is going on in all parts of your application! In this chapter, we'll spend the entire time really diving into and understanding the entire model for concurrency and parallelism behind Elixir. We'll explore:

- The difference between concurrency and parallelism
- What is OTP
- What is Elixir's model for concurrency and parallelism
    - Understanding supervisors
    - Understanding applications
    - Understanding workers
- Implementing each model:
    - Starting simple with task/await
    - Actors and agents
    - GenServers
    - GenStage

Introduction to Elixir's concurrency model

We talked a bit at the start about the concurrency and parallelism model at play in your standard Phoenix application but not really a lot about what it actually means. Sure, we get great scaling and performance right out of the box, but what is really going on? Phoenix is built to heavily lean on the BEAM VM's constructs, which allow multiple processes to be spun up at a moment's notice and discarded almost as quickly! The ability to spin up new processes with very low initial cost and toss them away without any repercussions to the rest of the system is a large part of what enables us to create such projects and architectures in Phoenix!

In Elixir, we typically try to divide up related bits of work into their own processes, much in the same way that in an object-oriented language you may try to separate functionality by object. We then rely on those processes to be able to communicate with each other and send/receive messages from each other, allowing pieces of state to be passed back and forth in a safe and immutable-friendly way! This also eliminates standard concerns around data access and data controls; side effects are isolated into their own processes to provide a safe way to get data in and out.

We also abstract away the strategies for dealing with process failure or destruction; the mantra of *let it die* becomes a way of life. We can quickly restart new processes since state should largely be isolated and can be tracked since there is no real *internal* or object state to worry about; a crash may destroy a process, but it can quickly be restarted through process handling through something like a *one for one* strategy.

 Elixir process handling strategies are broken out into multiple types; *one for one* is the most common strategy for dealing with processes and the one typically used in Phoenix. This just means that when a process is killed, it will be replaced with an identical process.

The difference between concurrency and parallelism

A quick note about the terms used as part of this chapter. There is a fundamental difference between concurrency and parallelism, and it is worth understanding what that difference is as we begin implementing some of the more complicated parts of our application. Concurrency refers to the ability to handle multiple tasks that are starting, stopping, and completing in some sort of overlapping manner. If we were to look at that like a list of tasks and results, it might look something like this:

In process 1

1. Task A starts
2. Task A begins computation
3. Task B starts
4. Task A completes
5. Task B begins computation
6. Task B completes

Run process 1

Parallelism, in the meantime, is more focused on tasks starting, stopping, and completing completely parallel to each other. This is a model that best takes advantage of a multiple core machine, and this is what Elixir is particularly great at:

In process 1

1. Task A starts
2. Task A begins computation
3. Task A completes

In process 2

1. Task B starts
2. Task B begins computation
3. Task B completes

Run process 1 and process 2 at the same time

In parallelism, processes 1 and 2 are able to execute at the same time and also operate completely independent of each other. This means that the steps involved in the concurrency example might end up delaying each other in some way (for example, if Task B is ready to begin right as Task A completes and is spitting back output).

We will talk in much greater detail about this, but the model behind Elixir makes it so that parallelism is the default state every time and is handled extremely efficiently. Also, you may notice that the definitions for concurrency and parallelism overlap each other a little bit; something that is concurrent is not necessarily parallel, but something that is parallel is necessarily concurrent!

In the Elixir world, if you're doing a lot of research, you may find that the two terms are used basically interchangeably, and even in this book we tend to stick to describing this problem as Elixir's concurrency model as opposed to Elixir's parallelism model. Part of this is related to community conventions and part of it is due to how these approaches and problems are described in a lot of other technologies. Ultimately, the important thing to note is that when we're talking about concurrency in Elixir, we're talking about its ability to do many things, all at the same time, and in an incredibly safe way that doesn't require us to implement crazy mutexes and semaphores and all kinds of other major headaches and nightmares!

Talking about OTP/understanding the model

For us to really begin implementing anything of note that fully utilizes the model behind Elixir, we need to understand a little more about what the model actually looks like. The main idea behind how Elixir is able to function so well with is that BEAM, the underlying Erlang VM that powers everything Elixir, runs on a model called the Actor model. Actors are simply just single-threaded processes that can send and receive messages, either from themselves or from other processes. They end up getting their own isolated memory, which also means that it is safe to let processes run and die independently without worrying about how it's going to start affecting other processes in your system all time. Each Actor runs independently, but there has to be some way for actors to be able to communicate with each other, right? They also need to be able to do so in a way that doesn't break this model for safety and parallelism, so instead it relies on something that anyone coming from a heavy object-oriented background will be comfortable with and appreciate: message passing!

Actors (or processes) each have their own independent mailbox that they can receive messages into, and any actor can send a message to another process, so long as it has a way to know where to send that message to. You can think of these as analogs of physical mail; you can send and receive mail from anyone, assuming they have your address. You can even send and receive messages from yourself if you're an enterprising individual, but expect weird looks from your local mail worker! You can think of the model as working something like this:

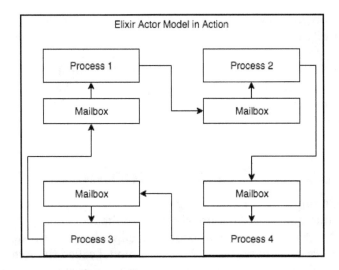

In the preceding example, **processes 1**, **processes 2**, **processes 3**, and **processes 4** all have their own respective messages that they can receive mail into. Each process sends its own message, however; there is no outbound mailbox. Each process can receive messages independently from any process and send to any process assuming they know its process ID (we'll talk more about this later).

Working with an example

Let's build out some code to see how this works and build upon it a little bit more. We'll start by building our first little process shell:

```
process = fn ->
  receive do
    {:msg, greeting} -> IO.puts("I received: #{greeting}")
  end
end
```

Now, if you just copy and paste that into an IEx window and try to run it (through `process.()`), you'll end up getting a process that just kind of hangs forever; something like this:

```
iex(1)> process.()
# ...a blank line followed by a whole lot of nothing
```

You'll end up having to interrupt it and kill the IEx session entirely. The reason for that is the line in there towards the top, the `receive do ... end` block. This will completely lock a process until it receives an actionable message. This part is especially important; notice that inside of the `receive` statement, we look for a message in the format of `{:msg, something}`; if we can't find that, the process will continue to wait. You can prevent this behavior by adding in a timeout, as well, using the `after` keyword:

```
process = fn ->
  receive do
    {:msg, greeting} -> IO.puts("I received: #{greeting}")
  after
    1_000 -> IO.puts("I give up")
  end
end
```

Now, if we call `process.()` inside of an IEx window, we'll see (after 1 second) the `"I give up"` message:

```
iex(2)> process.()
# ... One second has passed
I give up
:ok
```

How do we test this properly inside of our IEx window, then? We'll revert back to the version of the code that does not use the `after` statement, and this time, instead of running `process.()` directly, we'll use Elixir's `spawn/1` function, which itself takes in a function and executes it as a new process. Let's take a look at the help documentation for `spawn/1` to get a better sense of what it is and how it factors in:

```
iex(3) h spawn

def spawn(fun)

Spawns the given function and returns its PID.

# ...
```

Essentially, this is a helper macro that turns that function's execution into its own separate process and returns back the process ID for the new spawned process. Let's try using this inside of IEx. Open up a new IEx window, copy and paste this code into the window, and then we'll start messing around with things.

The code to copy in:

```
process = fn ->
  receive do
    {:msg, greeting} -> IO.puts("I received: #{greeting}")
  end
end
```

One thing that's worth mentioning is that IEx itself is considered a process as well! We can use another function in Elixir to get process information out from inside the process itself, via the `self/0` function. `self/0` will tell us information about the process, but we can expand this a little bit more by calling the `Process.info/1` function, which takes in as its single argument the process you want to inspect in greater detail. Let's look at an example of calling `self/0`, and then put it all together:

```
iex(8)> self()
#PID<0.84.0>
iex(4)> Process.info(self())
[current_function: {Process, :info, 1}, initial_call: {:proc_lib, :init_p,
5},
 status: :running, message_queue_len: 0, messages: [], links: [],
 dictionary: ["$ancestors": [#PID<0.59.0>],
   iex_history: %IEx.History.State{queue: {[{3, 'self()\n', #PID<0.84.0>},
     {2, 'pid = spawn(process)\n', #PID<0.91.0>}],
     [{1,
       'process = fn ->\n receive do\n {:msg, greeting} -> IO.puts("I
received: \#{greeting}")\n end\nend\n',
       #Function<20.99386804/0 in :erl_eval.expr/5>}]}, size: 3, start: 1},
   "$initial_call": {IEx.Evaluator, :init, 4}], trap_exit: false,
 error_handler: :error_handler, priority: :normal, group_leader:
#PID<0.53.0>,
 total_heap_size: 8370, heap_size: 4185, stack_size: 43, reductions: 13650,
 garbage_collection: [max_heap_size: %{error_logger: true, kill: true,
size: 0},
   min_bin_vheap_size: 46422, min_heap_size: 233, fullsweep_after: 65535,
   minor_gcs: 8], suspending: []]
```

Let's spawn a process and capture the resulting `pid`. We can then use `Process.info/1` to inspect the end result of our spawned process:

```
iex(5)> pid = spawn(process)
#PID<0.93.0>
iex(6)> Process.info(pid)
[current_function: {:prim_eval, :receive, 2},
 initial_call: {:erlang, :apply, 2}, status: :waiting, message_queue_len:
0,
 messages: [], links: [], dictionary: [], trap_exit: false,
 error_handler: :error_handler, priority: :normal, group_leader:
#PID<0.53.0>,
 total_heap_size: 610, heap_size: 610, stack_size: 9, reductions: 4001,
 garbage_collection: [max_heap_size: %{error_logger: true, kill: true,
size: 0},
  min_bin_vheap_size: 46422, min_heap_size: 233, fullsweep_after: 65535,
 minor_gcs: 0], suspending: []]
```

This is a pretty neat way to inspect processes that are in the middle of some form of the execution context and can give you a lot of information about what the process is, what it is doing, what state it is in, and so on. Looking at the preceding process information for our spawned process, we can see that it is in a status of *waiting* and has not received any messages. Before we start messing around further with this, though, we can also modify our process function to take in this information and display it out to the user as well; we'll need this for later iterations of this code:

```
process = fn ->
  receive do
    {:msg, greeting} ->
      me = self() |> inspect()
      IO.puts("#{me} => I received: #{greeting}")
  end
end
```

We're using `inspect/1` to create a string representation of the process information returned from calling `self/0`. This will allow us to see real differentiation if we end up spawning four of the same processes (which we will since we're trying to somewhat recreate the diagram from earlier). Finally, let's send a message to a spawned process:

```
iex(2)> pid = spawn(process)
#PID<0.93.0>
iex(3)> send(pid, {:msg, "Hello World"})
#PID<0.93.0> => I received: Hello World
{:msg, "Hello World"}
```

Awesome! We used the `send/2` function to send a message from the current process to a different process. `send` takes two arguments: the destination process ID and then the message itself. We want to send something that will match our receive block's pattern match statement, so we use a tuple of `{:msg, "String"}`. These match, so we get the message about the process ID saying `"I received: ..."`! Let's call `Process.info/1` on the process now and see what it looks like:

```
iex(4)> Process.info(pid)
nil
```

Uh oh! Where did our process go? Well, when the receive block finishes, the process is able to complete execution of its function, at which point it summarily closes! This means whatever state it is in when it completes is its final state; the process is done executing the function, so the whole thing ceases to be a process anymore. Let's also look at what happens when we try to send a message to the process that doesn't match anything in our receive block:

```
iex(2)> pid = spawn(process)
#PID<0.141.0>
iex(3)> send(pid, {:test, "Uh oh"})
{:test, "Uh oh"}
iex(4)> Process.info(pid)
[current_function: {:prim_eval, :receive, 2},
 initial_call: {:erlang, :apply, 2}, status: :waiting, message_queue_len:
1,
 messages: [test: "Uh oh"], links: [], dictionary: [], trap_exit: false,
 error_handler: :error_handler, priority: :normal, group_leader:
#PID<0.53.0>,
 total_heap_size: 4185, heap_size: 4185, stack_size: 9, reductions: 4015,
 garbage_collection: [max_heap_size: %{error_logger: true, kill: true,
size: 0},
  min_bin_vheap_size: 46422, min_heap_size: 233, fullsweep_after: 65535,
  minor_gcs: 0], suspending: []]
```

Notice here, after `status: :waiting`, we also see `message_queue_len: 1`! The process is still waiting, since it has not received a message it can process, but it cannot do anything with the message in the queue, so it will just continue to wait forever! We can fix this by implementing a looping function, but to do this we'll need to rewrite our code a bit for this to work. The first thing is that we need to refactor our code to be a module instead:

```
defmodule Msg do
  def loop do
    receive do
      {:msg, greeting} ->
        me = self() |> inspect()
```

```
        IO.puts("#{me} => I received: #{greeting}")
        loop()
    end
  end
end
```

If we copy and paste this code into our IEx window instead, we'll need to change how we call it via spawn, otherwise, it will halt our terminal again:

```
iex(2)> pid = spawn(fn -> Msg.loop() end)
```

And now, we can continue to call this as many times as we can:

```
iex(3)> send(pid, {:msg, "Hello World"})
#PID<0.144.0> => I received: Hello World
{:msg, "Hello World"}
iex(4)> send(pid, {:msg, "Hello World"})
#PID<0.144.0> => I received: Hello World
{:msg, "Hello World"}
iex(5)> Process.info(pid)
[current_function: {Msg, :loop, 0}, initial_call: {:erlang, :apply, 2},
 status: :waiting, message_queue_len: 0, messages: [], links: [],
 dictionary: [], trap_exit: false, error_handler: :error_handler,
 priority: :normal, group_leader: #PID<0.53.0>, total_heap_size: 752,
 heap_size: 376, stack_size: 3, reductions: 704,
 garbage_collection: [max_heap_size: %{error_logger: true, kill: true,
size: 0},
  min_bin_vheap_size: 46422, min_heap_size: 233, fullsweep_after: 65535,
  minor_gcs: 3], suspending: []]
```

If we send an unhandled message, we won't get any response as well:

```
iex(6)> send(pid, {:foo, "Hello World"})
{:foo, "Hello World"}
iex(7)> Process.info(pid)
[current_function: {Msg, :loop, 0}, initial_call: {:erlang, :apply, 2},
 status: :waiting, message_queue_len: 1, messages: [foo: "Hello World"],
 links: [], dictionary: [], trap_exit: false, error_handler:
:error_handler,
 priority: :normal, group_leader: #PID<0.53.0>, total_heap_size: 752,
 heap_size: 376, stack_size: 3, reductions: 904,
 garbage_collection: [max_heap_size: %{error_logger: true, kill: true,
size: 0},
  min_bin_vheap_size: 46422, min_heap_size: 233, fullsweep_after: 65535,
  minor_gcs: 4], suspending: []]
```

You can see in the messages key that the message will stay in that queue until the process itself shuts down (the lifespan of any message is until it is either processed or the process itself that owns that message is shut down).

This is a pretty common pattern (we'll see this frequently when dealing with Elixir GenServers, for example) where a function inside of a module recursively calls itself to turn itself into a loop. This process of using tail recursion is fundamental to Elixir applications, but if you're coming from another language, you may be wondering something along the lines of *Well, if I have an infinitely recursive function, isn't that just going to result in a stack overflow error?* Thankfully no, thanks to something called `Tail Call Optimization` in Elixir!

 Tail Call Optimization is where, because a function calls itself with different arguments, there's no need for the VM to keep adding new function calls onto the stack since the function itself is the same each time. Instead, it just returns back to the start of the same function, taking in account the new arguments but otherwise working with an identical function!

This allows a process to remain alive as it's necessary to receive and process messages and react to state changes, as well. We can finally implement a close approximation of the original diagram we drew:

```
iex(8)> pid1 = spawn(&(Msg.loop/0))
#PID<0.166.0>
iex(9)> pid2 = spawn(&(Msg.loop/0))
#PID<0.169.0>
iex(10)> pid3 = spawn(&(Msg.loop/0))
#PID<0.171.0>
iex(11)> pid4 = spawn(&(Msg.loop/0))
#PID<0.173.0>
```

Now we have four processes running that are able to handle spinning off each message. This is kind of messy, though, so let's add an `init/0` function that handles the spawn logic for us so we're not having to write that line of code over and over:

```
defmodule Msg do
  def init do
    spawn(&loop/0)
  end
  def loop do
    receive do
      {:msg, greeting} ->
        me = self() |> inspect()
        IO.puts("#{me} => I received: #{greeting}")
        loop()
    end
  end
end
```

Our implementation in IEx is much simpler now! Copy and paste that code preceding to declare the module and now we can test this out like so:

```
iex(2)> pid1 = Msg.init()
#PID<0.104.0>
iex(3)> pid2 = Msg.init()
#PID<0.106.0>
iex(4)> pid3 = Msg.init()
#PID<0.108.0>
iex(5)> pid4 = Msg.init()
#PID<0.110.0>
```

We can now send messages to each of these functions completely independently of each other:

```
iex(6)> send(pid1, {:msg, "Hello World"})
#PID<0.104.0> => I received: Hello World
{:msg, "Hello World"}
iex(7)> send(pid4, {:msg, "Hello World"})
#PID<0.110.0> => I received: Hello World
{:msg, "Hello World"}
```

Since we added the debug information about the current process to the receive message handler, we can see exactly which process is getting the information we're sending via the `send/2` function call! The overall diagram now looks something like this:

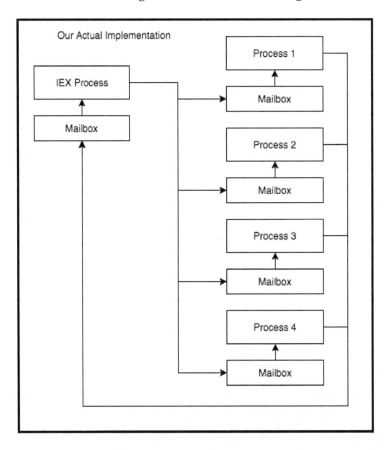

That's a pretty comprehensive example of the Actor model in Elixir/BEAM, so now we're ready to move on to diving even deeper into some of the definitions and explanations for a lot of what is going on here. We'll also continue to step through more complicated implementations that are more common in advanced Elixir applications, such as GenServer!

Diving deeper into the concurrency model

We've implemented a cool little bit of concurrency in the preceding example, but without a lot of the details about what we were doing behind the scenes. Let's spend a little bit of time really exploring and explaining each portion of the Elixir concurrency model. We'll define each term used and showcase a little bit of how to use each of them, in the hopes that this chapter becomes a handy little quick guide for how to implement different concurrency constructs in Elixir!

The model - what is a process?

A process is how Elixir is able to do so much all at the same time with no ill effects. As mentioned previously, processes are independent threads of work that BEAM manages. They're small, efficient, and memory-isolated. In fact, they're so small and efficient that even on relatively low-powered machines, you can safely run millions of processes all at the same time. They do not require copies of the entire language and ecosystem behind them for each one you spawn, so they end up being a currency that you can spend freely instead of having to ration them out and make trade-offs to implement and use them!

 Erlang processes and Unix processes are different concepts. A Unix process is much more like a running program (picture the whole thing), whereas an Erlang process is an actor responsible for sending/receiving messages. This model allows each process to be incredibly small and avoids needing to create new Erlang/Elixir processes for every single process we create!

When a process in Elixir is created, it also creates something called a *Process Identifier* (commonly referred to as a PID). Going back to our earlier example, the PID is the mail address to be able to send and receive messages from; it's also what Elixir uses to track the state and know when to restart or create a new one. The mailbox itself is something that BEAM provides for every process that it spawns over the course of time; they're the only reliable way for processes to communicate with each other in a side-effect-free way. We spent a little bit of time working with this structure when we implemented our Actors in IEx; we sent messages to each process by referencing its PID, and that gave us information about where we could send those messages to!

Working from the preceding example in our IEx terminal, when we call `Msg.init()`, what we're doing there is creating a process, so we're in a good place to really understand how processes work and what they are, but what about some of the other common implementations and terms that we'll see in the Elixir concurrent programming world?

The model - what if our process crashes?

We originally used `spawn/1` to spawn our process, but there is a better way to do it overall. The trouble with just using spawn is that if something happens to that for any reason, there's not really a good way to track it! Let's test this out by replacing our behavior in the `receive` to instead just raise an exception:

```
process = fn ->
  receive do
    _ -> raise "Oh no!"
  end
end
```

Now in IEx, if we spawn this and attempt to do anything with it by sending it a message, we'll get an error message about a raised exception inside of a process:

```
iex(2)> pid = spawn(process)
#PID<0.151.0>
iex(3)> send(pid, :test)
:test

18:08:16.958 [error] Process #PID<0.151.0> raised an exception
** (RuntimeError) Oh no!
    (stdlib) erl_eval.erl:668: :erl_eval.do_apply/6
```

But the calling process itself will remain fine. What if there was something mission critical in that process and we want to make sure that it either occurs successfully or terminates up the tree of processes that called it? We can instead use `spawn_link` for that, which spawns a process and then links it to the caller instead. If we do this from IEx, we expect IEx to also shut down when that exception is raised:

```
iex(4)> pid = spawn_link(process)
#PID<0.154.0>
iex(5)> send(pid, :test)
** (EXIT from #PID<0.84.0>) evaluator process exited with reason: an
exception was raised:
    ** (RuntimeError) Oh no!
        (stdlib) erl_eval.erl:668: :erl_eval.do_apply/6

18:10:04.065 [error] Process #PID<0.154.0> raised an exception
** (RuntimeError) Oh no!
    (stdlib) erl_eval.erl:668: :erl_eval.do_apply/6

Interactive Elixir (1.5.2) - press Ctrl+C to exit (type h() ENTER for help)
iex(1)>
```

Your IEx session will restart itself when this happens, you don't have to manually restart it!

That last bit is where IEx will restart itself if the process shuts down for any reason! Since we used `spawn_link` in our function that deliberately raised an exception, the process halted and took its parent process down with it! Ultimately, `spawn_link` is useful when you want to make sure that one process is aware of any sort of state changes in another process. If we wanted to instead trap the exception and exit from the block, we can call the following line before sending a message or implementing a receive block:

```
iex(3)> Process.flag(:trap_exit, true)
false
iex(4)> send(pid, :test)

18:23:26.023 [error] Process #PID<0.169.0> raised an exception
** (RuntimeError) Oh no!
    (stdlib) erl_eval.erl:668: :erl_eval.do_apply/6
:test
```

Finally, we can use the helper function `flush/0` to flush all of the messages out of the current process' mailbox:

```
iex(5)> flush()
{:EXIT, #PID<0.169.0>,
 {%RuntimeError{message: "Oh no!"},
  [{:erl_eval, :do_apply, 6, [file: 'erl_eval.erl', line: 668]}]}}
:ok
```

And there we are! We can see the exit message from our linked process that raised the exception, but this one did not kill our IEx process when it was called! `flush()` is a neat little function but one that is pretty specific to our IEx terminal:

```
iex(6)> h flush

def flush()

Flushes all messages sent to the shell and prints them out.
```

The model - what is a task?

Instead of directly calling the spawn and spawn_link functions, we have another option available to us as a part of the standard Elixir BEAM functions. We can instead use the functionality around calling tasks for our one-off processes instead of trying to call kernel-level functions to spawn things asynchronously. The task module in Elixir provides a couple of handy functions (and we'll dive into some of this functionality in greater detail when we start talking about supervisors as well), but we'll primarily be concerned with Task.async/1, Task.async/3, and Task.await/1.

Task.async/1 is very simple; it just takes in the function that you want it to run and executes it as if it were being executed via spawn. Let's look at a simple example that might represent some sort of longer execution:

```
iex(1)> Task.async fn -> Process.sleep(10000) && IO.puts("Hello World") end
%Task{owner: #PID<0.156.0>, pid: #PID<0.208.0>,
 ref: #Reference<0.3904235318.354418689.253235>}
iex(2)> "Now I will say..."
"Now I will say..."
Hello World
```

Here we create a new async task that will sleep for five seconds and then print "Hello World" out to the console. We can do other things while the task is executing and while we're waiting for a response. But what if I want the return value from a task? If I just do something like this:

```
iex(3)> result = Task.async(fn -> Process.sleep(10000) && (1 + 1) end)
%Task{owner: #PID<0.156.0>, pid: #PID<0.214.0>,
 ref: #Reference<0.3904235318.354418689.253348>}
iex(4)> result
%Task{owner: #PID<0.156.0>, pid: #PID<0.214.0>,
 ref: #Reference<0.3904235318.354418689.253348>}
```

That doesn't end up being very useful information to me at all! I want the result of that calculation, not information about the process that is being spawned and run. The good news is that we also have a function available to us that, given the information about a task, returns the information about what the end result of that function's execution is. Task.await takes in the task information as the only argument and then sits around and waits for the task to complete and store some information in it. What it is specifically waiting for is a DOWN message from the process, returning the final result of its function call as the return value.

It's important to note that this will block the current process necessarily. We can test this out by calling `await` after an async function with a `Process.sleep/1` call in it:

```
iex(1)> task = Task.async(fn -> Process.sleep(10000) && "Hello World" end)
%Task{owner: #PID<0.84.0>, pid: #PID<0.86.0>,
 ref: #Reference<0.4250898013.228065281.96611>}
iex(2)> Task.await(task)
"Hello World"
```

If we don't call `Task.await` on this task and just let it execute normally, we won't actually see the result of the function. Since we're in IEx, however, we get access to `flush/0`, which prints out all remaining messages in the mailbox. Let's see if we can use that information to pull the data out of task, since, remember that `Task.async` will link the current process to the asynchronous task:

```
iex(1)> Task.async(fn -> "Hello World" end)
%Task{owner: #PID<0.84.0>, pid: #PID<0.86.0>,
 ref: #Reference<0.2291378818.765460481.62316>}
iex(2)> flush()
{#Reference<0.2291378818.765460481.62316>, "Hello World"}
{:DOWN, #Reference<0.2291378818.765460481.62316>, :process, #PID<0.86.0>,
 :normal}
:ok
```

And there it is! We can see the result of our async function call from calling flush and printing out everything in our current process mailbox! `Task.await` is essentially just a wrapper around a receive block. This receive block is pattern matching each message it receives to find the reference (the `:ref` key in the result of the call to `Task.async`)! If you're concerned about the function taking too long to execute and don't want to be blocking your current process for too long, `Task.await` optionally takes in a timeout argument as the second argument. That allows you to say that if the execution and getting the result ends up taking too long, that you want to stop blocking the current process and raise it as an error instead. Let's try it:

```
iex(1)> task = Task.async(fn -> Process.sleep(999999) && "Hello World" end)
%Task{owner: #PID<0.84.0>, pid: #PID<0.86.0>,
 ref: #Reference<0.3203418017.1579941889.71050>}
iex(2)> Task.await(task, 1000)
** (exit) exited in: Task.await(%Task{owner: #PID<0.84.0>, pid:
#PID<0.86.0>, ref: #Reference<0.3203418017.1579941889.71050>}, 1000)
    ** (EXIT) time out
    (elixir) lib/task.ex:491: Task.await/2
```

Generally speaking, if you need simple one-off processes to do something and then not worry about it beyond that point, tasks are the way to go instead of calling `spawn` or `spawn_link` directly. If you end up needing something a bit more in-depth or something that should be more closely monitored, you might instead reach for something a little more robust like a GenServer or a similar concurrency construct.

The model - what is an agent?

Agents are another common implementation in the Elixir concurrency world, especially around the context of state management. agents are pretty much designed for that sole purpose: they exist to be simple wrappers around state! They're incredibly simple to work with. Let's open an IEx window (if we don't already have one open) and begin implementing a simple agent:

```
iex(1)> {:ok, agent} = Agent.start_link(fn -> %{} end)
{:ok, #PID<0.174.0>}
```

We start off by initializing our agent with `Agent.start_link/1`. This function takes in a single argument, which is the function that returns the agent's initial state. In the preceding case we're starting off with a completely blank map:

```
iex(2)> Agent.update(agent, fn state -> Map.put(state, :foo, "bar") end)
:ok
```

Then we can update the Agent's internal state with a call to the `update` function in the `Agent` module. This takes in a reference to our Agent PID (this ends up being a very similar implementation to the process spawning and returning a reference to the process via the process ID or PID). In the preceding case we're just blindly setting a `:foo` key to the value of *bar*, but we could be doing anything here, really. Note that the function called in update must supply the previous agent state as the single argument. Let's prove that out and try calling that without passing an argument to the update inner function:

```
Agent.update(agent, fn -> %{} end)
** (FunctionClauseError) no function clause matching in Agent.update/3

    The following arguments were given to Agent.update/3:

        # 1
        #PID<0.174.0>

        # 2
        #Function<20.99386804/0 in :erl_eval.expr/5>

        # 3
```

```
    5000

Attempted function clauses (showing 1 out of 1):

    def update(agent, fun, timeout) when is_function(fun, 1)

(elixir) lib/agent.ex:361: Agent.update/3
```

As expected, this blows up on us with an error about attempting function clauses on the update. It will check to see if the supplied function is a function with an arity of 1! That's the `when is_function(fun, 1)` guard clause being referenced!

Next, we have a means of getting the data back out of the Agent's internal state:

```
iex(3)> Agent.get(agent, fn state -> state end)
%{foo: "bar"}
```

The `Agent.get/2` call takes in the Agent reference (the PID of the agent) and the function, again, must take in a single argument and return out something back to the caller. In our case, we're just arbitrarily returning the whole thing!

Finally, we stop the Agent, since we're done setting and getting data out of our Agent process:

```
iex(4)> Agent.stop(agent)
:ok
```

We'll close down the process since we have no more we want to do here.

The model - what is a supervisor?

A Supervisor is in charge of managing the various child processes that may be a part of your larger Application. The Supervisor is where the list of children is managed, as well as the strategies for dealing with what happens when one of those child processes decides to break down during the course of your application getting work done.

The Supervisor typically provides an initialization function and can perform a few other random functions, such as being able to look up a child process and report back on data about that child process when necessary. If we were to think about Elixir projects in terms of a hierarchy, it would look something like this:

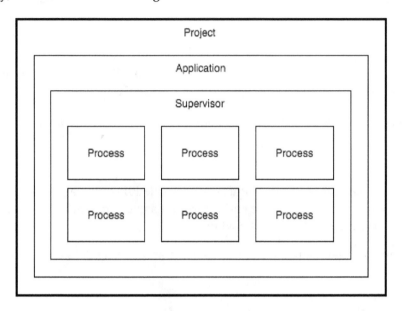

We'll talk a little bit more about the remaining parts of this puzzle (**Application** and **Project**) now! But what if we wanted to actually write our own Supervisor, since we're in the process of stepping through all of this currently? The good news is that is actually a really simple thing to do, again, thanks to Elixir's built-in helpers and macros! Our Supervisor will need something to actually supervise, so we're going to create a dummy `logger` function to start:

```
defmodule MyLogger do
  use GenServer

  def start_link do
    GenServer.start_link(__MODULE__, [], name: __MODULE__)
  end

  def init(_) do
    {:ok, []}
  end

  def log(message) do
    GenServer.cast(__MODULE__, {:add_log, message})
```

```
  end

  def print do
    GenServer.call(__MODULE__, :get_log)
  end

  def explode do
    GenServer.cast(__MODULE__, :explode)
  end

  def handle_cast({:add_log, message}, state) do
    new_state = state ++ [message]
    {:noreply, new_state}
  end

  def handle_call(:get_log, _from, state) do
    Enum.each(state, &(IO.puts(&1)))
    {:reply, :ok, state}
  end

  def handle_cast(:explode, _state) do
    raise "I am undone"
  end
end
```

We create a basic GenServer and expose a few simple public functions to the user, `log/1`, `print/0`, and `explode/0`. `log/1` adds a new message onto the logs being stored as part of the GenServer's state. `print/0` prints out all of the logs currently stored, and `explode/0` exists solely to raise an exception and terminate the process. We'll explore writing a GenServer in much greater detail later, but those are really the important pieces. Copy and paste this code into your IEx window to create our instance of `MyLogger`. Let's try working with this a little bit before we implement our server:

```
iex(2)> MyLogger.start_link
{:ok, #PID<0.135.0>}
```

We start off by starting up our GenServer via the `MyLogger.start_link/0` function. Next, we'll add two strings to the logs through calls to the `MyLogger.log/1` function call:

```
iex(3)> MyLogger.log("hello")
:ok
iex(4)> MyLogger.log("world")
:ok
```

Finally, we'll print out the current state of the logs via the `MyLogger.print/0` function:

```
iex(5)> MyLogger.print()
hello
world
:ok
```

Here is where it gets interesting: let's call `MyLogger.explode/0` and then try to print out our log:

```
iex(6)> MyLogger.explode()
** (EXIT from #PID<0.130.0>) evaluator process exited with reason: an
exception was raised:
    ** (RuntimeError) I am undone
        iex:35: MyLogger.handle_cast/2
        (stdlib) gen_server.erl:616: :gen_server.try_dispatch/4
        (stdlib) gen_server.erl:686: :gen_server.handle_msg/6
        (stdlib) proc_lib.erl:247: :proc_lib.init_p_do_apply/3

Interactive Elixir (1.5.1) - press Ctrl+C to exit (type h() ENTER for help)

11:44:14.543 [error] GenServer MyLogger terminating
** (RuntimeError) I am undone
    iex:35: MyLogger.handle_cast/2
    (stdlib) gen_server.erl:616: :gen_server.try_dispatch/4
    (stdlib) gen_server.erl:686: :gen_server.handle_msg/6
    (stdlib) proc_lib.erl:247: :proc_lib.init_p_do_apply/3
Last message: {:"$gen_cast", :explode}
State: ["hello", "world"]
```

And then we'll try to call `MyLogger.print/0`:

```
iex(1)> MyLogger.print()
** (exit) exited in: GenServer.call(MyLogger, :get_log, 5000)
    ** (EXIT) no process: the process is not alive or there's no process
currently associated with the given name, possibly because its application
isn't started
    (elixir) lib/gen_server.ex:766: GenServer.call/3
```

Well, this is no good! Our process died from a raised exception, it took out our parent, and then it failed to return back to us! If we had a Supervisor in place, however, we could gracefully handle the crash and restart the process without a significant lift! Let's write up a MyLogSupervisor module that will act as the main Supervisor for our logger! We'll start off by using the Supervisor macros:

```
defmodule MyLoggerSupervisor do
  use Supervisor
end
```

Next we'll need a method for starting up the supervisor itself, so we'll create a `start_link/0` function that we can use to start up the Supervisor:

```
def start_link do
  Supervisor.start_link(__MODULE__, [], name: __MODULE__)
end
```

There's not really much new here except we're calling `start_link` from the Supervisor module instead of GenServer! Finally, we create our init function, which is responsible for setting up and linking the children to the main process:

```
def init(_opts) do
  children = [
    worker(MyLogger, [])
  ]
  supervise(children, strategy: :one_for_one)
end
```

We tell Elixir that we're going to supervise these child processes and use a restart strategy for them called `:one_for_one`, which means when a process crashes, we will restart a new process in its place. Let's step back through what we used to test our GenServer, except our `start_link` call is going to start with MyLoggerSupervisor instead of MyLogger:

```
iex(6)> MyLoggerSupervisor.start_link()
{:ok, #PID<0.148.0>}
iex(7)> MyLogger.log("hello")
:ok
iex(8)> MyLogger.log("world")
:ok
iex(9)> MyLogger.print()
hello
world
:ok
```

Everything is working as expected! Note that we didn't need to call `start_link` on MyLogger now, because our Supervisor is already in charge of making sure the process is up and running for us. Now, let's call the explode function and observe the results:

```
iex(10)> MyLogger.explode()
:ok
13:45:05.291 [error] GenServer MyLogger terminating
** (RuntimeError) I am undone
    iex:35: MyLogger.handle_cast/2
    (stdlib) gen_server.erl:616: :gen_server.try_dispatch/4
    (stdlib) gen_server.erl:686: :gen_server.handle_msg/6
    (stdlib) proc_lib.erl:247: :proc_lib.init_p_do_apply/3
Last message: {:"$gen_cast", :explode}
State: ["hello", "world"]
```

Okay, it explodes like we're expecting it too, sure. But what about the process itself? If we call print, is it going to give up because the process doesn't exist anymore?:

```
iex(11)> MyLogger.print()
:ok
```

Hooray! The process is back (albeit without its state) and calls are being made without errors anymore! This is the beauty of Supervisors in Elixir; they give your code a significant amount of robustness that allows your processes to just die with no ill effects on the rest of the system!

The model - what is an application?

The Application is the single largest unit of work in your Elixir application. A Project is what organizes your Application (or Applications) into a single functioning piece of work, but ultimately the Application is the largest unit that ends up getting built, assembled, and run for the BEAM VM.

You can think of the Application as the big piece that gets compiled and executed by the BEAM VM and the Project as everything that glues that Application together! Applications can also work in conjunction with other Applications, so they can also be isolated nicely by their functionality. This is a pretty common model for libraries that get pulled into Phoenix applications (Poison and HTTPoison being immediate examples of that)!

Using GenServers

Let's go back and look at the GenServer we implemented for the previous chapter:

```
defmodule Vocial.ChatCache do
  use GenServer
```

We started off by declaring that we wanted to use the GenServer macros as a starting point for building off our ChatCache Genserver. `GenServer.start_link/0` should take in the module that is running as the server, the arguments to starting the link, and the list of options for starting the server itself. In the following case, we're going to register this running process as a name, using its module name as the name:

```
def start_link do
  GenServer.start_link(__MODULE__, [], name: __MODULE__)
end
```

Next, we need to declare an entry point for our GenServer. This is how our Supervisor knows how to start up our GenServer and keep it running in its list of child processes. We'll now need to implement an init function; this is what sets up the initial state of our GenServer. init functions should always take in an argument, which is typically a keyword list of options that is passed in. It must return out a standard Elixir tuple of `{:ok, initial_state}`, which in our case is a map indicating what the ETS table is:

```
def init(_) do
  table = :ets.new(@table, [:bag])
  {:ok, %{table: table}}
end
```

The next function that we have as part of our implementation is not a GenServer-specific function, but it does contain a GenServer module call, so we're going to include that as an opportunity to talk about the way GenServers handle incoming messages and how they respond to them:

```
def write(topic, username, status) do
  row = %{
    topic: topic,
    username: username,
    status: status,
    timestamp: DateTime.utc_now()
  }
  GenServer.cast(__MODULE__, {:write, row})
end
```

The `GenServer.cast/2` is the important bit. Cast tells Elixir that we want to send a message to a running GenServer but that we don't necessarily care about the results, so it will make the message being sent be handled entirely asynchronously. That makes this a non-blocking call and our execution can continue on its merry way! The downside to this call, however, is that it makes it very difficult to track down if something goes wrong and you don't really have a good way to react to things when they do fail. In the preceding case, we're specifically sending a tuple with our message in the form of an atom as the first value in the tuple and the row we want to write as the second value in the tuple.

The counter to cast, as you'll see below, is `GenServer.call/2`. Whenever we use call, we're using the same structure of arguments as we use in cast, but the major difference is that call is synchronous, so that means our process is going to sit and wait until it gets a response from the server. We might be okay with that, because it's probably information that is critical in some way to the execution of our current process:

```
def lookup do
  GenServer.call(__MODULE__, {:lookup})
end
```

Next, we move on to some more GenServer-specific code. Any time we want our server to actually be able to handle and respond to casts and calls from other processes, we need to write the code that is responsible for handling those. The macros we're expecting to implement out as functions are `handle_cast(message, state)` and `handle_call(message, state)`. To get a better feel for how these are expected to be structured, let's take a look at a sample implementation of a `handle_cast/2` function:

```
def handle_cast({:write, row}, %{table: table}=state) do
  :ets.insert(table, {@key, row})
  {:noreply, state}
end
```

In the case preceding, we're pattern matching for a tuple where `:write` is the type of message and we're pulling the `row` of data out. We end up returning a `{:noreply, new_state}` tuple, which tells Elixir we're not expecting anyone to be waiting on a reply from this call and to supply the new state that we're in now. We're also pattern matching against the GenServer's state, but this can seem a little magical if you're not expecting how the GenServer macros play out.

GenServers are ultimately stateful, but remember that we're not working with an object-oriented language, so we don't really have an internal state that is clearly represented by object properties and a collection of data in memory. Instead, GenServers rely on maintaining their state by adding state as one of the arguments to each of its handling functions. You could think of the way it's working behind the scenes as looking maybe something a little bit like this:

```
def loop(state) do
  receive do
    {:cast, message} ->
      {:noreply, new_state} = handle_cast(message, state)
      loop(new_state)
    {:call, message} ->
      # ... etc
  end
end
```

Notice how the message is handled via receive, a new state is returned from the result of the call to `handle_cast/2`, and then we pass that new state back into the loop function to wait for our next message. Through this recursive call behavior, we are able to make our functional construct *stateful* but in a way that properly respects all of the rules that we've seen, such as remaining immutable and not setting object states. Finally, let's look at the implementation for the `handle_call` function:

```
def handle_call({:lookup}, _, %{table: table}=state) do
  case :ets.lookup(table, @key) do
    [] -> {:reply, [], state}
    data ->
      results = Enum.map(data, fn {_k, v} -> v end)
      {:reply, results, state}
  end
end
```

This is largely the same as what you've already seen, except this takes in a second argument before the final state argument. This argument is used to tell Elixir who to send the information back to (it's even called *from* in the standard documentation). We don't actually care who, since we're replying back with the data anyways. The return value from this call should be a `{:reply, response, state}` tuple where response is the data we want to send back as the result of the `GenServer.call` function.

Summary

In this chapter, we spent a lot of time talking in great detail about what's really going on behind the scenes in our Phoenix application. There are a lot of pieces of functionality that we tend to take for granted, even in our relatively simple Phoenix applications! GenServers, Processes, and Supervisors all power significant portions of our Phoenix application that we've written so far.

This is so pervasive that even before we got to this chapter designed around explaining a lot of these core concepts, we ended up having to implement one of the pieces of this puzzle (the ETS cache GenServer), because of how critical it is to the overall implementation and ensuring that we're building our Phoenix application the right way the first time around!

Understanding the concurrency building blocks behind Phoenix applications also goes a long way to give you both an appreciation for how simple and clean Elixir has made things when trying to think and plan around taking full advantage of every single core on your server and how much thought and planning really went into this language! For once, you have a language where the functionality is designed around the idea of concurrency instead of in spite of it!

This will enable you to build better applications that are thoughtful, fast, and most importantly, as scalable as humanly (or perhaps computerly) possible! You will be building your application using your processes as currency for scaling instead of just money or even worse, your sanity!

In the next and final chapters, we'll be diving into the last steps of getting our Phoenix application out into the world. We'll also spend a little bit of time talking about an often-neglected topic in the Phoenix world: how to design and build an API. The good news is that implementing an API is an incredibly simple topic in Phoenix and it works and scales great right out of the box! In fact, Phoenix has become my framework (and Elixir my language) of choice when it comes to implementing a good API in the fastest time. It has yet to fail me and is consistently a joy to work with!

11
Implementing OAuth in Our Application

We now have a working application with a lot of special features and some pretty cool internal tweaks based off the deep down internals of Elixir and Phoenix! We'll want to spend just a little bit of time polishing up our application and turning it into something that we're ready to push to production!

One thing that we don't have currently is a better system for creating an account on our system, so before we start talking about a way to actually ship this out into production, we'll spend a little bit of time shoring up our login system and including support for OAuth flows, such as support for Twitter and Google!

This is a significant part of preparing an application: to go from an idea in your head to something that is a viable platform and product that people actually want to use! The reality is that most people don't want another login for something. The advantage of introducing an OAuth flow into your site is that it allows people to just keep the logins they already have, which is a nice feeling when you don't have to remember yet another login.

In this chapter, we'll spend a good bit of time at the start introducing another library into our application: Ueberauth. This will give us everything we need to be able to implement some OAuth support for a few different providers. We'll also very quickly include guides on setting up those OAuth applications for development so we can verify the results. There is a lot involved, not just in the implementation phase, but also in the configuration phase before you even crack open your code editors, so we'll include a lot of screenshots as references to help you navigate around those screens and get the information you need to be able to set up OAuth properly in your Phoenix application.

By the end of this chapter, we will have covered:

- Final tweaks to our application to make it production ready
- Adding OAuth Account Support for Twitter
    - Registering our application and signing up for OAuth with Twitter
    - Hooking up Ueberauth
- Adding OAuth Account Support for Google
    - Registering our application and signing up for OAuth with Google
    - Hooking up Ueberauth

Solidifying the new user experience

As mentioned previously, we'll want to do a bit more to really make our application production ready. Typically, when people think of something being production ready, they tend to associate that term and idea around hardening the product: making it more secure, making it perform better, cleaning up old spaghetti code, or other types of cleanup and polishing work. That's a very important thing to do as part of getting your application ready to live in a production environment, to be sure, but it's also not the whole thing. We'll start off by cleaning up some more of our application's layout and navigation issues, and then we'll move from there into cleaning up the user signup page (since we'll need to clean it up from our current default and boring design) to allow users to sign up via some OAuth provider.

We'll start off by hopping into our main display on the page and adding a link that will help users find where the user signup page is. If we open up our browser window right now, we'll just see a pretty barebones page and nothing that really helps guide the user.

This is a very confusing first experience for our user. They navigate to our site for the first time and then see... nothing? There's no way to sign up, so everything seems confusing. You can really lose people who visit your site when they see no clear way to sign up for an account or start doing anything, so let's clean up that first experience. Open up `lib/vocial_web/templates/page/index.html.eex` and we'll modify the code inside of the `jumbotron` class to include two new links to get the user moving: a user signup link and a most recent polls link:

```
<div class="jumbotron">
  <h2><%= gettext "Welcome to %{name}!", name: "Vocial" %></h2>
  <p class="lead">A social voting app!</p>
  <p>To create a new account, <%= link "click here", to: user_path(@conn,
:new) %></p>
```

```
    <p>To view the most recent polls, <%= link "click here", to:
poll_path(@conn, :index) %></p>
    </div>

    <%= render(VocialWeb.SharedView, "_chat.html", messages: @messages,
chatroom: "lobby") %>
```

Now, when the user navigates to our site for the first time, they will have a pretty clear call to action for either creating a new account or for viewing some of the polls on the site! All we did is add two new links to the page, but that's already an incredibly different new user experience and one that helps pull the user in a little bit better. Compare our previous, boring page to this:

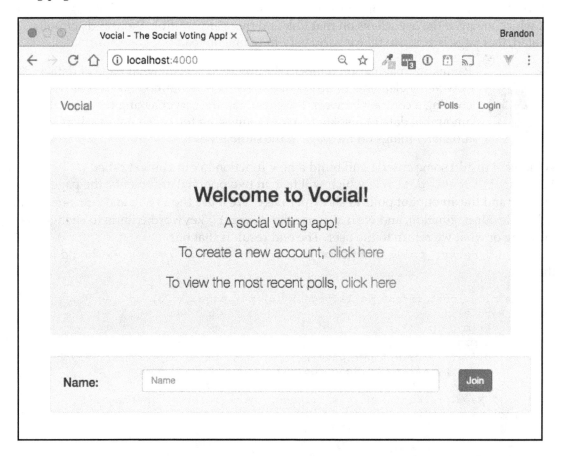

Unfortunately, we still have one more quick tweak to implement, since our *most recent polls* link is actually a little bit dishonest right now. Think back to our polls Controller; the index function actually calls out to the Votes Context and calls the `list_polls/0` function. Let's look at that:

```
def list_polls do
   Repo.all(Poll) |> Repo.preload([:options, :image, :vote_records,
:messages])
  end
```

There are a few minor issues with this in terms of what we'll see in our polls listing. First off, we're not actually sorting by anything here, so we're just relying on the database to return data to us in whatever order the database sends it back. We're also not paginating at all, which means if the user clicks on that link and there are multiple thousands of polls created, that page is going to take a very, very long time to load up!

 Paginating/pagination refers to the ability to specify what page of data and how many elements to display per page; it is a common method of creating a contract between the client and the server asking for a specific amount of data to display to avoid requesting too much data or displaying too many things on the page at the same time.

We'll want to add some criteria and build a new function in our context called `list_most_recent_polls/2`, which will take in two optional arguments: the page number and the amount of polls to show per page. We'll use the `limit` and `offset` criteria to handle our pagination, and we'll also use the `order_by` keyword criteria to change the ordering of what we return to the user. The end result is that our `list_most_recent_polls/2` function in `lib/vocial/votes/votes.ex` should look like this:

```
def list_most_recent_polls(page \\ 0, per_page \\ 25) do
  Repo.all(
    from p in Poll,
    limit: ^per_page,
    offset: ^(page * per_page),
    order_by: [desc: p.inserted_at]
  )
  |> Repo.preload([:options, :image, :vote_records, :messages])
end
```

We'll write up a few quick tests to make sure our function is going to work and returns the results the way that we expect it to. Let's hop over to `test/vocial/votes/votes.exs` and start fixing up our tests! First, we'll quickly need to make sure our `poll_fixture/1` function includes `:messages` as part of the preload statement or else a good number of our tests for reasons totally unrelated to our change:

```
def poll_fixture(attrs \\ %{}) do
  with create_attrs <- Enum.into(attrs, @valid_attrs),
       {:ok, poll} <- Votes.create_poll(create_attrs),
       poll <- Repo.preload(poll, [:options, :vote_records, :image,
:messages])
    do
      poll
    end
end
```

Shoring up our tests

Next, we can move on to actually writing our tests. We'll want to test two things, specifically:

1. When we have multiple polls, we want to return them in the order of most-recently created to least-recently created.
2. When we are including pagination params (`page` and `per_page`), we should get the correct results (also respecting ordering).

We'll start with a test to cover the first scenario, since that should be pretty simple to write:

```
test "list_most_recent_polls/2 returns polls ordered by the most recent
first", %{user: user} do
  poll = poll_fixture(%{user_id: user.id})
  poll2 = poll_fixture(%{user_id: user.id})
  poll3 = poll_fixture(%{user_id: user.id})
  assert Votes.list_most_recent_polls() == [poll3, poll2, poll]
end
```

What we're doing here is creating three polls specifically, and then verifying that when we call our new `list_most_recent_polls` function with no arguments, that we just get back the default page size and first page, and that the results are ordered correctly. The end result should be `poll3`, `poll2`, and then `poll`. Run the test, verify the result, and then we'll move on to our next test, which should be a little bit more complicated:

```
test "list_most_recent_polls/2 returns polls ordered and paged correctly",
%{user: user} do
  _poll = poll_fixture(%{user_id: user.id})
  _poll2 = poll_fixture(%{user_id: user.id})
  poll3 = poll_fixture(%{user_id: user.id})
  _poll4 = poll_fixture(%{user_id: user.id})
  assert Votes.list_most_recent_polls(1, 1) == [poll3]
end
```

This is a little bit stranger. We're creating four polls instead of three, and we're prefixing some of the variables with an underscore! The reason for the underscores is that we don't actually need the variable, but it's still worth us keeping track of which poll is which.

> An underscore prefixing any variable in Elixir means that the variable will not be used later.

We also create four polls instead of three because if we left the number of polls at three, we wouldn't actually be able to tell that our polls were ordered correctly (since `poll2` would be the first offset poll after the first page in either order). This allows us to verify all of the behavior at the same time without making a bunch of extra weird assumptions!

Run the tests for this file, verify that they are green and passing, and we can move on to hooking this up to the controller and templates!:

```
$ mix test test/vocial/votes/votes_test.exs
.............

Finished in 4.2 seconds
13 tests, 0 failures

Randomized with seed 906033
```

Building a good development seeds file

We're confident that our Votes Context can provide us with the data we need in the format and expectations that we need, so now, we should move on to shoring up the implementation and making sure that everything matches as well. One thing that will help our development of this is to build a good seeds file that will allow us to reset our development instance whenever we need to. Let's open up `priv/repo/seeds.exs` and start building out a seeds file so that we can reset whenever we need to without impacting our development flow:

```
alias Vocial.Repo
alias Vocial.Votes
alias Vocial.Votes.Poll
alias Vocial.Votes.Option
alias Vocial.Votes.VoteRecord
alias Vocial.Votes.Image
alias Vocial.Votes.Message
alias Vocial.Accounts
alias Vocial.Accounts.User
```

We just straight up need a bunch of aliases, so we set these up here just in case. Next, we'll want to wipe out our existing data before we move on further, so the next few lines in our `seeds` file is going to be a chunk of `Repo.delete_all/1` calls:

```
Repo.delete_all(Option)
Repo.delete_all(VoteRecord)
Repo.delete_all(Image)
Repo.delete_all(Message)
Repo.delete_all(Poll)
Repo.delete_all(User)
```

We'll also want to create a test user account, since we'll need one anyway to be able to create any sample Polls. We'll want to track whether there are any errors or if the user was created successfully as well:

```
user_attrs = %{ username: "testuser", email: "testuser@test.local", active:
true, password: "test1234", password_confirmation: "test1234" }
user = case Accounts.create_user(user_attrs) do
  {:ok, user} ->
    IO.puts("User created successfully!")
    user
  {:error, changeset} ->
    IO.puts("Failed to create user account!")
    IO.inspect(changeset)
    nil
end
```

Finally, if we have succeeded at everything else, we'll move on to checking for our user and creating a bunch of polls associated with that user's account:

```
if user do
  polls = [
    %{ title: "Test Poll 1", options: ["Choice 1", "Choice 2", "Choice 3"]
},
    %{ title: "Test Poll 2", options: ["Choice 1", "Choice 2", "Choice 3"]
},
    %{ title: "Test Poll 3", options: ["Choice 1", "Choice 2", "Choice 3"]
},
    %{ title: "Test Poll 4", options: ["Choice 1", "Choice 2", "Choice 3"]
},
    %{ title: "Test Poll 5", options: ["Choice 1", "Choice 2", "Choice 3"]
}
  ]
  Enum.each(polls, fn p ->
    case Votes.create_poll_with_options(%{title: p.title, user_id:
user.id}, p.options) do
      {:ok, _poll} ->
        IO.puts("Poll created successfully!")
      {:error, changeset} ->
        IO.puts("Failed to create poll!")
        IO.inspect(changeset)
    end
  end)
end
```

Now, we can run our seeds file against our local development database and verify that we have a nice, fresh set of data to work with:

```
$ mix run priv/repo/seeds.exs
# ...tons of output from deleting/inserting a bunch of data
```

 Remember that this is, by design, a destructive operation! It will wipe out all of your development database's data for this application and rebuild the data!

Fantastic! Now, we can move on to the controller portion of the implementation!

Hooking up our polls index

We need to hook this amazing new logic up to our Vote controller's `index` function if we'd like to start taking advantage of it! We'll start it off simply enough and not worry about hooking up the paging portions of our code and verifying the end results. Our new `index` function in `lib/vocial_web/controllers/poll_controller.ex` should look something like this:

```
def index(conn, params) do
  %{"page" => page, "per_page" => per_page} = Map.merge(%{"page" => 0,
"per_page" => 25}, params)
  polls = Votes.list_most_recent_polls(page, per_page)
  render conn, "index.html", polls: polls
end
```

The first line in this controller (other than us changing the function arguments to actually care about `params` again) is the `Map.merge` statement. The reason behind this is that we want to be able to pull out the `page` and `per_page` arguments that a user may pass in, and handle them appropriately. This allows us to set up sane defaults for our `page` and `per_page` arguments and map them back out to the appropriate variable, which we then pass into the `Votes.list_most_recent_polls/2` call.

> `Map.merge/2` takes in two arguments; the first is the map that we want to start with, and then the second is the map that will overwrite any duplicate information in the first. Given a base of `%{ message: "Hello World", color: "red"}` and a second map of `%{ message: "Good morning!", age: 23 }`, the resulting map would be `%{ message: "Good morning!", color: "red", age: 23 }`.

Other than that, the controller function remains identical! Let's take a look at the results (which if you ran your seeds file should actually look exactly like this):

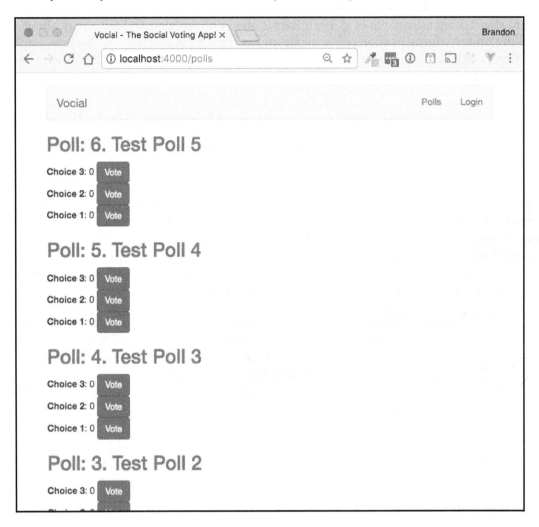

But what if we want the paging stuff to actually function the way we're expecting it to? This is where things are going to start getting significantly more complicated! If we want this to be a bit more usable, we're going to have to make this logic significantly more complicated, I'm afraid!

The first issue we have to approach and deal with is how we're going to deal with pagination in general. First, we need to normalize out our `page`/`per_page` params before we can start doing anything with them since by default they're going to be typed as strings. We'll start off by building a helper function that will make sure the end result we pass along to our query will end up as integers when it gets to the database (still in `lib/vocial_web/controllers/poll_controller.ex`):

```
defp paging_params(%{"page" => page, "per_page" => per_page}) do
  page = case is_binary(page) do
    true -> String.to_integer(page)
    _ -> page
  end
  per_page = case is_binary(per_page) do
    true -> String.to_integer(per_page)
    _ -> per_page
  end
  %{"page" => page - 1, "per_page" => per_page}
end
```

We'll anticipate this working by just passing the `params` variable along to this function and getting a resulting map. If this page is `is_binary` (that is, if the page variable is storing a string), we'll want to convert it to an integer via `String.to_integer/1`. This will guarantee that our paging params are being passed to us in a format that we're expecting and can properly use. We'll create another helper function that will call out to `paging_params`, which will be responsible for normalizing the paging params entirely, including setting up default values for both the current page and the `per_page` size. One thing to note in the preceding function however, is that after we convert the page value to an integer, we decrease the value by 1. We do this so that the URL the user sees is page 1 for the user, instead of page 0 for the first page. Let's take a look at what our `normalize_paging_params/1` function will look like:

```
defp normalize_paging_params(params) do
  %{"page" => 1, "per_page" => 25}
  |> Map.merge(params)
  |> paging_params()
end
```

What we're doing here is we're taking in the `params` passed to that page. We're including a default state of our `params` map that includes paging data, and then we're using that as the base to merge against `params`. This means that any values in the `params` map will be preserved, and if `page`/`per_page` do not exist, they will get values. Finally, the resulting map is sent off to the `paging_params/1` function. This prevents us from needing multiple pattern match clauses for our function since we're normalizing everything first!

Next, we'll need to include some options to pass along to the template so that it knows what page we're on and whether it should include the previous/next page links on the page. Similar to the previous function's strategy, we'll use a default map and build values on top of that:

```
defp paging_options(polls, page, per_page) do
  %{
    include_next_page: (Enum.count(polls) > per_page),
    include_prev_page: (page > 0),
    page: page,
    per_page: per_page
  }
end
```

At the top, we check the number of polls and see whether they're larger than the `per_page` value. The reason why we do this will be very clear later, but the short version is that we're actually going to request one more item than our `per_page` size. If we do this, using 25 as our example value, we'll request 26 items but limit what we actually get back to 25. This means that if we know there's at least one more object, there should also be at least one more page! This prevents us from doing extra count queries against our database and performing quick operations to build out pagination logic.

We'll set up the rest of our default arguments simply enough; by default, we determine whether the previous page link should be displayed by determining if we're on page 0 or not. Additionally, we include the `page` and `per_page` values to be passed along as the previous/next links.

Finally, let's take a look at our index function, which will actually be decently short because we already broke the logic out into a few separate helper functions:

```
def index(conn, params) do
  %{"page" => page, "per_page" => per_page} =
normalize_paging_params(params)
  polls = Votes.list_most_recent_polls(page, per_page)
  opts = paging_options(polls, page, per_page)
  render conn, "index.html", polls: Enum.take(polls, per_page), opts:
opts
  end
```

So, we start off by pattern matching out our `page` and `per_page` values from our call to `normalize_paging_params/1`. Next, we get the list of polls out of the database. Next, using the list of polls, we set up our options for displaying the page. Finally, we render the whole thing, now including our opts variable in addition to the polls. We also make sure that we only take the `per_page` amount for the polls. After all, we don't want to display 26 items if we say we're only including 25 items. If you go back and test out your UI, everything should mostly work, right?

Unfortunately not! If you test it out, you'll probably notice that as you're paging through, it's not actually giving us another page! The reason for this is that the logic in our context doesn't match what we're trying to accomplish exactly. What we need to do is modify our query in the context to include the extra item to make our pagination work correctly, but in a way that doesn't affect our limits or offsets. We'll write a new function for this in the context to keep our logic a little bit separate. In `lib/vocial/votes/votes.ex`, we'll create a new function:

```
def list_most_recent_polls_with_extra(page \\ 0, per_page \\ 25) do
  Repo.all(
    from p in Poll,
    limit: ^(per_page + 1),
    offset: ^(page * per_page),
    order_by: [desc: p.inserted_at]
  )
  |> Repo.preload([:options, :image, :vote_records, :messages])
end
```

Notice that the big difference here is that we're setting the limit to the `per_page` value plus one! We keep this function separate since we may want the original behavior, but since we only want to modify the `per_page` value once, we'll keep this functionality separate! We'll also write a quick test in `test/vocial/votes/votes_test.exs` to cover this behavior:

```
test "list_most_recent_polls_with_extra/2 returns polls ordered and
paged correctly", %{user: user} do
  _poll = poll_fixture(%{user_id: user.id})
  poll2 = poll_fixture(%{user_id: user.id})
  poll3 = poll_fixture(%{user_id: user.id})
  _poll4 = poll_fixture(%{user_id: user.id})
  assert Votes.list_most_recent_polls_with_extra(1, 1) == [poll3,
poll2]
end
```

Finally, we'll modify our controller
(`lib/vocial_web/controllers/poll_controller.ex`) to use the new function instead:

```
def index(conn, params) do
  %{"page" => page, "per_page" => per_page} =
normalize_paging_params(params)
  polls = Votes.list_most_recent_polls_with_extra(page, per_page)
  opts = paging_options(polls, page, per_page)
  render conn, "index.html", polls: Enum.take(polls, per_page), opts:
opts
  end
```

Save it and we can move on to the final portion of this work, which is modifying the
template. Open up `lib/vocial_web/templates/poll/index.html.eex` and add some
pagination logic to the bottom:

```
<br/>
<div>
  <%= if @opts.include_prev_page do %>
    <div class="pull-left">
      <%= link "<< Previous Page", to: poll_path(@conn, :index, [page:
(@opts.page - 1), per_page: @opts.per_page]) %>
    </div>
  <% end %>
  <%= if @opts.include_next_page do %>
    <div class="pull-right">
      <%= link "Next Page >>", to: poll_path(@conn, :index, [page:
(@opts.page + 1), per_page: @opts.per_page]) %>
    <div class="pull-right">
  <% end %>
</div>
```

If we go back to our page and append the pagination params (I used `page=2` and
`per_page=2`), we should see a proper pagination, just like we expect! The end result should
be a page that looks something like this:

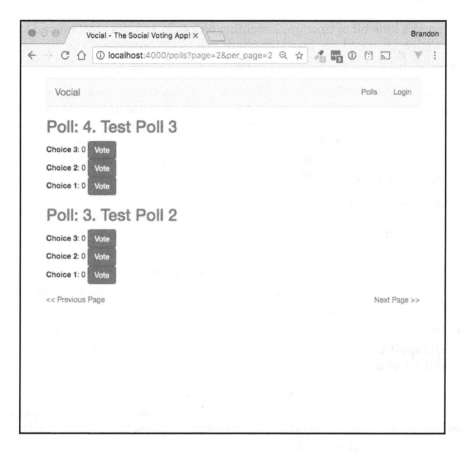

That's a pretty good user experience! I think we can move on to some further optimization and polishing!

Adding Ueberauth support

A common thing that people want to implement into their applications is some form of login support through some sort of external provider. The big advantage of this is that when people then want to create their account, they can avoid having to create yet another login to deal with. This can remove a major blocker from people wanting to sign up to your site, so this is always a great thing to do, but it's also something that's a bit complicated! Based on that, let's demystify this feature a little bit and implement a Twitter account creation and login system in our application!

We'll also spend a little bit of time implementing a Google account creation and login system just to demonstrate how easy Ueberauth makes it to add new OAuth strategies to your application without having to reimplement a bunch of things over and over!

Part of the reason for including this is that this is probably one of the most commonly requested features for implementations on a lot of new startups. This is also something that tends to be very difficult to figure out the first time you try and tackle it. If you've never attempted to create an OAuth sign in before, it can be difficult to navigate each of the site's various workflows to get an application up and running, and then taking that information and applying it to your application is even harder!

The way OAuth works is as follows:

1. The user makes a request to log in via their OAuth provider of choice
2. The application makes a request on behalf of the user asking for permission
3. The OAuth provider returns a request token and a secret token
4. The user is redirected with the token and secret back to the OAuth provider to approve the login request
5. The user approves the request and returns the access token and secret token
6. The application then finalizes the login with the provider with the access token and secret token

The hope is that by the end of this chapter, you have a firm grasp on at least two OAuth providers and can apply what you've learned should you also decide to implement something like Facebook or some other provider that supports OAuth2! Let's take a look at our first implementation: Twitter sign in!

Adding OAuth login support for Twitter with Ueberauth

We're going to start off by implementing Twitter, as this is actually one of the simplest to find, configure, and implement, and is also one of the most common OAuth providers. We'll need to start off by actually setting up and configuring our application in Twitter itself.

Twitter provides a "Twitter Apps" UI for developers, which you can use to set up your application. We're going to walk through the process of creating and configuring an application in this UI and talk about where each of the values needs to go in our Phoenix application to enable us to properly use the Twitter OAuth strategy with Ueberauth!

Setting up our application with Twitter

First, you'll need to go to `https://apps.twitter.com`, and click on the **Create New App** button at the top. Shown here is my own `apps.twitter.com` page (you can see I already have a custom OAuth development environment that I tend to use for a lot of my projects that need to implement OAuth). We're going to start from scratch instead of using my pre-existing configuration, so we'll click on that **Create New App** button!:

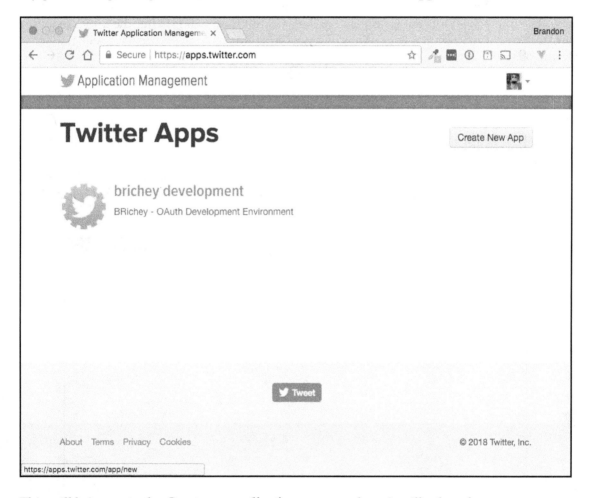

This will bring us to the **Create an application** screen, where it will ask us for some information. Most of this is just the information that will be displayed in the *Authorize this application* interstitial page that you'll see when creating a new account or logging in via Twitter.

One thing that is very helpful is to include the environment you'll be running your application in if it is not being run in Production. Since we're running in Development, we'll call this *Vocial Development* for the Application Name. The description is simple enough; just have it describe your application to the user!

Next, you'll fill out the user. Note that this field needs to be an actual site; if you don't have a domain for your project just yet, you may need to use something like your own personal site. I just used my personal site for now. Moving on, the next field is the most important one. The callback URL is the URL that Twitter's OAuth flow will hit after the initial request and authorization from the user. We will set up our route as (don't worry, we will implement this later):

```
scope "/auth", VocialWeb do
  get "/:provider/callback", SessionController, :callback
end
```

This will be wrapped underneath an `"auth"` scope, so the full URL for something like Twitter would be `http://(whatever we're working in locally)/auth/twitter/callback`, so that is the pattern we'll follow here. We'll end up with `http://localhost:4000/auth/twitter/callback`. Finally, check that box and we're ready to go!:

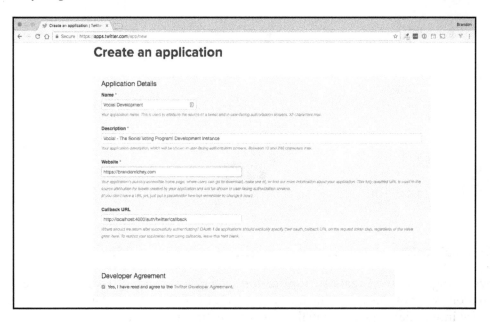

Creating an application in the Twitter Developer Center

Hit the save button, and of course, take note of the Callback URL we're using! Assuming everything was filled out successfully, we should be able to move on to actually managing the configuration of this. Click on your new application that you've created and navigate over to the **Keys and Access Tokens** tab. Here, you can see the Consumer Key and Consumer Secret values. Keep track of the values, and more importantly, **do not store these values in source control!** Should you ever accidentally commit them into your git repo or anything, the good news is that you can regenerate your key and secret values very quickly using the **Regenerate Consumer Key and Secret** button at the bottom! I've provided a screenshot of the page (with all the good stuff edited out, I'm afraid) to use as a reference:

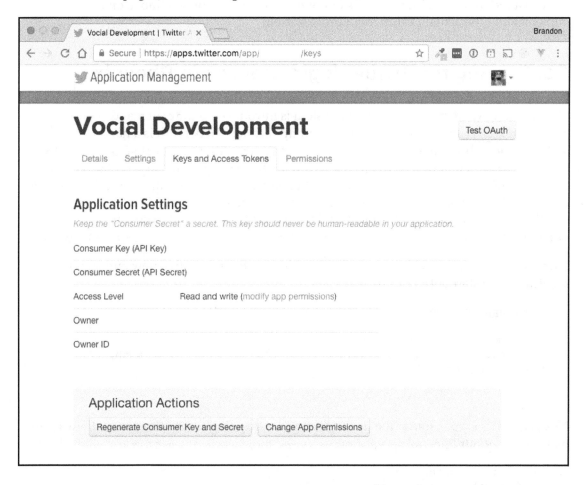

As mentioned previously, I've edited my values out of this screenshot, but you'll use the **Consumer Key** for the `TWITTER_CONSUMER_KEY` environment variable and the **Consumer Secret** for the `TWITTER_CONSUMER_SECRET` environment variable! (I edited out the **Owner** and **Owner ID** values as well; you should see these populated as your own Twitter username and user ID). We'll use these environment variables later on, but it's important to note that these values are best placed as environment variables for the system that your app is going to be running on. This will allow you to change them quickly should they ever get exposed or anything else happens that requires you to change them.

Now that the configuration process is out of the way, we're going to move on to implementing the actual OAuth login process itself!

Configuring the Twitter login process in Phoenix

We're ready to start moving on to actually hooking up the configuration to some real code! The first thing we're going to do in our system is introduced `ueberauth` and `ueberauth_twitter` as dependencies to our application. Ueberauth is a handy authentication library that supports logging in via a few different `strategies`. The idea behind it is that the underlying code that supports the strategies are largely similar, and only a few of the minor details for each need to be modified behind the scenes. This allows us to spend a little bit of up-front development cost to get our first login system working and then spend incredibly little effort getting each additional OAuth provider implemented! Let's start by using `ueberauth` with an `ueberauth_twitter` strategy.

First off, in `mix.exs`, modify the application function to include two new entries for applications to start with our Phoenix application `:ueberauth` and `:ueberauth_twitter`:

```
def application do
  [
    mod: {Vocial.Application, []},
    extra_applications: [:logger, :runtime_tools, :ueberauth,
:ueberauth_twitter]
  ]
end
```

Next, still in `mix.exs`, under the `deps` function, we're going to add three more libraries to make a part of our Phoenix application: `:ueberauth`, `:ueberauth_twitter`, and `:oauth`:

```
{:ueberauth, "~> 0.4"},
{:ueberauth_twitter, "~> 0.2"},
{:oauth, github: "tim/erlang-oauth"}
```

We've added our dependencies, so now we're ready to pull them into our application! We're going to quickly run the following command in the Terminal:

```
$ mix do deps.get, compile
```

After this is successful, we're going to move on to managing the initial configuration for our application. Next, in config.exs, add the following configuration blocks:

```
config :ueberauth, Ueberauth,
  providers: [
    twitter: {Ueberauth.Strategy.Twitter, []}
  ]

config :ueberauth, Ueberauth.Strategy.Twitter.OAuth,
  consumer_key: System.get_env("TWITTER_CONSUMER_KEY"),
  consumer_secret: System.get_env("TWITTER_CONSUMER_SECRET")
```

The first configuration block tells the Ueberauth application that it is running as a part of our main application's workflow that one of our Ueberauth providers is going to be called *Twitter*, and this is going to use the Ueberauth Twitter strategy! After that's in our config, we need to also tell the Twitter OAuth strategy what to use for the consumer_key and the consumer_secret values. This combination helps Twitter understand where our OAuth requests are originating from, which application they should be used with, and how to verify that information. Since we set these values in our environment variables, we'll use System.get_env/1. Let's take a quick look at the help page for this:

```
iex(1)> h System.get_env

def get_env()

Returns all system environment variables.

The returned value is a map containing name-value pairs. Variable names and
their values are strings.


def get_env(varname)

Returns the value of the given environment variable.

The returned value of the environment variable varname is a string, or nil
if
the environment variable is undefined.
```

Perfect, just what we need! Now, we can start our implementation and write some real code! We'll start off by modifying the users' schema to include some OAuth details so that we can tie this information back to the appropriate accounts and code.

Modifying the users schema

We'll start off by generating the migration that we'll need to use to add more data to our user accounts. Specifically, we'll need to keep track of which user account is using which OAuth provider and what the external OAuth user ID is. Let's start by generating our OAuth schema migration:

```
$ mix ecto.gen.migration add_oauth_data_to_users
* creating priv/repo/migrations
* creating priv/repo/migrations/20180114145743_add_oauth_data_to_users.exs
```

Then, we need to actually pull up and modify that migration file. We can't be 100 percent sure what the format of the returning OAuth user ID may be, so we'll use a string to keep it simple and easy. The OAuth provider will also be a string:

```
defmodule Vocial.Repo.Migrations.AddOauthDataToUsers do
  use Ecto.Migration

  def change do
    alter table(:users) do
      add :oauth_provider, :string
      add :oauth_id, :string
    end
  end
end
```

Finally, we'll run our migration with:

```
$ mix ecto.migrate
[info] == Running Vocial.Repo.Migrations.AddOauthDataToUsers.change/0
forward
[info] alter table users
[info] == Migrated in 0.0s
```

Now that our database table is set up and we have the columns we need, we'll also need to add those as fields on the schema! In `lib/vocial/accounts/user.ex`, add the following to the schema:

```
field :oauth_provider, :string
field :oauth_id, :string
```

And add in our new fields to `cast` so that we can create users with them:

```
|> cast(attrs, [:username, :email, :active, :password,
:password_confirmation, :oauth_provider, :oauth_id])
```

And change `:email` so that it is no longer be required, since Twitter won't send that back, in our changeset function:

```
|> validate_required([:username, :active, :encrypted_password])
```

Implementing the Twitter login in Phoenix

We'll move on to implementing our actual login and authentication code in Phoenix! First, we'll need to set up our routes. Ueberauth is expecting us to provide a route for each provider and a callback for each provider as well. In `lib/vocial_web/router.ex`, we'll add a brand new scope for our Ueberauth routes called `/auth`. This means all OAuth-specific routes will be in the format of `/auth/....`. This also helps us segment away the code that deals specifically with Ueberauth's login details:

```
scope "/auth", VocialWeb do
  pipe_through :browser

  get "/:provider", SessionController, :request
  get "/:provider/callback", SessionController, :callback
end
```

Next, we'll need to modify the aforementioned SessionController. Open up `lib/vocial_web/controllers/session_controller.ex` and add the following to the top, somewhere near the aliases and import statements:

```
plug Ueberauth
```

And then at the bottom of the file, we'll start implementing our callbacks. The first important callback for us to implement is the one that occurs when the OAuth login attempt fails. Should that happen, we'll just redirect out of this and send a `Failed to authenticate` message:

```
def callback(%{assigns: %{ueberauth_failure: _fails}} = conn, _params) do
  conn
  |> put_flash(:error, "Failed to authenticate.")
  |> redirect(to: "/")
end
```

That's a simple enough implementation, so the next thing we'll work on is the good stuff: what happens when the authentication works! Remember that Ueberauth plug that we placed at the top of our Session Controller? That places a special key in the `conn` object that's been assigned, under the `:ueberauth_auth` key. We'll pattern match against that and move on. Next, we'll attempt to either find the right user or create a new user account in the case of a user signing up with an OAuth provider. If the user is found or created, we'll return that user as part of the `conn` objects:

```
def callback(%{assigns: %{ueberauth_auth: auth}} = conn, _params) do
    case find_or_create_user(auth) do
      {:ok, user} ->
        conn
        |> put_flash(:info, "Logged in successfully!")
        |> put_session(:user, %{ id: user.id, username: user.username,
email: user.email })
        |> redirect(to: "/")
      {:error, reason} ->
        conn
        |> put_flash(:error, reason)
        |> redirect(to: "/")
    end
  end
```

Let's take a look at that `find_or_create_user/1` function that we talked about there. We know a couple of things about it: it takes a single argument, which should be the `auth` map from Ueberauth:

```
defp find_or_create_user(auth) do
  user = build_user_from_auth(auth)
  case Accounts.get_user_by_oauth(user.oauth_provider, user.oauth_id) do
    nil ->
      case Accounts.get_user_by_username(user.username) do
        nil -> Accounts.create_user(user)
        _ -> Accounts.create_user(%{ user | username:
"#{user.username}#{user.oauth_id}" })
      end
    user -> {:ok, user}
  end
end
```

This function will first attempt to build a user struct from the `auth` information. Then, we'll need to call out to another new function, `Accounts.get_user_by_oauth/2`, to find out whether there are any existing user accounts that look like they're based on the `oauth_provider` and the `oauth_id`. If that gives us no existing user, then we'll check to see if the username is available first before we attempt to create a new user. The reason for this is to avoid us getting into a weird scenario where a user signs up with one username, finds another account, and logs in as that person instead. We'll either create the user with the returned username, or with the username plus the OAuth user ID appended to it! Let's take a look at `build_user_from_auth/1` for the Twitter implementation:

```
defp build_user_from_auth(%{provider: :twitter}=auth) do
  password = random_string(64)
  %{
    username: auth.info.nickname,
    oauth_id: auth.uid,
    oauth_provider: "twitter",
    password: password,
    password_confirmation: password
  }
end

def random_string(length) do
  :crypto.strong_rand_bytes(length) |> Base.url_encode64 |> binary_part(0,
length)
end
```

We'll pattern match specifically for the Twitter provider, since that's the implementation we're working towards first. We'll create a random password for creating the user account first of all since we'll need to have a user account with a working password. Twitter will send us back the person's username in the info hash as the nickname. We'll then return back the appropriate user map.

We'll also quickly create the `Accounts.get_user_by_oauth/2` function. This will need to be implemented in the Accounts Context (`lib/vocial/accounts/accounts.ex`):

```
def get_user_by_oauth(oauth_provider, oauth_id) do
  Repo.get_by(User, oauth_provider: oauth_provider, oauth_id: oauth_id)
end
```

We can now move on to working with our templates to get everything else set up in `lib/vocial_web/templates/user/new.html.eex`:

```
<%= link "Sign Up with Twitter", to: "/auth/twitter" %>
```

We'll also need to add something to log in
(`lib/vocial_web/templates/session/new.html.eex`):

```
<hr />
<%= link "Login with Twitter", to: "/auth/twitter" %>
```

Now, when we go back to our app and create a new account, we should see the following
User Signup page:

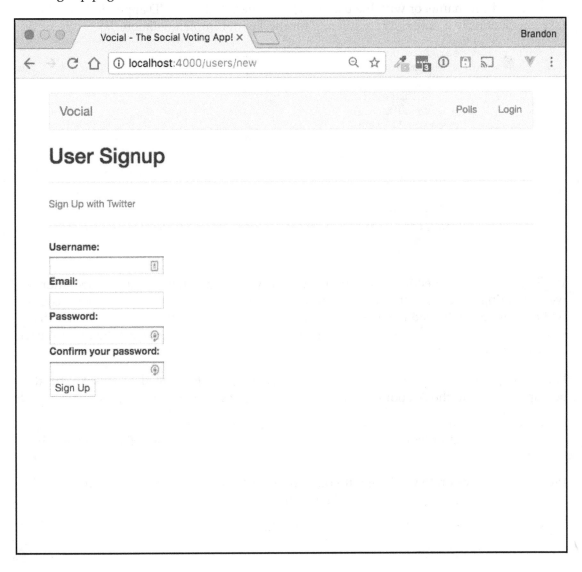

If you click the **Sign Up with Twitter** link, you should then see:

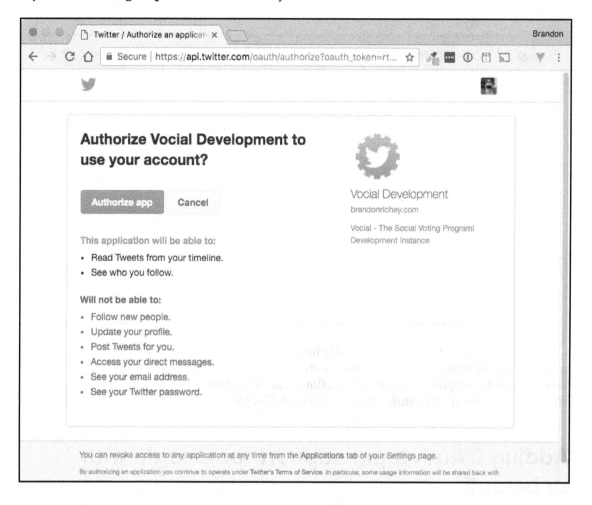

And then you should be all logged in! You should also be able to log in after creating your account:

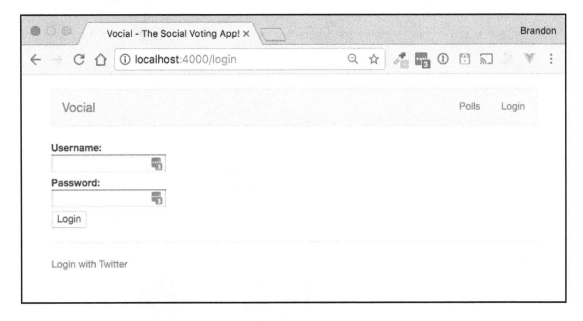

...And that's it! We have now successfully implemented OAuth login with Twitter! I spent a good amount of time talking about how powerful the ability of Ueberauth is when it comes to being able to support multiple OAuth flows out of the box, so let's jump into implementing our next OAuth support provider, Google!

Adding OAuth login support for Google with Ueberauth

With all of the hard work of the initial setup ready to go, it should be pretty easy to add a new OAuth provider flow into this! We'll go through a few of the same steps that we went through with Twitter, except this time we're going to target Google. It's always important to include a list of other options when you do include login or account creation via some third party, because not every person is going to have the same sources for accounts. Some people don't like one site or another, so it's always a good idea to include a list of options!

We'll have to set up our project in Google first so that we can get the necessary login OAuth details to configure our app.

Configuring Google to allow OAuth

First, under the Google developer console, you'll want to create a new project (if you don't already have one). This is what allows you to associate an OAuth flow with your Phoenix application. You can name it whatever you like, but again, you should try to keep your development (or otherwise non-production) environments named in such a way that you can pick them out easily enough:

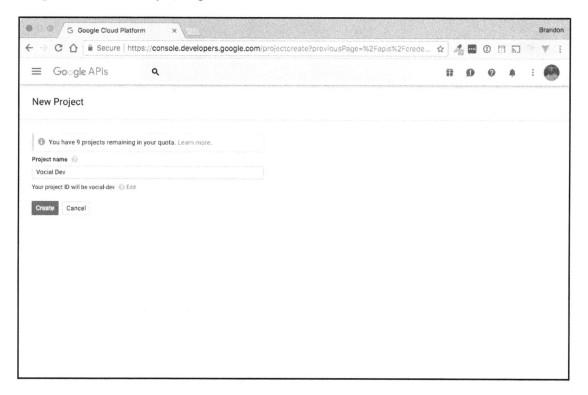

The next step after you've created your project is to navigate to the application's **Credentials** screen. Here, you'll click on **Create Credentials** (if you don't already have credentials set up and ready to go). You will be presented with a list of options for what sort of credentials you want to create. In our case, we want to create the OAuth client ID, which allows us to log in on behalf of a user with their consent:

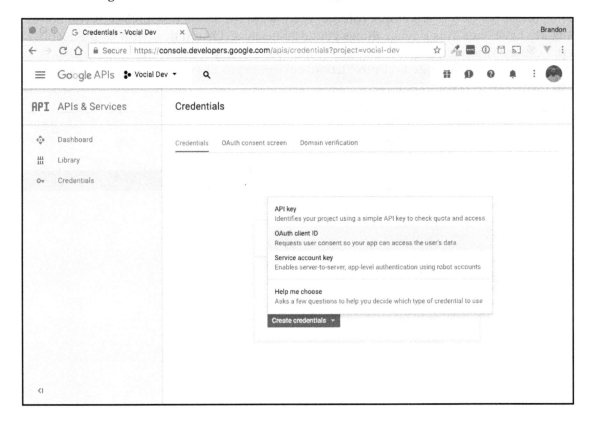

When we attempt to do this, however, we're going to get a message on our screen that tells us that we need to configure a consent screen first to at least include a product name. The good news is that it's very easy for us to get to that point; just click that big blue button on the page:

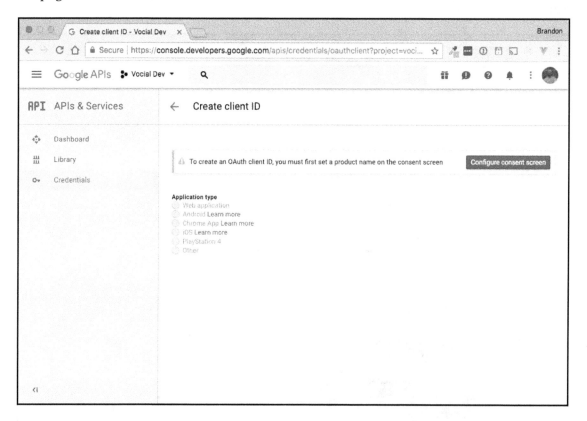

Under the project credentials page, we'll be in the OAuth consent screen. We'll enter in our product name that will be shown to our users. Again, I'm choosing **Vocial Dev** to work as my product mame; this tells me the product and the environment that this product is running under. We can include our homepage URL as an added safety measure, but it's not actually required:

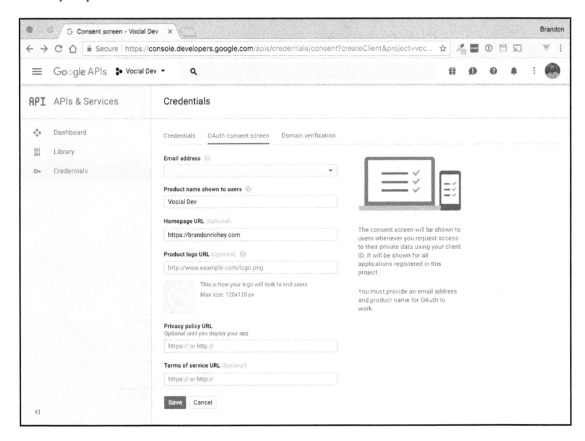

After we click **Save** there, we will finally have the option to go back and create our client ID. Go back to the previous page where we originally tried to create our OAuth client ID and this time, we'll get that screen but without the error at the top telling us that we need to configure a product name! Since we're building off of our development environment, we'll include that under the `Restrictions` section. We'll set the *Authorized JavaScript origins* field to be `http://localhost:4000` and our Authorized redirect URIs should be set to the Ueberauth Google callback route, which is `http://localhost:4000/auth/google/callback`:

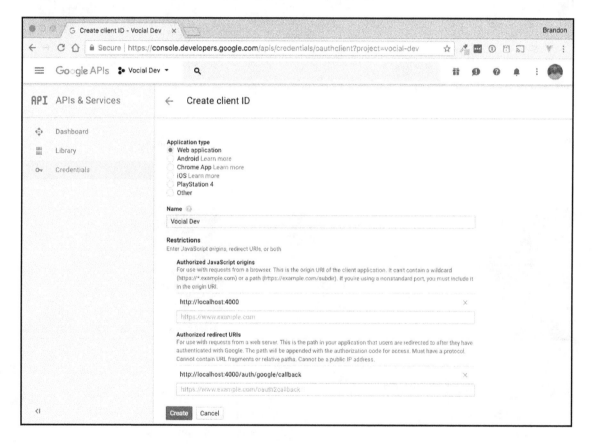

Finally, we'll be presented with the client ID and the client's secret values! Take note of these (and again, don't check them into source control), and we'll have everything we need to start our implementation of Google OAuth:

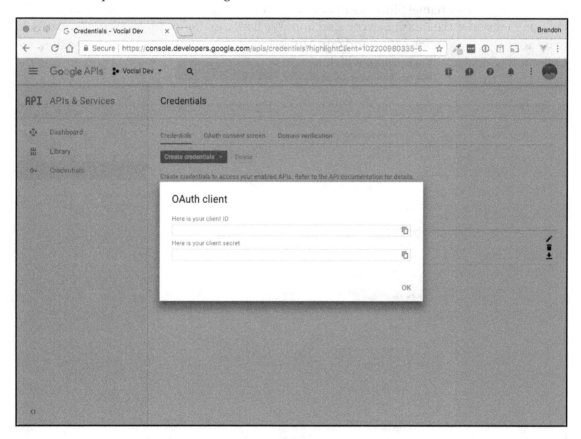

Configuring Ueberauth in Google

We'll begin by configuring `mix.exs`, first with the list of running applications. This is the same as what we had to do to get Ueberauth and Ueberauth's Twitter strategy installed:

```
extra_applications: [:logger, :runtime_tools, :ueberauth,
:ueberauth_twitter, :ueberauth_google]
```

Of course, we'll also have to add it to our list of dependencies under the `deps` function:

```
{:ueberauth_google, "~> 0.7"}
```

Now, we'll modify our `config/config.exs` file to include a new provider for Ueberauth. The providers key is just a list of the different providers and which strategy they use to log someone in, so we'll add Google to our list:

```
config :ueberauth, Ueberauth,
  providers: [
    twitter: {Ueberauth.Strategy.Twitter, []},
    google: {Ueberauth.Strategy.Google, []}
  ]
```

Finally, we'll configure the Google OAuth strategy directly. When you sign up, you'll be presented with both the client ID and the client's secret values. We'll keep the environment variables named in a similar fashion to our Twitter key and secret to make our lives easier:

```
config :ueberauth, Ueberauth.Strategy.Google.OAuth,
  client_id: System.get_env("GOOGLE_CONSUMER_KEY"),
  client_secret: System.get_env("GOOGLE_CONSUMER_SECRET")
```

Implementing Google OAuth for Ueberauth and Phoenix

We'll start off simply enough by modifying our templates. We're going to add links to login with Google in both our login page and our new user account page. We'll start in `lib/vocial_web/templates/session/new.html.eex`:

```
<br />
<%= link "Login with Google", to: "/auth/google" %>
```

And then modify our account creation page as well with a very similar link in `lib/vocial_web/templates/user/new.html.eex`:

```
<br />
<%= link "Sign Up with Google", to: "/auth/google" %>
```

Finally, in the session controller (`lib/vocial_web/controllers/session_controller.ex`), we'll need to add a `build_user_from_auth/1` that accounts for Google being the provider instead of Twitter. Google doesn't give us back a username, so we'll use the email address as both the email address and the username:

```
defp build_user_from_auth(%{provider: :google}=auth) do
  password = random_string(64)
  %{
    username: auth.info.email,
    email: auth.info.email,
    oauth_id: auth.uid,
```

```
            oauth_provider: "google",
            password: password,
            password_confirmation: password
        }
    end
```

And that's it, the rest of this should just work! Let's try it out really quickly. If you go to account creation and click the **Sign up with Google** link, you should be presented with a screen that looks something like this (slightly different, of course, depending on how many email accounts you have):

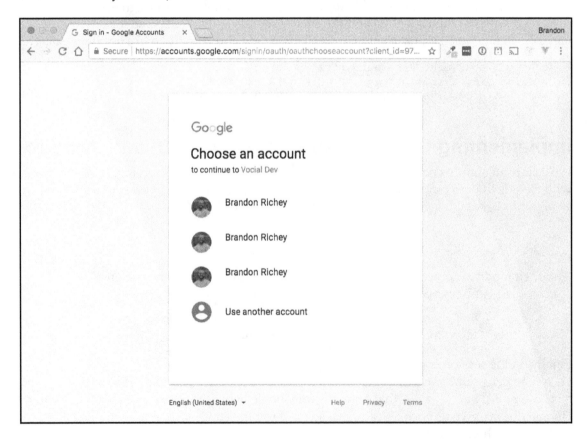

Choose an account, log in, and then you should see the blue **Logged In Successfully!** message at the top of the screen! Congratulations, you just implemented a second OAuth provider for your application with almost zero fuss (just a lot of configuration)!:

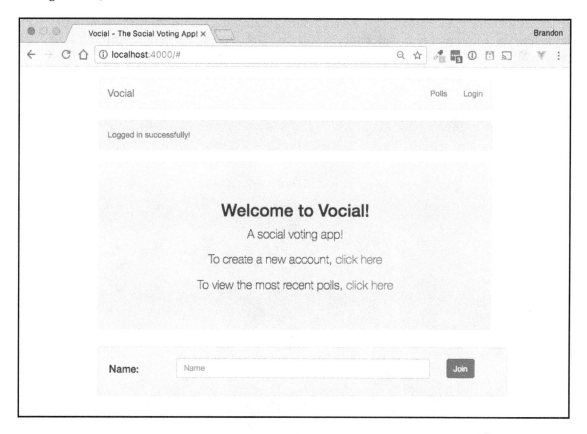

Summary

This chapter was very information heavy, but knowing how to properly implement OAuth in your application can help you go a long way towards making your application more accessible and pulling more people in to use your application! It's a very difficult thing to just get started and configure it, which is a big part of why we spent so much time detailing the configuration process with the two separate providers!

The good news is that Ueberauth makes the entire process so simple and easy to swap out providers whenever you need to that it becomes surprisingly trivial to add support for new OAuth providers at any given point in time (assuming there's already an Ueberauth Strategy package that you can use, of course)!

In the next chapter, we'll cover the last two parts of building our application: adding an API layer and handling API authentication, modifying/configuring logging for our application, and finally, deploying and running our application out in the real world in production!

12
Building an API and Deploying

In the last chapter, we focused on implementing OAuth logins through a few separate providers to give a concrete example of developing a social media login system. Here in our final chapter, we'll build out an API for our users to use to get Poll and Vote data out in JSON format. For the final portion of work, we'll talk about different deployment and production running strategies to take your application the last few steps across the finish line!

In this chapter, we'll cover:

- Implementing an API in Phoenix
    - Building API-specific pipelines
    - Building API-specific controllers
    - Working with JSON views instead of HTML views
    - Setting up rules for error handling
    - Setting up plugs for API key authentication
- Deploying a Phoenix Application to Production
    - Logging Best Practices
    - Running the application in Production
    - Common deployment gotchas
    - Alternative Deployment Strategies

Building our API

If we try to run API requests against our application right now using a tool like a cURL or a Postman we will (rightfully) get an error message since we have no real framework in place to serve API requests. The good news is that Phoenix makes everything incredibly simple to build a new API with very, very little dependency on extra libraries to get everything put together.

In fact, building an API in Phoenix is such a simple endeavor that it has completely replaced my usual defaults of other languages and tools! Everything is given to you in some way or another without requiring a lot of extra work or configuration, and having an API live seamlessly side-by-side with the rest of your application is a breeze!

If we start off by making a request to our non-existing API routes, we will (as expected) get an error message. For purposes of this chapter, I'll be using Postman to make and showcase the API functionality, but you could easily use another tool or just plain old cURL!

The following screenshot is an example of using Postman to send our API requests. You can see the URL we're hitting, as well as any configuration and headers we may be set as well, so this tool makes it especially easy to follow along:

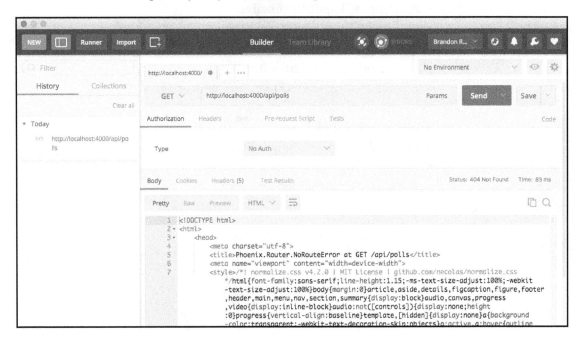

Building an API in Code

Phoenix comes default with an API Pipeline that we can start with as part of our application. They do this to highlight how easy it is to introduce new pipelines in Phoenix to be able to handle different paths that a request needs to take to build a valid response. Let's open up our router file and take our first peek at API-specific code, which sets up our base API pipeline. Instead of going through the normal browser pipeline (which has other work it needs to do to make the browser even work), the API essentially just needs to make sure that the format being sent is what the API can accept. For purposes of our API, all we need to accept is JSON.

Let's open up `lib/vocial_web/router.ex` and take a peek:

```
pipeline :api do
  plug :accepts, ["json"]
end
```

If you've been scrolling around and reading the files as we've been working on them, you've probably seen this commented out block of code at the bottom of our file as well:

```
# Other scopes may use custom stacks.
# scope "/api", VocialWeb do
#   pipe_through :api
# end
```

This is a good example of setting route scopes! This means that any requests that happen with the starting path of `"/api"` will run through the API pipeline that we set up! Let's start by un-commenting out that block that we talked about before. Then, we're going to add a new line to it that will set up to be able to start serving out our first API requests.

```
scope "/api", VocialWeb do
  pipe_through :api

  resources "/polls", Api.PollController, only: [:index]
end
```

Next, create a new directory in `lib/vocial_web/controllers` called `"api"`, and in that directory create `poll_controller.ex`. This will be the start of the workhorse for our API development!

```
defmodule VocialWeb.Api.PollController do
  use VocialWeb, :controller

  def index(conn, _params) do
    render(conn, "index.json", [])
```

```
      end
  end
```

Also, create a new directory in `lib/vocial_web/views` called `"api"`, and in that directory make `poll_view.ex`. This file will be responsible for all of the serialization logic necessary to convert outbound data to JSON in a way that our API consumers should be able to follow:

```
defmodule VocialWeb.Api.PollView do
  use VocialWeb, :view

  def render("index.json", _data) do
    %{
      message: "Hello World"
    }
  end
end
```

Now let's rerun out postman request and see if it's working:

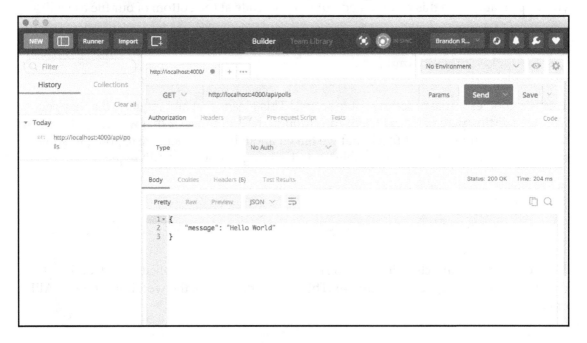

Awesome! Let's build on this a little bit more, since this is all just boiler-plate code right now.

Expanding Our API Request

We have a good start to our code, but we should really expand on this a little bit more. In order for us to do that, we'll need to start off by modifying our controller. This should actually be very similar to what you've already seen in the past when displaying regular information to normal templates. We'll alias our Votes Context, grab the list of polls from our `list_most_recent_polls/0` call, and then send that information on to our views! Let's take a look at the changes to `lib/controllers/api/poll_controller.ex`:

```
alias Vocial.Votes

def index(conn, _params) do
  polls = Votes.list_most_recent_polls()
  render(conn, "index.json", polls: polls)
end
```

Next, we'll need to set up the process for our data to go from the database into JSON output! There's a function call here that calls out to a function that we will write later. We'll send the polls variable off to a function that will render each poll that you have. In `lib/views/api/poll_view.ex`:

```
def render("index.json", %{polls: polls}) do
  %{
    polls: render_many(polls)
  }
end
```

Next, we'll need to implement our first render function. This will be the render call that is utilized by the `render_many/1` function. All this does is take in a poll struct and convert it into a normal Elixir map. We'll also map through the list of the options available for each poll and grab the title and the vote count from each.

 `Map.take/2` takes in the map that you want to grab the information out of as the first argument and a list of keys and returns the result out as a map of only the keys you requested!

```
def render_one(poll) do
  %{
    id: poll.id,
    title: poll.title,
    options: Enum.map(poll.options, fn o -&gt; Map.take(o, [:title,
:votes]) end),
    image: %{
      url: poll.image.url,
```

```
      alt: poll.image.alt,
      caption: poll.image.caption
    }
  }
end
```

After that, we can start to implement our `render_many/1` function that we had originally started implementing. All this function even needs to do is take in the list of polls, which it will then map over and call the `render_one` function on each poll. The resulting function should look like this:

```
def render_many(polls) do
  Enum.map(polls, &render_one/1)
end
```

We can then refactor this a little bit since it's a little ugly right now. We'll start off by writing a `render_options/1` function, where if you supply a `nil` value it will just return out an empty array. If there are any options, we'll iterate over them again using the same logic from the `render_one` function:

```
def render_options(nil), do: []
def render_options(options) do
  options
  |&gt; Enum.map(fn o -&gt; Map.take(o, [:title, :votes]) end)
end
```

We'll also want to separate out the logic for rendering our image data for each poll to keep our initial render call nice and lean. Our implementation of the `render_image/1` function is shown as follows, with the same nil-handling logic as in the `render_options` function:

```
def render_image(nil), do: nil
def render_image(image) do
  %{
    url: image.url,
    alt: image.alt,
    caption: image.caption
  }
end
```

That should leave us with refactoring our original `render_one` function to be much, much simpler and cleaner:

```
def render_one(poll) do
  %{
    id: poll.id,
    title: poll.title,
```

```
        options: render_options(poll.options),
        image: render_image(poll.image)
    }
  end
```

That's it! So with our views all nice and refactored, when we make our API request we
should see:

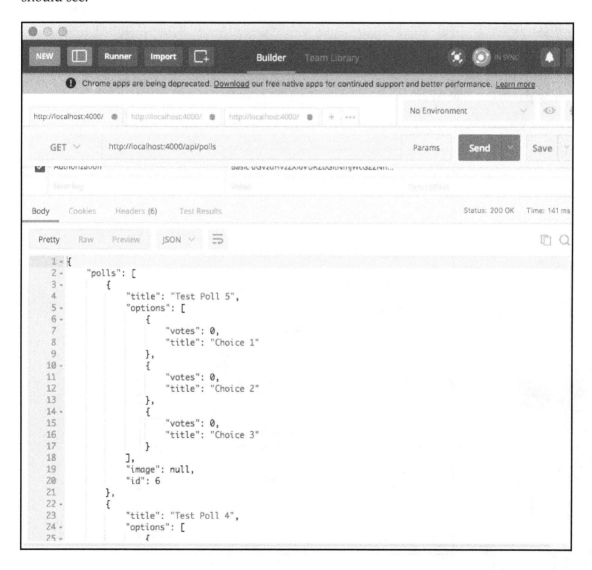

Now that we have our API responding back the way we expect it to for the data that we're sending it, let's start requiring an API key to work without API!

Authenticating Against our API

Allowing API access without any sort of restrictions or authentication can actually be very dangerous for the long-term health of your application. Without a means of restricting access, you are very prone to bad actors coming along and disrupting the experience of your application and API for all of the legitimate users of your API, so let's implement a simple HTTP Basic authentication mechanism using the already-established usernames and a new password-like API key.

The flow of our Phoenix application's flow should look something like this:

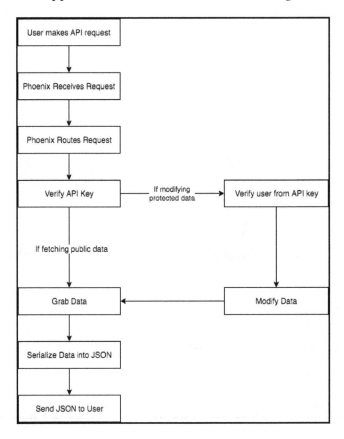

The good news is that this remains a very simple thing to implement in Phoenix. We'll need to take a quick sidebar first, though, because actually navigating to a user's profile page (where they will be able to generate their API key or regenerate it if necessary) is borderline impossible if you don't know your own unique user ID (which they won't). We're going to modify the nav bar up at the top to allow us to quickly get into our user profile page!

Allowing a user to navigate to their profile page

Right now it's actually difficult to navigate to the user's profile page to actually be able to generate our API key, so we'll take a quick sidebar to implement that. We'll start off by returning to the main application layout, `lib/vocial_web/templates/layout/app.html.eex` and modify the render call for `_nav.html` to pass in the `conn`:

```
<%= render "_nav.html", conn: @conn %>
```

Then we'll hop over to the `_nav.html.eex` template, where we'll change the *login* link to instead be conditional based on information that should be in the session:

```
<%= if user = Plug.Conn.get_session(@conn, :user) do %>
  <li><%= link "Welcome #{user.username}", to: user_path(@conn, :show, user.id) %></li>
<% else %>
  <li><a href="/login">Login</a></li>
<% end %>
```

This should make it a lot simpler for the user to find their way back to the user profile! After the user logs in, at the top (in the navigation bar), they should see a **Welcome ____** link. Clicking that will bring us to the user profile page!

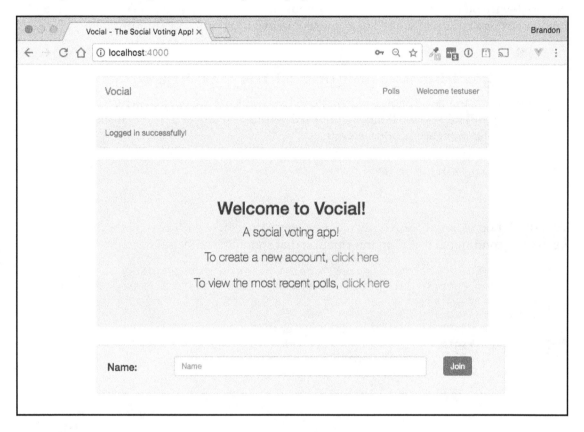

Now we can actually direct a user easily to their profile page, which will be necessary for the next steps! As I mentioned, this is a pretty easy thing for us to implement and will be well worth the small amount of effort for the next bit of work and testing that we'll need to do!

Introducing API keys to the database

The next step, now that we have a good way to get to the user profile page, is to actually store these keys in the database. We're going to stick with a few simple design decisions first:

- Users can have 1 API key
- API keys are not shared
- API keys should just be strings

We will be based on that criteria, just create API keys as strings on the users' table and not worry about creating a separate table that joins to users. If you ever wanted to expand out this system too, for example, allow a user to create multiple API keys, you would want to instead store those in a separate table. You could probably use a table that stores the user ID and the API key to keep it simple, for perhaps make it more complicated by allowing users to deactivate/reactivate API keys.

For us, however, we'll just stick to the simplest implementation, as that will enable us to get this out and working. Remember to always start small and build up!

```
$ mix ecto.gen.migration add_api_key_to_users
* creating priv/repo/migrations
* creating priv/repo/migrations/20180125221425_add_api_key_to_users.exs
```

Next, open up that migration file. Since we just need to add a single string column to the users' table, we'll just have a single `alter table` statement for the `users` table, adding `api_key` as a string. Open up the migration file that was created after running the last terminal command and update the change function to the code as follows:

```
defmodule Vocial.Repo.Migrations.AddApiKeyToUsers do
  use Ecto.Migration

  def change do
    alter table(:users) do
      add :api_key, :string
    end
  end
end
```

Run the migrate command to catch everything up:

```
$ mix ecto.migrate
[info] == Running Vocial.Repo.Migrations.AddApiKeyToUsers.change/0 forward
[info] alter table users
[info] == Migrated in 0.0s
```

We'll also need to tell our users schema to be able to handle this. Any time we add any new columns, we have two things we need to do at a minimum to be able to support those new columns. First, we need to modify the list of fields in the schema block itself. Open up `lib/vocial/accounts/user.ex`, and in the schema, block add the following line:

```
    field :api_key, :string
```

The next thing we need to do to be able to support the new database column is to make sure that we can actually write to it through changesets. To do that, we'll need to update the `cast` call in the `changeset` function in our users file. In the `changeset` function, change that cast call to include `api_key`:

```
|&gt; cast(attrs, [:username, :email, :active, :password,
:password_confirmation, :oauth_provider, :oauth_id, :api_key])
```

Now we'll need to make a form to tie it all together. Go to `lib/vocial_web/templates/user/show.html.eex` and we'll take this from being a considerably useless page to something that is actually functionally useful for the user! We'll add a new API key section. We're using a little bit of template logic inside our new section that verifies that the user's API key exists before displaying it, and then we have a form that will actually submit the request to generate the user's API key. One thing to note is that we have not actually created this form action yet! We'll get to that very soon. Open up that template and add the block as follows:

```
&lt;br /&gt;
&lt;div class="api-key-section"&gt;
  &lt;h3&gt;API Key&lt;/h3&gt;
  &lt;hr/&gt;
  &lt;%= if api_key = @user.api_key do %&gt;
    &lt;strong&gt;Key:&lt;/strong&gt; &lt;%= api_key %&gt;
  &lt;% end %&gt;
  &lt;%= form_for @conn, "/users/#{@user.id}/generate_api_key", [as:
:user], fn _f -&gt; %&gt;
    &lt;%= submit "Generate API Key", class: "btn btn-primary" %&gt;
  &lt;% end %&gt;
&lt;/div&gt;
```

This won't work without the appropriate route, so open up `lib/vocial_web/router.ex`. Since this is a browser operation and action, we will want to add this under the `"/"` scope with the rest of our routes:

```
post "/users/:id/generate_api_key", UserController, :generate_api_key
```

We'll also need to build up the implementation for the controller action. Move into the controller (`lib/vocial_web/controllers/user_controller.ex`), and we'll start implementing our controller action (but again, with the absolute simplest initial implementation). To keep it simple, we'll start with:

```
def generate_api_key(conn, %{"id" => id}) do
  conn
  |> put_flash(:error, "Not implemented yet")
  |> redirect(to: "/")
end
```

Let's take a look at the flow now to make sure it's working before we move on. If you navigate to your user profile, you should see something resembling the UI as follows:

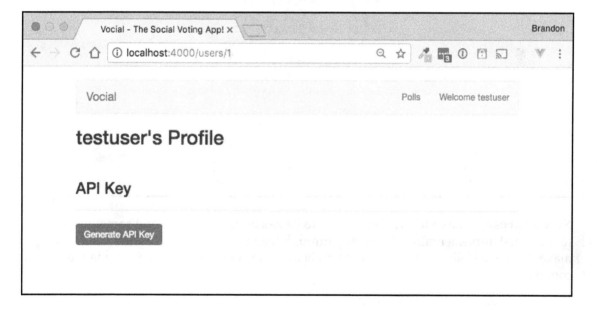

And then when we try to generate the API key, we're expecting to see an error message pop up about that route not being implemented yet:

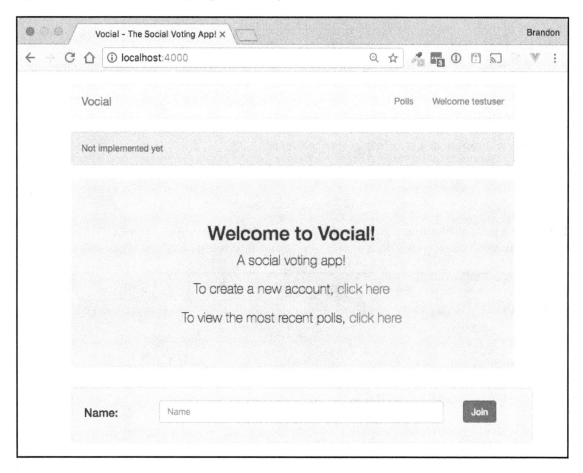

Now let's change the controller code again to be less boilerplate code and something closer to the actual implementation. We'll step through the implementation block by block to make it easier to follow. Let's start with grabbing the user out of the database via the context:

```
user = Accounts.get_user(id)
```

Next, we'll want to set up our general case statement for dealing with the function call to generate the API key request. We don't know precisely what that will look like yet, but designing things this way allows us to essentially design this feature by contract.

```
case Accounts.generate_api_key(user) do
  # ...
end
```

The first clause we'll add to our case statement is for when everything returns successfully. We'll use the standard Elixir pattern of sending back `{:ok, something}`, so that is precisely what we'll look for! If it is successful, we'll just want to set a flash message letting the user know that we were able to update the API key for the user, and then we'll redirect them back to their user profile page where they can see the new API key!

```
{:ok, _} ->
  conn
  |> put_flash(:info, "Updated API key for user!")
  |> redirect(to: user_path(conn, :show, user)
```

We'll also want to implement an error clause, since bad things can happen to our applications, no matter how thoughtful we are about our design up front! If we receive an error, we'll again set the flash message and we'll redirect out to the user profile page:

```
{:error, _} ->
  conn
  |> put_flash(:error, "Failed to generate API key for user!")
  |> redirect(to: user_path(conn, :show, user))
```

We've written our action, but remember that along the way we called a function called `generate_api_key/1` that doesn't actually exist in our Accounts Context yet! Let's take the time to write our boilerplate code for that function now. In `lib/vocial/accounts/accounts.ex`:

```
def generate_api_key(user) do
  user
  |> User.changeset(%{api_key: "ABCDEF"})
  |> Repo.update()
end
```

Now let's go back to the profile page and try this all again:

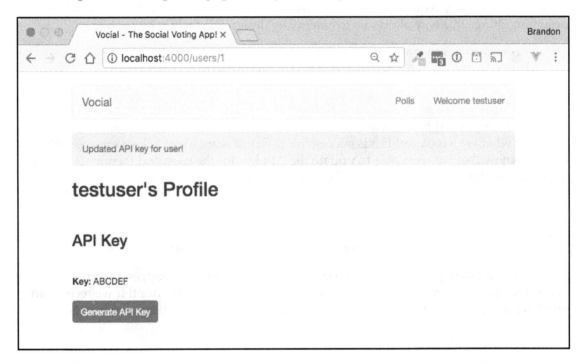

Much better! But we probably want to modify our API key to be a bit more random than what it is, otherwise, this would be the least secure API in the history of APIs! We'll need to reuse the random_string function that we've used elsewhere (for the session token handling with OAuth providers). We're going to move the random_string/1 function from the session controller to here to make it a little more reusable. The new generate_api_key/1 function should now look like this:

```
def generate_api_key(user) do
  user
  |&gt; User.changeset(%{api_key: random_string(32)})
  |&gt; Repo.update()
end
```

So again, we're going to move that `random_string/1` function over into the context here. The following function is, just in case you want to double check the body of that function!

```
def random_string(length) do
   :crypto.strong_rand_bytes(length) |&gt; Base.url_encode64 |&gt;
binary_part(0, length)
   end
```

Then we can refactor some old code sitting in `lib/vocial_web/controllers/session_controller.ex`, since we moved where the `random_string/1` function lives into the Accounts Context instead of it living as a function inside of our Session Controller:

```
defp build_user_from_auth(%{provider: :twitter}=auth) do
   password = Accounts.random_string(64)
   %{
      username: auth.info.nickname,
      oauth_id: auth.uid,
      oauth_provider: "twitter",
      password: password,
      password_confirmation: password
   }
end

defp build_user_from_auth(%{provider: :google}=auth) do
   password = Accounts.random_string(64)
   %{
      username: auth.info.email,
      email: auth.info.email,
      oauth_id: auth.uid,
      oauth_provider: "google",
      password: password,
      password_confirmation: password
   }
end
```

If we head on over back to our UI, we should now be able to click that **Generate API Key** function and expect to receive some results back! We should get something like: `JCXg1jNNogNttRsrV8k5JazoxdcGtvHX` This will work for our API key, so we can now move forward a bit and implement a check to make sure the API key is valid.

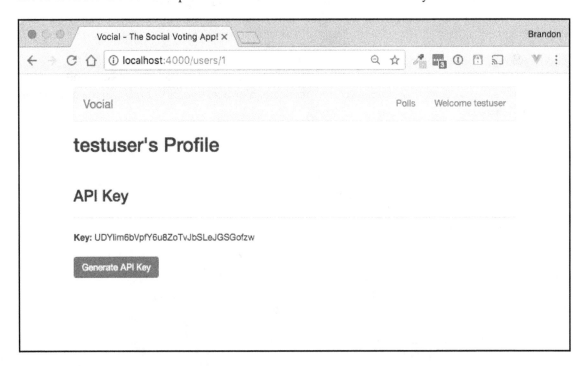

Validating API Keys

We're moving along at a great pace so let's try to keep it up and implement an API key authentication mechanism so that all of our work here was not in vain! We'll use the username as the username for the user making API requests and the API key as the password for an HTTP Basic Authentication scheme. This is generally a good method for authenticating your API and will serve our purposes nicely.

We'll start off by implementing a new plug that will be responsible for handling our API key checks. We'll call this one `VerifyApiKey` to keep things consistent with our other custom plug. Create `lib/vocial_web/verify_api_key.ex` and we'll start building this out:

```
defmodule VocialWeb.VerifyApiKey do
  def init(opts), do: opts

  def call(conn, _opts) do
    conn
  end
end
```

We'll also need to hook it up to our API pipeline in the router. Open up `lib/vocial_web/router.ex` and in it, we're going to add a new call to plug that will pass in the preceding new module that we started to write:

```
pipeline :api do
  plug :accepts, ["json"]
  plug VocialWeb.VerifyApiKey
end
```

Right now we're not doing anything particularly interesting; this is just our initial Plug template starter. Let's make this a little more interesting, though. Since we don't have a means of checking an API key yet, let's just make this always return a message saying that the API key was invalid!

```
def call(conn, _opts) do
  conn
  |&gt; put_status(401)
  |&gt; render(VocialWeb.ErrorView, "invalid_api_key.json")
  |&gt; halt()
end
```

To make this work, we'll also need to import our `put_status/2`, `render/3`, and `halt/1` calls. Up at the top of the file, add our imports:

```
import Plug.Conn, only: [halt: 1, put_status: 2]
import Phoenix.Controller, only: [render: 3]
```

This won't work until we also edit the `ErrorView` to include an `invalid_api_key.json` render clause. Open up `lib/vocial_web/views/error_view.ex` and add the following function:

```
def render("invalid_api_key.json", _assigns) do
  %{ message: "Invalid API Key" }
end
```

The beauty of Phoenix for writing an API is that all of the difficult serialization logic is already handled for us! We just need to return out the appropriate data structure and the rest is handled for us! Let's run our API request again and we should be able to validate that we're now receiving an error message!

Let's expand this functionality a little bit more by making it actually implement an API key check! We'll need to do a couple of things in order to verify the API key:

1. Fetch the `Authorization` header out of the `conn` (this is a header coming from the client making the API request)
2. Decode the Authorization header from Base64 into a regular string
3. Split the string apart into a username and API key, separately
4. Verify the username and API key passed in

Let's implement each of these functions in turn. We'll start with fetching the authorization header out of the passed-in conn. We then convert the list of headers into a map to make fetching values out of them simpler, and fetch the "authorization" key:

```
def fetch_authorization_header(conn) do
  conn.req_headers
  |&gt; Enum.into(%{})
  |&gt; Map.fetch("authorization")
end
```

Next, we'll implement the function that will be responsible for decoding the Authorization header from Base64 into plain text. I'm going to step through this piece-by-piece to make it a little easier for me to explain:

The first piece is our function signature. We're expecting this to be a function that will just take in the fetched "authorization" header from before:

```
def decode_authorization_header(auth_header) do
  # ...
end
```

Next, we'll split apart the auth header into two parts. Generally an authorization header looks something like this: `Basic AbCd1Efgh54319` so we'll need to split the auth header apart by splitting on spaces. This will give us the type of authentication (the first string) and the encoded authorization information:

```
[type, key] = String.split(auth_header, " ")
```

Next, we'll convert the type to lowercase to avoid any sort of weird issues where each client sends the authorization information differently each time, and we'll do a case statement on that to make sure we're only ever dealing with basic auth:

```
case String.downcase(type) do
  # ...
end
```

Finally, as we mentioned, we want to decode the authorization information if it is indeed basic auth, so we'll include that as our first clause and an error message as our second clause:

```
"basic" -&gt; Base.decode64(key)
_ -&gt; {:error, "Invalid Authorization Header Format"}
```

The fully-finished function should look like this:

```
def decode_authorization_header(auth_header) do
  [type, key] = String.split(auth_header, " ")
  case String.downcase(type) do
    "basic" -&gt; Base.decode64(key)
    _ -&gt; {:error, "Invalid Authorization Header Format"}
  end
end
```

We'll also need a function in our Accounts Context that will be responsible for verifying the username/API key. Since they're both stored as plain text values in our users' table, this becomes a simple check using `Repo.get_by/2`. In `lib/vocial/accounts/accounts.ex`:

```
def verify_api_key(username, api_key) do
  case Repo.get_by(User, username: username, api_key: api_key) do
    nil -&gt; false
    _user -&gt; true
  end
end
```

Finally, we can go back and finish writing our plug out. First, at the top of the plug, add an alias for the Accounts Context:

```
alias Vocial.Accounts
```

Then we'll refactor a little bit to keep our functions small and purpose-specific. We'll start by writing a function to handle dealing with the conn when the API key check fails:

```
def invalid_api_key(conn) do
  conn
  |&gt; put_status(401)
  |&gt; render(VocialWeb.ErrorView, "invalid_api_key.json")
  |&gt; halt()
end
```

We'll also need a check for verifying the API key itself is valid. This is a long function overall, but nothing terribly complicated. This is essentially a pipeline, where we take the request headers, fetch the authorization header out of those, decode the authorization header from Base64 encoding, then split the authorization information. In our case, we expect the user to send their authorization information by using their username as the username for HTTP Basic auth and their API key as the password:

```
def is_valid_api_key?(conn) do
  with {:ok, header} <- fetch_authorization_header(conn),
       {:ok, decoded_header} <- decode_authorization_header(header),
       [username, api_key] = String.split(decoded_header, ":")
  do
    Accounts.verify_api_key(username, api_key)
  else
    _ -> false
  end
end
```

Finally, we'll need two functions to handle what to do with the actual conn. One for when the key is valid, and one for when the key is invalid:

```
def handle_conn(true, conn), do: conn
def handle_conn(_, conn), do: invalid_api_key(conn)
```

That's it! Now we can go back to our `call/2` function implementation and refactor it:

```
def call(conn, _opts) do
  is_valid_api_key?(conn)
  |> handle_conn(conn)
end
```

That's it! We're left with a very clean `call/2` function implementation since we split apart our functions and kept the functionality of each super lean!

Dealing with Error Handling in APIs

A good API that does everything right but completely ignores how to handle errors in a sane, graceful way is many things, but not actually a good API! You need to treat dealing with errors, exceptions, and issues in a way that makes it easier for your end users and consumers to be able to appropriately deal with the error and resolve things in meaningful ways. For us to do that, we'll again need to take a quick sidebar and implement another route, since that will make building up our API error handling a lot simpler in the long run.

Implementing an API Resource Show

We'll need to next a resource show API route since that will make it easier for us to demonstrate how to build custom error handlers for your APIs.

Open up `lib/vocial_web/router.ex`:

```
# Other scopes may use custom stacks.
scope "/api", VocialWeb do
  pipe_through :api

  resources "/polls", Api.PollController, only: [:index, :show]
end
```

We'll also need to implement a Show action in `lib/vocial_web/controllers/api/poll_controller.ex`:

```
def show(conn, %{"id" => id}) do
  poll = Votes.get_poll(id)
  render(conn, "show.json", poll: poll)
end
```

And of course our View needs to be implemented as well for the JSON to get back out to the user:

```
def render("show.json", %{poll: poll}) do
  %{
    poll: render_one(poll)
  }
end
```

When you request a single poll resource back you should get something like this back:

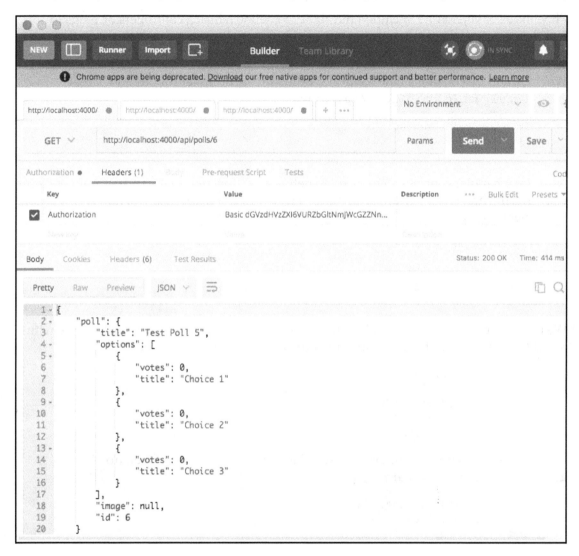

With that out of the way, we can start working on some better custom error handling for our API!

Adding an Error Handler for 404s for JSON

Phoenix, as of version 1.3, included the ability to define fallback controllers or plugs to handle scenarios where a conn is not returned back out. We can harness this to write custom error handling code for our API to catch these scenarios!

We'll start off by creating a new controller called ErrorController for our API. Create `lib/vocial_web/controllers/api/error_controller.ex`:

```
defmodule VocialWeb.Api.ErrorController do
  use VocialWeb, :controller
end
```

Next, for a handler controller, you need to define a call function that will attempt to look for a conn as the first argument and pattern match against the second argument. We'll just implement a simple 404 handler for purposes of this example:

```
def call(conn, {:error, :not_found}) do
  conn
  |&gt; put_status(:not_found)
  |&gt; render(VocialWeb.ErrorView, "404.json")
end
```

We'll also implement a general fallback to cover other situations that may occur since with an API you don't want to just be spewing out whatever errors come your way.

```
def call(conn, _) do
  conn
  |&gt; put_status(500)
  |&gt; render(VocialWeb.ErrorView, "500.json")
end
```

We'll also need to update our error view to handle these templates. Open up `lib/vocial_web/views/error_view.ex`:

```
def render("404.json", _assigns) do
  %{ message: "Resource not found"}
end

def render("500.json", _assigns) do
  %{ message: "An unhandled exception has occurred" }
end
```

Next, we'll need to tell the API PollController to use this as our fallback. In
`lib/vocial_web/controllers/api/poll_controller.ex` under our alias statement,
add the following line:

```
action_fallback VocialWeb.Api.ErrorController
```

We'll also quickly want to refactor our show function to take advantage of our new
functionality:

```
def show(conn, %{"id" => id}) do
  case Votes.get_poll(id) do
    nil -> {:error, :not_found}
    poll -> render(conn, "show.json", poll: poll)
  end
end
```

We'll also need to change the `Accounts.get_poll/1` function in the Votes Context to not
use `Repo.get!` for this to work, so back in `lib/vocial/votes/votes.ex`, modify that
function:

```
def get_poll(id) do
  Repo.get(Poll, id)
  |> Repo.preload([:options, :image, :vote_records, :messages])
end
```

And there we go! If we try to do something crazy like making an API authenticated request
for a poll with an ID of 1234567890 we should see a response from the server with a status
code of 404 and a body of:

```
{
    "message": "Resource not found"
}
```

From here we could implement all kinds of other error handlers or use manual error
renders, similar to what we did with our API key handling function! And that's it, our API
is ready to go (and it would be simple for us to add new API endpoints later)!

Deploying Phoenix applications to production

The last step in getting our application ready to go and ready to run in production is for us to finally deploy our application to production! We're not going to cover absolutely every delivery method available to us because there are frankly a ton of them. You can use Docker and deploy an image, or you can deploy a binary release with a tool like a distillery. You can just upload the source to a server that has Elixir already installed on it and ready to go as well. For sake of simplicity, we're going to stick with the last option as a means of keeping the deployment process as simple as possible, since this is probably the safest fallback option for deployment.

Initial requirements for deployment into production

If we want to deploy our application to Production, we're going to need a few things installed on the target server first. The deploy requires us essentially taking our code from our machine and throwing that onto a target server where it will run. The advantage of this process is that if we have our code on a server, doing things like running migrations becomes a much simpler ask than if we do binary releases or docker releases.

If we want to deploy our application for production, we will need:

- A suitable target production environment
- A suitable production database with the correct permissions
- A completed application (which we now have)

The simplest implementation requires us to have a server with SSH access and git installed, although there are even a number of different ways for us to approach even this one way to deploy our application!

We'll start off by checking our code into some sort of source control, whether it's git or something else. This will allow us to log in to our server and deploy our code! We'll start by logging into our server (the deployment target we mentioned previously).

```
$ ssh [username]@[server]
... Logging in
$ cd [applications directory]
$ git clone [application]
$ cd [created application directory]
```

```
$ MIX_ENV=prod mix deps.get --only prod
$ MIX_ENV=prod mix compile
```

The next step, having logged into our server and started running our application, will be to start working on setting up all of the pertinent connection information and secrets information! You'll need to create your `prod.secret.exs` file in the config directory to set up the connection information for your production environment. This is also where you will set up the production secret that will be used for things like token creation and encryption. If you're using postgres, you'll also likely want to create a user, a database, and set up the appropriate password and permissions:

```
$ sudo -u postgres createuser vocial
$ sudo -u postgres createdb vocial_prod
$ sudo -u postgres psql
$&gt; alter user vocial with encrypted password '...'
ALTER ROLE
$&gt; grant all privileges on database vocial_prod to vocial
GRANT
```

We'll also want to generate a new secret that we can use in production! You'll get a different secret key every time you run this:

```
$ mix phx.gen.secret
GtLKgzRJpAnSt15...8G6313RsTwWG4e9lfZl
```

Using all of this information, our `prod.secret.exs` file should look something like this:

```
use Mix.Config

config :vocial, VocialWeb.Endpoint,
  secret_key_base: "somegeneratedsecret"

config :vocial, Vocial.Repo,
  adapter: Ecto.Adapters.Postgres,
  username: "vocial",
  password: "somepw",
  database: "vocial_prod",
  pool_size: 25
```

You'll want to tune the `pool_size` depending on the resources available to you and your database. The bigger this number is the less likely you'll run into issues where your Phoenix application is waiting for a worker in the poll to service its request, but it also means more strain on your database, so there is a fine line to walk for how this should be tuned overall.

Next, we'll create the prod database environment by running `mix ecto.migrate` in a production environment:

```
$ MIX_ENV=prod mix ecto.migrate
13:47:36.912 [info] == Running
Vocial.Repo.Migrations.AddPollsTable.change/0 forward
13:47:36.912 [info] create table polls
13:47:36.924 [info] == Migrated in 0.0s
13:47:36.969 [info] == Running
Vocial.Repo.Migrations.AddOptionsTable.change/0 forward
13:47:36.969 [info] create table options
13:47:36.973 [info] == Migrated in 0.0s
```

We'll also want to make sure that we've set up everything for the front end code as well, so we'll go into the assets directory and run the `deploy` command, and then run the production Phoenix digest command:

```
$ cd ./assets && npm install
$ npm run deploy && cd -
$ MIX_ENV=prod mix phx.digest
```

And finally, you're ready to run this in production mode!

You'll want to set the `RUN_ERL_LOG_MAXSIZE` and `RUN_ERL_LOG_GENERATIONS` environment variables since the default that any Erlang application uses is 10,000 bytes (roughly 10kb), which is far too small for use in a production environment! I typically will use something like this:

```
RUN_ERL_LOG_MAXSIZE=10000000 RUN_ERL_LOG_GENERATIONS=10
```

This makes sure that the logs generated are actually big enough that I can catch any issues that do occur! Finally, let's run our application:

```
RUN_ERL_LOG_MAXSIZE=10000000 RUN_ERL_LOG_GENERATIONS=10 MIX_ENV=prod
PORT=4001 elixir --detached -S mix do compile, phx.server
```

And that's it! Our application is now officially deployed and running in production!

Alternative Deployment Strategies

There are other ways to deploy as well! You can build a docker image for your application and then deploy that image to an environment that can run containers, for example. This is a great deployment method for being able to reliably deploy your environment, but it carries a number of other gotchas associated with it, such as having to deal with having docker running on your target environment which may not be an option. It can also be tricker to allow multiple separate Phoenix instances to communicate with each other.

You can also deploy BEAM binaries using tools like the fantastic Distillery. Distillery is centered around creating release files that can include the entire Erlang runtime and all dependencies, allowing you to deploy your application to an environment that may not have the full stack of running applications available to it!

In addition, another approach is to deploy your application in a managed environment such as Heroku. This carries with it its own set of concerns and advantages which could easily eat up most of this book on its own. Ultimately, there are a lot of different alternate strategies for deployment that are worth investigating if you're concerned about the approach of running your application directly!

Summary

It has been quite the journey! We've started with literally nothing, no code, no framework, nothing to build our application. From there, we've tackled and, more importantly, made sure we thoroughly understood each piece that went into building our Phoenix application!

We've implemented a social application from scratch, allowing real-time communication and live results viewing. We've implemented means of allowing the users to log in using popular social media OAuth providers so they don't have to create new accounts to start taking advantage of our platform!

We know and have practiced working with our database and working with Ecto over and over, and learned the ins and outs of setting up and configuring each step in the process along the way. We've explored turning our application into an application that supports API integrations in the span of single chapter thanks to the simplicity of Phoenix.

Finally, we've delved into some of the more advanced concepts and fundamentals behind the scenes powering our Phoenix application with GenServers, OTP, and more, and moved on to actually bringing our application from nothing to actually running on a real production machine!

I hope you can take this time to sit and be proud of what you've done and what you've achieved. I can't wait to see what wonderful new projects you will build in the future on top of Elixir and Phoenix. These wonderful technologies have made a lot possible in web development that have typically been the most difficult things to plan and design for. Thank you for coming along with me on this journey!

Other Books You May Enjoy

If you enjoyed this book, you may be interested in these other books by Packt:

Mastering JavaScript Functional Programming
Federico Kereki

ISBN: 978-1-78728-744-0

- Create more reliable code with closures and immutable data
- Convert existing methods into pure functions, and loops into recursive methods
- Develop more powerful applications with currying and function composition
- Separate the logic of your system from implementation details
- Implement composition and chaining techniques to simplify coding
- Use functional programming techniques where it makes the most sense

ECMAScript Cookbook
Ross Harrison

ISBN: 978-1-78862-817-4

- Organize JavaScript programs across multiple files, using ES modules
- Create and work with promises using the Promise object and methods
- Compose async functions to propagate and handle errors
- Solve organizational and processing issues with structures using design patterns
- Use classes to encapsulate and share behavior
- Orchestrate parallel programs using WebWorkers, SharedMemory, and Atomics
- Use and extend Map, Set, and Symbol to work with user-defined classes and simulate data types
- Explore new array methods to avoid looping with arrays and other collections

Leave a review - let other readers know what you think

Please share your thoughts on this book with others by leaving a review on the site that you bought it from. If you purchased the book from Amazon, please leave us an honest review on this book's Amazon page. This is vital so that other potential readers can see and use your unbiased opinion to make purchasing decisions, we can understand what our customers think about our products, and our authors can see your feedback on the title that they have worked with Packt to create. It will only take a few minutes of your time, but is valuable to other potential customers, our authors, and Packt. Thank you!

Index

www.ingramcontent.com/pod-product-compliance
Lightning Source LLC
Chambersburg PA
CBHW060651060326
40690CB00020B/4603